To The C...

...

...ovans

John Franklin Phillips

9-24-1988

ISBN 0-9618289-1-9 Hardcover
ISBN 0-9618289-2-7 Paper

The cover picture is "The Appeal To The Great Spirit." This is made from a photograph of the statue at The Boston Museum of Fine Arts. The sculptor was Cyrus Edwin Dallin.

Printed and bound by the Parthenon Press
of The United Methodist Publishing House, Nashville, Tennessee

INTRODUCTION

The American Indian in Alabama and Southeast

Church's Involvement of Native Americans

The Reverend Franklin Phillips, out of deep Christian compassion, is dedicated to the needs of the Native American peoples of this nation.

The history of the inhuman treatment of Native Americans by European settlers in the Americas is filled with tragedy and injustice. Unfortunately, such injustice continues in a number of places in the Western Hemisphere.

Franklin Phillips' fine book, *The American Indian in Alabama and the Southeast,* is an attempt to make us all aware of the existance of American Indians among us, to show the ways in which the Church has ministered with them, and to point out additional ways in which the Church may bring the ministry of Christ's love to the original peoples of this land.

May we feel the hurts of the American Indians and be inspired by this unique book to find creative and redemptive ways to serve and to communicate the Gospel in all its fullness to the Native Americans.

Franklin Phillips is to be commended for excellent work in this field.

J. Lloyd Knox
Bishop, Birmingham Area
The United Methodist Church

DEDICATION

This Book—*The American Indian in Alabama and the Southeast*—is dedicated to my dear wife, Frances Madry Phillips, and my beloved family, who have loved me and sustained me through this long and tiring, but exciting experience!

Franklin Phillips

Author: Franklin Phillips

REMEMBRANCES

I am grateful for the love and encouragement of my beloved family!

The Congregations of The Langdale, Trussville, Hamilton, and Fayette United Methodist Churches for their love and support of my ministry.

To Reba Duke, the faithful secretary of The First United Methodist Church of Trussville, and Dot Crutcher, the devoted secretary of The First United Methodist Church of Fayette who have helped me immeasurably!

To Margaret Lawless whose typing and expertise of manuscript preparation has been invaluable!

To a dear Friend, J. W. Vickers, who gave much of the inspiration to this interest!

PREFACE

There is something hauntingly beautiful about such words as Chattahoochee, and such terms as, The Great Council Fire. The American Indian endures!

The American Indian lives on in the names of many of our states—such as Alabama, Mississippi, and Tennessee; in the foods of our kitchens, the produce of our fields, and marts; in the Democracy that has evolved; and yes, even through the larger society where his blood flows by intermarriage. There is much we, who are regarded as non-Indian, can learn of them, and from them, and come to appreciate about them.

My purpose in writing this book is to tell the story of the great drama—evolution of The American Indian in Alabama and the Southeast—in a way that would be both readable and provocative. I hope thereby to help create a new consciousness, or greater awareness of the Indian and something of the great significance of his contribution to our National Heritage. Hopefully, such will stimulate us to help bring these fellow Americans more fully into the action, life, and returns of the life of America.

It is my purpose also, to help create a new self-awareness in the American Indian. We have gone through a period in our national development that did not encourage the Indian to have pride in his heritage. I have long felt the importance for these people of the idea expressed by Dr. Martin E. Marty in *Toward a Usable Past.* When the American Indian can gain a sense of pride in his heritage—like the thesis in *Roots* by Alex Haley—he will find new or additional strength that will better enable him to confront life—frustration, challenge, hope, and opportunity—as an American! To this end we all gain and America will be the stronger for it too! To this end this book is written and dedicated!

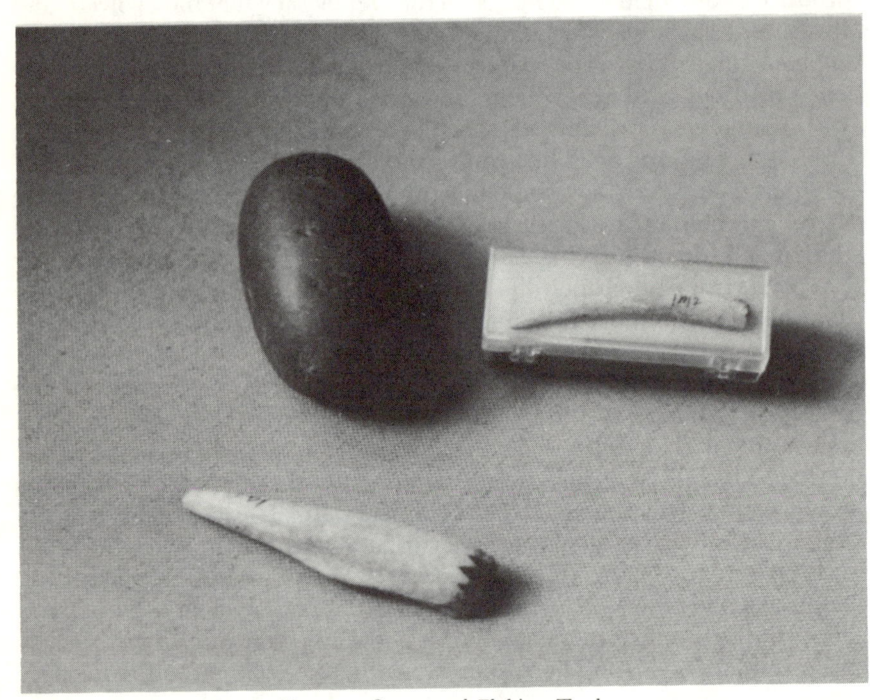

Hammer Stone and Flaking Tool.

CONTENTS

I

WHENCE THEY CAME?

Since the earliest encounter of the 'Red Man' by the first European Explorers, such as Christopher Columbus, the questions of who these folk are and where they came from have been pondered and researched. And many different theories have evolved, or have been developed.

The best theory, it seems to me, is that of 'The land bridge between North America and Asia in the 'Bering Strait'. This bridge was created by the 'Ice Age'. As the icebergs formed—especially the polar ice caps—and grew larger and larger over many, many centuries, it took up more and more of the earth's surface water, thus lowering the level of the sea. In the process the highest mountain ranges that had been covered by the sea emerged as dry land. Thus the Bering Strait land bridge was formed.[1]

During the period of time the 'land bridge' existed (probably thousands of years), some of the 'Asians', who in their hunting expeditions happened to roam into the area of the 'land bridge', crossed over it into North America. The tundra area of the 'land bridge' seems to have been heavily used by animals of the area. So that in the natural pursuit of game using the tundra area, in time, some of these 'Asians' would have ventured onto the tundra, across it, and into the North American Continent![2] Thus man—The American Indian—had arrived to conquer and populate the continent! And from Alaska all the way to the tip of South America they would conquer and populate every area. They would populate it rather sparsely in vast sections of it, but the noteworthy point is they successfully adapted to every part—swampland, desert, mountain range, etc. There are various influences that might possibly have been contributing factors in these Asian hunting parties crossing over into North America. One is simply the pursuit of game for food. Another would be the search for better areas in which to live—'the grass looks greener on the other side'. And I am sure these hardy folk had an adventurous spirit.

Such influences resulted in some family groups or simple hunting parties crossing over the bridge into a new hunting—living area, which was also a new world—a new hemisphere! The most reasonable theory, it seems to me, for these people to cross the land bridge, and thus become the first to discover, and to inhabit the North American Continent, was they were in search of food. As hunting groups saw the various animals from North America on the tundra and pursued them they would be naturally drawn or lured on toward the rich source of these animals. In time these hunting parties are across the bridge and spreading out and onward across the hemisphere.

Once across, it seems three forces would interplay to lure them ever southward—the ice-snow-cold barriers that formed a narrow passage, the warmer climate farther south, and the more abundant food supply to be found southward.[3]

Some evidence indicates the land bridge existed some 20 thousand years ago, and for a period of many, many thousands of years. Evidence of man having crossed this land bridge into North America in this, the paleo era, has been found. According to Jesse D. Jennings, author of Across an Arctic Bridge, which is part of The National Geographic Society's book, *The World of the American Indian,* evidence of the Indian was found in Old Crow Flats in Canada's Yukon Territory. A scraper, made from an animal leg bone, that was undeniably the work of human hands, was found that carbon dated at about 25,000 B.C. This would indicate that man had crossed the land bridge fairly soon after it became a possibility.[4]

Waves of Indians crossed by the land bridge from Asia into North America. There were ice caps over Greenland and another or two over much of Alaska. There was one or two corridors between these ice caps that led toward the south or warmer areas. The Indian moved through these corridors, where strangely enough the temperature was such that he could adapt to it.

It seems that from the ending of the corridors of the ice caps the

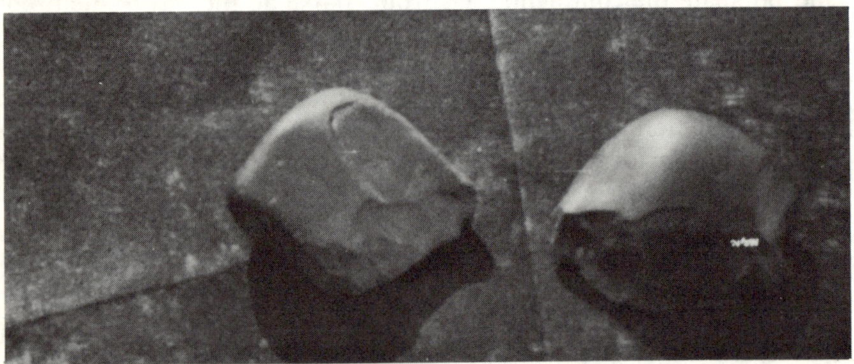

Pebble stone complex chopper tools—Most primitive tools of Stone Age Peoples.

Indians fanned out all across the area of presentday United States. This evolved across a span of time of thousands of years.

Author C. W. Ceran in *The First American* says, "it is significant that scholars no longer discuss the question of whether the first Americans came from Siberia; today that is regarded as conclusive.[5]"

The primary tools of the early people were the spear or projectile point, the spear thrown by the aid of atl-atls, or spear thrower, the clubs, knives, scrapers, choppers, grinders, nutting stones, hammer stones and antler flakers.

The atl-atl or spear thrower is one of the most significant tools in man's long struggle to survive. It is the earliest significant development in human technology. It greatly increased the efficiency of the hunter. The Indian could by using the spear thrower throw a spear for 50 or 60 yards with lethal force. It also enabled him to take game such as the saber tooth tiger or wooly mammal etc. without getting so dangerously close to the prey. Therefore, it increased both safety and efficiency. There is evidence that this tool became virtually an universal tool among the Indian for some 10,000 years.

Atlatl-spear thrower. Courtesy of Russell Cave National Park.

II

WHO ARE THEY?

There are several theories as to who the American Indian is. One is that he is simply a creature God uniquely created for this hemisphere. To be sure, he was the first people in this area of the world. I feel the people of both North and South America, called Indian, were the first in this hemisphere and are, it seems, of the same stock. They are of one common racial background, though the eons of time, climate, living conditions, and developing cultures have resulted in some differences and variations. Many family groups evolved based particularly on different language, such as Muskogees, Algonkian, Iroquois, etc. and varied ceremonies.[1]

Another theory of who they are, specifically held by author James Adair, is that the American Indian is of the Hebrew or Jewish stock of people. Adair argues, and I feel with considerable basis, that a segment of the pre-Hebrew stock were those wandering hunters of Eastern Asia who happened to cross the 'land bridge' of the Bering Strait and came into North America. Thus, they became the first of the American Indian. Adair's principal argument is the many, and some very strong, similarities to be found in the religious expression of the American Indian and that of The Hebrews of The Old Testament era.

According to Adair, "The Hebrews had various ablutions, and anointings, according to the Mosaic ritual-and all the Indian nations constantly observe similar customs from religious motives. The law of purity, bathing in water, was essential to the Jews, and the Indians to this day would exclude the men from religious communion who neglected to observe it. The Indian sings Yo He Wah, the divine essence, as they run along at dawn to purify themselves by ablution."[2]

Adair argues these folk were Jews or of common origin with them. He argues that thesis primarily on the basis of common elements in their worship expressions. It may only indicate their closeness to, their harmony with nature, and the God of nature. This thesis—'You see I stand in good relation to the earth, to you, and to the gods' is beautifully expressed in *The World of The American Indian.*[3]

Governor William Penn and the New England theologian Cotton

Mather held views similar to that of James Adair that the Indian was of pre-Hebrew stock.[4]

The soundest theory, I believe, is that The American Indian is the decendant of the ancient people that inhabited the area of Asia near the Bering Strait. Certainly the most widely held view of 'Who The Red Man is', is that they are decendants of ancient Asians. There may be a good basis for the racial subtitle of 'American Indian', but ultimately that subdivision needs to be placed under the larger division of Asian or Mongollian.[5]

Though there are many differences in the Indian, such as variations of complexion, there seems also to be much uniformity. As Peter Farb in Man's Rise to Civilization as Shown by the Indians of North America says, "The American Indian actually represents one of the most homogeneous populations on earth."[6]

III

CAVE DWELLERS

The very earliest of The American Indian were roaming hunters. They were relatively small hunting groups that followed the movement of the game in order to secure their food. The availability and the securing of food was the most basic element of their primitive existence. This food supply would be primarily the animals they were able to capture or kill. But this food supply would also include seasonal fruits and nuts, etc. that they could gather as they needed it.

These earliest arrivals to this hemisphere would have brought the traditions, skills, and tools of their ancestral people, who were of the 'Stone Age'. Thus, their total belongings, which they brought with them across the land bridge, was probably clubs, stone and bone tipped spears, stone and bone scrappers, knives or cutters, and hand axes; and skins for clothing and for covering at night and in severe weather. They would have done so, because in following the movement of game the entire group would break camp and carrying all belongings, endeavor to keep their camp in close range of the game.

These hunting groups, roaming in search of food, sought shelter in caves and under ledges or overhanging bluffs from the elements and dangers that might threaten them. These dangers might be ferocious animals such as the saber tooth tiger, giant sloth, herd of buffalo or bison, as well as bears. Or it might be the danger of other hostile hunting parties, who did not want any hunting competitors in the area. Many of the caves, with small openings, the use of fires, and guards, would offer excellent protection to such hunting family groups. There is much evidence, such as chips from the manufacture of artifacts, that indicates the common and widespread use of such caves and ledges as shelter or home for these early Indians. Such shelter provided this most basic need of these people.

In Alabama there are many fine examples of this era of the Indian life here. The Russell Cave in Jackson County, near the town of Bridgeport, and the Stanfield-Whorley Bluff-shelter north of Cedar Creek Lake are the earliest known of such shelters in the State of Alabama and the Southeastern United States. These caves, or really they are rock ledges

Trapp Ledge Shelter-home

Sun Cirles

Foraging era grinding bowl

are known, through intensive archeological research, to have been used by the Indian fairly continuously for some ten thousand years. This stretches back into the Paleo or the dawning period of Indian history in the area to become Alabama. In Russell Cave the investigations, especially by The Smithsonian Institute and The National Geographic Society, found evidence of the use of part of a leg bone as an oil lamp. The evidence indicated its use some 5,000 years ago. There was also evidence of the use of fires under the ledge, in the living areas some 9,000 years ago. Some of the bowls under these ledges may have been cooking pots for use with hot pebbles from the fire. Others may have been used to prepare acorn bread.[1]

Another such shelter, very much like Russell Cave, is the Stanfield-Whorley Bluff. This bluff is located in the southern part of Colbert County. It is also near the north side of the new lake created by The Tennessee Valley Authority on Cedar Creek. This shelter or home of these early Indians in Alabama was researched by archeological teams from The University of Alabama.

In the DeSoto State Park, along the bluffy areas of the gorge or canyon of Little River there are several cave or ledge shelters that were used by the Indian. The ledge under Noccalula Falls in Gadsden is another such shelter.

In Franklin County, the 'Trapp Ledge' is an interesting and beautiful example of an early Indian shelter or habitation. Under this rock ledge, which is like a large natural bridge, is to be found pictographs-cut or scratched into the rock by these early Indians. Some of these pictures are of various 'Sun Circles' which relates to their religious expression. There is also a picture of a possible pre-historic water creature that they might have seen or encountered in an underground lake a few miles away. There are also two large grinding bowls that are carved or ground out in huge rocks or boulders along the floor of this shelter.

Another such shelter, and a famous one at that, is Kymulga or DeSoto Cave near Childersburg. This cave was visited and explored by the DeSoto Expedition. And it is the first such cave to be reported on to The United States Government. Indian Agent Benjamin Hawkins reported on it in 1796.

Another example is Manitou in Fort Payne. This cave was supposedly home for awhile for Sequoyah, who developed the Cherokee syllabary, and where he did part of this work.

Growing populations or enlarging hunting parties would begin to put space pressure on such cave and ledge dwelling places. Also the need to be more mobile to find sufficient game for food caused the need for other and more suitable or mobile type shelter. This was probably a

DeSoto Cave

contributing factor in the evolvement of tent or skin devised shelters. These in turn were very adaptable or accommodating to the increasing need to be on the move, in search of adequate sources of food. Many areas that could provide fine sources of food had no natural shelter such as caves or ledges for the Indian to use, thus making crude 'lean to' or skin devised shelters to be a necessity.

The earliest man simply found his shelter in a cave or under a ledge and used it as it was. The length of time he used it would depend upon the availability of food and water in the near vicinity, and to its desirability for such use. Many elements would be significant in determining its desirability for continuing use. Among these would be such factors as the amount of water dripping down from the ceiling. It is reasonable to assume that even in the earliest times, though conditions were most primitive, the creature comfort of those trying to sleep would be affected by cold water dripping on them. At first they probably moved or pulled a skin up over themselves. But suppose they were sleeping near the fire, the skin over them could cause them to be too hot to be comfortable. Hence, such a problem might cause the pondering, of a resourceful person, to find a possible solution. And such an irritation might well result in the evolvement of a crude lean-to shelter of skin to keep the water from dripping on them. Thus, such might have been part of the evolvement of tents or skin shelters that enabled them to be more mobile, and to use areas where there were no natural shelters. This would certainly open up good hunting-fishing-foraging areas that provided little or no natural shelters for these roving bands.

Lean-to shelter done by Joe B. Vann

Art work by Benny Yates

IV

ROAMING HUNTERS AND FORAGERS

The American Indian has been influenced and impacted by many things, but none so much as by his involvement in hunting. It was hunting for food, as the primary of all factors, that brought him out of eastern Asia into this continent or hemisphere. Thus, the American Indian is first and foremost a direct product of his hunting.

Hunting shaped his early life style. In the search for food, especially the pursuit of roaming herds, he was of necessity very mobile. Thus, to be fully mobile and make use of all areas with abundant food sources, the Indian needed to provide or carry his own shelter such as a quickly prepared 'lean to' with skins or bark covering or wigwam type shelters.

John E. Pfeifer in an article, "The Mysterious Rise and Decline of Monte Alban," in Feb. 1980 Smithsonian Magazine, says, "The Valley of Oaxaca's first migrants from a nearby valley—perhaps 50 persons—arrived some 10,000 to 15,000 years ago. They were nomads, taking nature pretty much as they found it, living on what the good earth offered, wild plants and wild animals. When local resources became scarce, they moved on to another part of the valley, rarely camping in one spot more than a month or so. This was the ancestral way of the hunter-gatherer, dating back at least two million years to the earliest members of the Genuo Homo."[1]

Between the period of primary dependence upon hunting, to the period of dependence upon agriculture, is a period known as 'foraging'. I suppose several factors influenced this development, such as the growing population, less game available in an area, and the growing awareness of the forageable food. Thus a period evolved in which foraging was very significant in the supply of food for the group.

The 'Shell Mound Culture' along the rivers of the area to become Alabama evolved and flourished prior to the 'Foraging Era'. It declined and faded away with the beginning of the Foraging Era.

The simple fact of supplying the food needs of the group was important, but an equally important thing was happening as they foraged. They were learning about more and more edible plants, herbs, seeds, and nuts. They were also developing skills of food preservation, such as the extraction of oil from nuts and the drying of fruits, etc. They were also gaining the interest, curiosity, and knowledge that was the foundation for the evolvement of the agriculture era.

Being so dependent upon hunting and so deeply involved in it, it is natural that he developed so many skills of the hunt. He learned the animals, their habitat, and their habits. He learned the signs that told him of the development of weather. He learned the lay of the land and became a master of direction. He developed a keen sense of danger. He developed the ability to track and stalk all kinds of animals, and even man too. He took the primary materials available to him-stone, bone, wood or plant and developed efficient tools to meet his needs. Surely one of the first feats of human technology—in the Paleo-era at that—was the Indian's development of the atlatl for far greater efficiency in throwing a spear. In *The First American* the author Robert Claiborne says,

> The invention that revolutionized Indian hunting was not an improved spear point but an innocent-looking wooden handle with a hooked tip: the spear thrower, generally called by its Aztec name of atlatl. It enabled a hunter to throw his spear hard enough to kill big game from a distance—instead of having to creep up on it and stab it.
>
> The atlatl in effect lengthened the throwing arm and, in a snap-the-whip action, increased the velocity of the spear, adding to its range and impact. The ring weights on the atlatl shaft were presumably added to adjust the "feel" to suit the hunter.
>
> Whether the Indians invented the atlatl themselves or acquired it from Asia is unknown, but it was used by them more than 10,000 years ago.[12] (Reprinted from The First American by Robert Claiborne, Time-Life Books, Inc., Alexandria, Va.)

The next most significant development in weapon or tool making, for the Indian, occurred about 3,000 years ago with the development of the bow and arrow. There is some indication that the Indian's bow and arrow raises an interesting possibility. It was re-invented by the Indian a thousand years or more after the Asians and Europeans had invented it. Or it is something learned from some visitors or explorers who came to these shores long, long before Columbus came.

The American Indian became deeply sensitive to the balance of nature. In awareness of the abundance of, or scarceness of game, and the presence of other hunters in the area, he would determine his stay. As a people the American Indian became very sensitive to any deterioration of the strength and beauty of the land. I have been deeply appreciative of the television spot of the Indian, in a canoe, looking at the litter along the shoreline, the dirty water, and the barren lake, and we see the sadness he feels and 'the teardrops fall'. The American Indian had a profound love and respect for 'Mother Earth'.

The hunting techniques the Plano period hunters used for such large scale killing required bands of perhaps 50 people. This would imply that some sort of rudimentary social organization with a sense of discipline had been developed, and that the concept of leadership had taken hold.[2]

Much of the leadership of The American Indian developed in the hunt. The skills directly involved in the kill or in the satisfaction of the needs of the group were part. But added to that the skill of working with others, the building of a team, the development of self reliance and we see how these often influenced the choice of leaders or chiefs.

Tragically, the Indian's love of, and involvement in hunting would be used as a corrupting force by the shrewd European traders. The traders took advantage of the Indian's love of trinkets, etc, and the lure of the relieving of some of the pressure of a difficult way of life to persuade the Indian to supply them furs. The great pressure of this demand for furs

Display of paint pot, skinning tool, pottery sherds, fishing weight, hoe, flaker, celt, part of atlatl, war clubs etc, from the author's collection, often used in programs.

would in time cause the near destruction of herds, especially deer, that had never been so threatened by the Indian prior to the coming of the white man. This pressure of the white man for furs corrupted the Indian from one of the world's finest conservationist into a hunting force that was destructive.[3]

V

CHANGING STYLES OF LIFE

Many things like the extinction of mammal herds, may influence changes in styles of life. Such has been the case in the long, and colorful span of Indian history in Alabama. In the dawning of civilization, the style of life was quite simple, though doubtlessly very rugged or difficult. The trappings or possessions were few and simple because the group was constantly on the move, or pursuing some herd for food and skins. The only way of transporting these few belongings was to carry them. (The first horses or beast of burden these Indians ever saw being used were probably those of the De Soto Expedition in 1540.) At this time there were two basic guiding principles influencing the Indian's life. These were (1) necessity, and (2) make use of what is available. The Indian no doubt knew the best quality of stone to work for tools, but if it were not available they would make use of what was at hand.

There is a flint quarry on Flint Creek near Decatur where it is supposed the Indian came over a period of eons, and dug or quarried flint for spears, blades or knives, arrows, etc. There is evidence that this flint was carried over a very large surrounding area. This flint was scattered across the area in several ways. Hunters would naturally lose spears and arrows in the hunt. Roving hunter bands might trade with other bands they encountered. And some teams may have come from far off places to quarry flint for their tribe's use.

These teams, at first on a special assignment to meet a need of the tribe, would, in time, evolve into a specialty or trade. Some of these would develop a special interest in this kind of thing and see in it a medium of livelihood. Thus trading would evolve as a matter of specialization and with it would develop a trade language such as the Maubilian Trade language.

In time there would be persons who traded in flint, others who traded in sea shells, others in furs or copper, etc.[1]

It was to these Indian traders that the first white traders related. They would be the primary ones who would seek to supply the demands for furs, etc.

In *Sun Circles and Human Hands* the authors speak of the significant items of various areas that became part of a trade system. These items include "obsidian from the Rocky Mountains region, pipestone from the great red pipestone quarries of Minnesota or Wisconsin, steatite and mica from the Appalachians, copper from the region of the Great Lakes and elsewhere, shells from the Gulf of Mexico and the Atlantic, dentalium and abalone shells from the Pacific Coast."[2]

A part of the development of traders was the evolvement of a trade language. In this area and across the Southeast it was the Maubilian Trade language. It seems to have been widely used in the Gulf area. It was an important and common means of communication. A part of this, no doubt, was the evolvement of a fairly universal sign language which was the most basic of all inter-tribal communication. The Indian evidently used sign language extensively in trading.

The Indian regulated his stay in an area by the availability of seasonal nuts and fruits and game. He also regulated his family—the number of children and the size of the hunting party or groups—on this basis. The size of the hunting group was also influenced by the game sought and the weapons to be used. In the era of the very large animals, and of very crude tools the hunting party needed to be quite large to be efficient. It would be necessary for several hunters, maybe a dozen or more, to work together with such tools as clubs, spears, and traps to kill a large elephant, sloth, saber tooth tiger, or other large Paleo period animal. On the other hand a hunter equipped with a throw stick-spear and atlatl was much more efficient in the kill and thus the hunting group might be reduced. And equipped with the bow and arrow the hunter was still more efficient and was able to stalk such game as deer, bear, and turkey, etc. alone.

Group leadership would be influenced by the skills of the hunt and of guiding. Those who developed great efficiency in knowledge of game and of the hunt, and of leading a group often became the chief of the group. After white men came, many Indians became famous because of, or through their great skills as guides.

Agriculture development and permanent settlements

When the Indian began to develop the skills of agriculture, he also began to further change his style of life. Through even limited farming, the Indian was able to supplement his food supply derived from hunting-foraging. But this pursuit of agriculture would make it necessary to stay in one area, at least through the growing season. It probably evolved to a ten to twenty year stay, depending on the strength and lay of the land being cultivated. Evidence indicates the first farming was the

Temple Mound at Moundville, Alabama

growing of maize or corn probably in Mexico about 7000 years ago.[3] As the Indian took seeds of the maize and planted it and cultivated it, he realized more return of food than when gathering wheat that chanced to grow wild. In time from this he would learn that other wild plants he used for food as beans, peas, squash, etc. would also produce more food if he cultivated them. I believe agricultural knowledge and skills spread from group to group in a similar manner to that of the building of various mounds. In fact, I believe most social or cultural skills spread in such manner, which we call acculturation.

In time the area that was to become Alabama was 'dotted with mounds of all manner of shapes and sizes, and everywhere smoke rose from the eternal fires of the Council House, in stately columns through leafy canopies to the heights above.[4]

As he stayed in one place, he began to develop better, or more comfortable and livable housing or shelter. In time this housing in Alabama and the Southeast seems to have been generally the style of the simulated village at Moundville, or like that to be seen at the Oknaluftee Living Indian Village in Cherokee, North Carolina. It seems, from the early colonial writers, that this was the style of homes the Indians were

This picture is of The Indian Mound in Florence, Alabama. This mound is the only one left here, where once there were probably several, such as at Moundville. This particular mound is thought to have been primarily a site of a chief's residence.

generally using when the first white men came into this area. These huts were made of logs being placed side by side with one end in the ground, and interwoven with cane and vines. It was then plastered over inside and out with mud. The tops were made of small poles covered with swamp grass or reeds, or bark. This development of better housing resulted in larger families and many more living together in one area or village. Now, instead of the simple, roving hunter-forager bands of a few dozen, the villages might have a hundred or so, or even thousands.

The Council House and The Great Council Fire

The evolvement of villages or towns, resulted in the need for new styles of leadership to that which led the old roving hunter-forager bands. This called for greater skills to develop and sustain community. To be sure the skills of the hunter and warrior continued to be important in selecting the

Simulated Village at Mound State Monument

village leaders or chiefs. As the village developed there evolved with it a council square and council house. The arrangement of these villages around the council square and council house was somewhat like towns, of the present day, developed around the courthouse in county seat towns. The council square was the place for such social affairs as dancing, or athletic activities, or contests such as ball play or chunky. The council house was the place where the men, who were in good standing in the village or tribe, met regularly, in some cases even daily, with their leaders or chiefs to discuss the concerns and needs of the village.

The village council met to discuss all concerns of the community and decide on a course of action. The decision had to be virtually unanimous before the course of action was determined. Thomas Jefferson was a serious student of the Indian style of government and was obviously impressed with it.[5]

Thomas Jefferson in describing the Indian style of government says, "The several towns or families that compose a tribe, have a chief who presides over it, and the several tribes composing a nation have a chief who presides over the whole nation. These chiefs are generally a man advanced in years, and distinguished by their prudence and abilities in council. The matters which merely regard a town or family are settled by the chief and principal men of the town: those which regard a tribe, such as the appointment of head warriors or captains, and settling differences between different towns and families, are regulated at a meeting or council of the chiefs from the several towns; and those which regard the whole nation, such as the making war, concluding peace, or forming alliances with the neighboring nations, are deliberated on and determined in a national council composed of the chiefs of the tribe, attended by the head warriors and a number of the chiefs from the towns, who are his counsellors. In every town there is a council house, where the chief and old men of the town assemble, when occasion requires, and consult what is proper to be done. Every tribe has a fixed place for the chiefs of the towns to meet and consult on the business of the tribe: and in every nation there is what they call the central council house, or central council fire, where the chiefs of the several tribes, with the principal warriors, convene to consult and determine on their national affairs. When any matter is proposed in the national council, it is common for the chiefs of the several tribes to consult thereon apart with their counsellors, and, when they have agreed, to deliver the opinion of the tribe at the national council: and as their government seems to rest wholly on persuasion, they endeavor, by mutual concessions, to obtain unanimity."[6] (Reprinted from notes on Virginia by Thomas Jefferson, edited by William Peden. Permission granted by The University of North Carolina Press.)

In the *History of Alabama* the author, A. B. Moore says the Indian tribes developed social structures very much like the early Germanic Tribes.[1]

In the case of the Creeks, and not unlike many other tribes, the village began to feel the need to consult with and to cooperate with other nearby villages. In time the very large and formidable Creek Confederacy was intact and spreading across most of central Alabama and Georgia.

One of the interesting things, that seemed to be universal among the Indian, was that a small group within a village or of a tribe might decide to move into, and become a part of another tribe or nation. Such moves might be influenced by security concerns, economic interests, religious or political ideas or concerns. A small band of the Natchez left central Mississippi, probably for security reasons, and came into the Creek Confederacy and settled near presentday Talledega. This was one of the ways that ideas or concepts and skills spread among the Indians. In the colonial period the Creek Confederacy included quite a list of small tribes or parts of tribes, such as the Natchez, Coushattas, Yamasees, Alibamos, Yuchi, Eufalas, and Hitchitis, etc.

Thomas Jefferson observed that the Indian lived somewhat in a state of anarchy in that, "their only controuls are their manners, and that moral sense of right and wrong, which, like the sense of tasting and feeling, in every man makes a part of his nature. An offence against these is punished by contempt, by exclusion from society, or where the case is serious, as that of murder, by the individuals whom it concerns. Imperfect as this species of coercion may seem, crimes are very rare among them; insomuch that were it made a question, whether no law as among the savage Americans, or too much law, as among the civilized Europeans, submits man to the greatest evil, one who has seen both conditions of existence would pronounce it to be the last."[8]

Codwallader Colden says, "One of the strong traits that developed among the Indian was the rule of revenge. It became a matter of great honor to carry out very severe revenge on those who seriously offended, as murderors and enemies."[9]

In the development of Indian Nations or states, the laws or resolutions were not carried out by compulsion or force and their punishments mere shame and to be despised. Each nation is an absolute Republic by itself, governed in all public affairs of war and peace by the Sachem or Old Men, whose authority and power is gained by and consists wholly in the opinion the rest of the nation have of their wisdom and integrity.[10]

Cultural and Sports Events

The development of the villages also involved the time to develop other interests and skills that could not be pursued in the earlier, more demanding culture of the hunter-forager. Artistic, games, and religious ceremony pursuits were particularly part of this evolvement. With more leisure time on hand it was natural that games might be developed that would replace some of the excitement of the hunt and kill as well as develop physical strength and prowess. Ballplay and chunkey were two such games. Surely the most famous such games ever played in this area was that of the Creek village at or near Fort Mitchell, who so entertained General LaFayette, who had come for a visit in Alabama.[11]

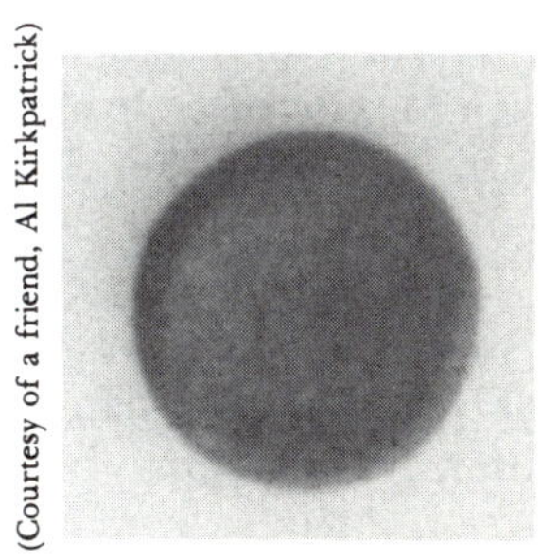

(Courtesy of a friend, Al Kirkpatrick)

Chunkey

According to some, chunkey was played by rolling a round disk of stone and the braves would throw spear-like shafts at it. This provided them an opportunity to show their hunter and warrior skills.

Ballplay on the other hand was played with a ball made of deer skin and stuffed with hair. Two groups of men played a contact sport somewhat as our football or soccer in an effort to get the ball over a goal line. This was a very rough and tumble sport and was often played between villages or tribes and drew large crowds from the villages to watch the games. It was a very social event, often involving much ceremony, pomp, and celebration.

This was also the period of the development of the burial and ceremonial mounds and temples. There are many mounds all across the state that give evidence of the universal impact of this stage of evolvement of Indian life styles or cultures. Many of these mounds have been completely destroyed by farming, construction, or by treasure hunters. Two such mounds my Father-in-law, William Dupree Madry, dug into some half-century ago, were completely obliterated by treasure hunters. Mr. Madry found a pipe somewhat like the pipe illustrated in the picture I made of one made by the Cherokee in Oknaluftee or Living Indian Village in Cherokee, North Carolina. He also found what he was sure was a bar of gold. These mounds were on the Basden farm between the Trinity Mountain and the Tennessee River. Some years later these mounds were utterly destroyed, evidently by some out of state treasure hunters.

The finest example of the evolvement of the Mound Builders Culture in Alabama is Moundville State Monument. We owe a great debt of gratitude to those who with great foresight worked to preserve and develop this fine park for the benefit and enjoyment of all. Evidence indicates this was the principal village of a chiefdom consisting of a number of other villages scattered across the area of about fifty miles around. It seems these villages were deserted when the DeSoto Expedition came through the area, for otherwise his chronicler would surely have made some mention of them. Some hold these Mound Builders had migrated from Mexico or an area closeby that was strongly influenced by the Mexican culture about 1000 or 1100 A.D. That chiefdom lasted some 300 years. I believe the building of mounds in general, not the Moundville village in particular, was a great cultural impact or influence that swept through most of the groups and tribes. There may be, and probably was, an originating group for whom it was far more significant and intensive, and it may be this group developed the Moundville Village.

There is no single way to describe an individual Indian. They, like all

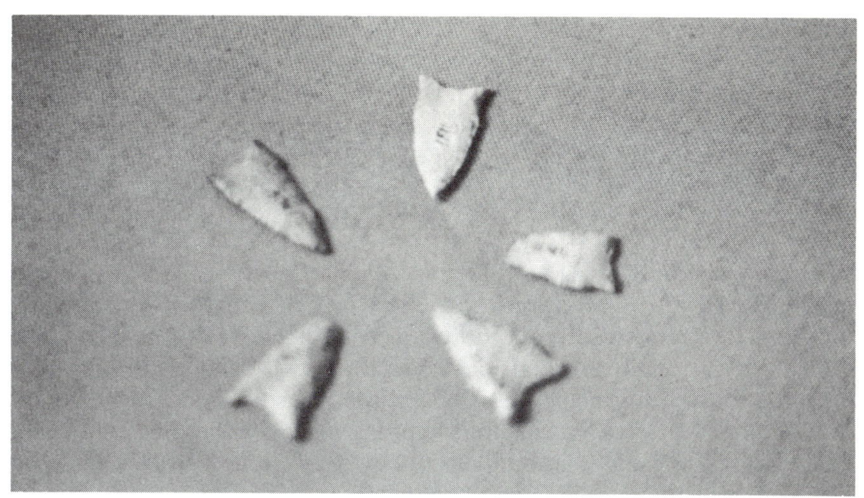

Dalton points from the author's collection.

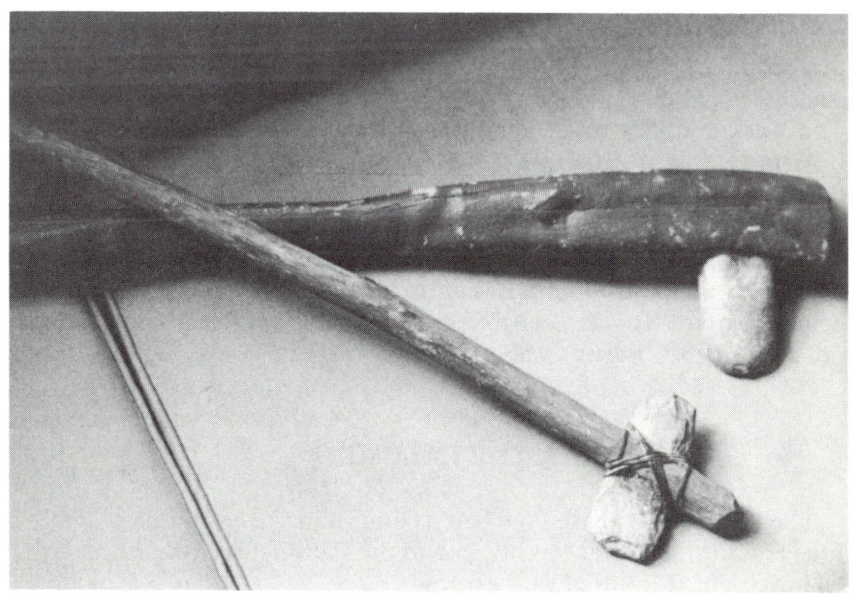

Ax and warclub from the author's collection.

other people are varied, some were noble, others were evil. Each needs to be judged according to the culture that influences his life. There were customs influencing the Indian that white people had difficulty understanding. One of the most significant of these being that the Indian could not conceive of individual ownership of land.

Religious Rituals

I believe from the earliest time the Indian expressed faith in a Higher Being or Spirit, a Great Spirit, or The Giver of Breath. From my own infancy, I have been influenced by a picture, 'The Appeal to The Great Spirit'—that hung by my bedside. It was the picture of an Indian man on horseback with uplifted arms as in prayer or praise to God. By the time of the Mound Temples the religious expression under the direction of the Shaman or medicine man had become quite elaborate. One of the most significant of these religious ceremonies was 'The Green Corn Dance.' This was a harvest or Thanksgiving Ceremony. It took place at the time the corn first became ready for use—the roasting ear stage I believe. It was a time of feasting, of dancing, and great rejoicing, and a time of Thanksgiving unto God. James Adair held the view that this ceremony was very much like a harvest time feast of the ancient Hebrews.

The Green Corn Dance or Busk Celebration was of several days duration. It began with a fast and included the Shaman or priest rebuilding the fire of the Temple. This was a high moment in which all the people of the chiefdom or nation were to participate, for fire was considered a gift of, or even the very Presence of their God with them. The Busk ended with all joining in a feast of the new corn.[12]

Alvin M. Josephy, Jr. In *The Indian Heritage of America* says as a part of the Green Corn Ceremony, "Old fires were extinguished, worn pottery was broken, villages were cleaned, and most old feuds and animosities were ended."[13]

It was from the traditions of ending old feuds that the term 'bury the hatchet' comes. It was probably ritualized, but was also very real and practical in the Indian village.

THE CALUMET

The Calumet or Peace Pipe had its origins in the distant past. There is little historical record of its origin and the Calumet Song and Dance that were part of the Ritual that evolved.

Among some of the tribes a secret Rite of The Calumet evolved.

This Hopewell platform pipe—Calumet—was given to me by my neighbor, Mrs. T. L. Lindsey, Sr. that I might share it with many persons in speaking engagements.

The Calumet became part of The Celebration of The Green Corn Dance. At a high moment—the real climax—an honored elder of the Tribe would come forth and smoke a few puffs on the Calumet and then offer it unto The Great Spirit.

The Calumet was used in personal quiet time or communion experiences with The Great Spirit. And it was used in making agreements. When William Penn began the Pennsylvania Colony he developed a close, friendly relationship with the Indians of the area. He worked out an agreement with the Indians to buy land for the colony and they smoked the Calumet as a seal. This same kind of thing was done between the Indian leaders of the Mobile area and Bienville about 1703.

The smoking of The Calumet between persons or groups sealing the agreement was a most solemn event. It meant in part—"His word is his bond." There is no record, I know of, of an Indian who thus smoked The Calumet—giving his pledge—ever violating it.

CELEBRATION OF THE AMERICAN INDIAN

This was a Program written and directed by the author for The North Alabama Conference School of Mission.

A high moment has come. The time of Celebration has come. We have gathered to Celebrate the strong life, the noteworthy achievements, The Great Spirit of Hope of The American Indian.

We welcome you! We invited each of the seven Bands or Tribal Groups of Indians of Alabama, The Alabama Commission of Indian Affairs, leaders of The North Alabama Conference of The United Methodist Church, The School of Mission, and the public to share in this Celebration. We are glad you are here!

Our purpose in this Celebration is to bring leaders of The Indian

Groups, The United Methodist Church, and the community together to get to know each other, to talk with each other, and to work together for the good of all. Here we would do well to remember, 'Love is a two way street'.

Our immediate purpose is to Celebrate one aspect of the common life of The American Indian—The Celebration of The Busk. This Celebration was one of the most common or universal to all the Indians. The Busk, or Green Corn Dance, was, I believe, the most sacred, most universal, most significant ceremony of The Indian World.

The Busk was an annual celebration of the harvest of green corn or roasting ears. It was a Thanksgiving Celebration of The Gift of Corn. Early in The Celebration an offering of corn is made as a Burnt Offering unto The Great Spirit, The Giver and Sustainer of Life!

Tom Queen, Director of The United Methodist Mission to The Cherokee Indian of Cherokee, N. C. will lead our Invocation in his native Cherokee language. Those who have seen The Cherokee Drama, "Unto These Hills" were touched by the moving scene of the execution of Tsali, and the last moment allowing of the little son of Tsali to be spared. That little boy was the forefather of my dear friend, Tom Queen. Tom, come now and lead us in a time of prayer.

The Busk was usually of four to eight days. Today we are doing The Busk in scenes of short glimpses. Our intent is to do in sacred fashion the most significant parts of The Busk to help us get a better feel for, and appreciation of The American Indian's life and culture.

In the First Day, The Shaman or Beloved Man comes early in the morning to The Ceremonial Plaza to begin the Busk. The first step is to extinguish the old Sacred Fire. He then directs young braves in sweeping and cleaning The Ceremonial Plaza. As the cleaning is finished two young braves will come bringing four logs for The Sacred Fire. These four logs will be placed in the four Cardinal Directions. Then two more young braves will come bringing four ears of new corn as an offering of The First Fruits unto The Great Spirit, The Giver and Sustainer of Life! These young men now help The Beloved Man to prepare The Sacred Fire.

In the Second Day, Honored, older Women of The Tribe come forth to The Ceremonial Plaza and prepare the Pot of Black-Drink. This Sacred Drink was used in preparation for strenuous activities and ceremonies, etc. to purify their bodies and clear their minds as they begin their Council Meetings, and especially as part of The Busk. In this Ritual, in The Busk, all the men would participate in this cleansing experience. Today we are asking The Chiefs to symbolize this sacred event. As the Ritual of The Black-Drink ends, The Beloved Man comes forth to admonish all the people to spend some time in fasting as further preparation. The Beloved

Man as the village or Tribal Spiritual Leader strongly recommended fasting as a significant spiritual discipline.

Then there was time for dancing. We have asked Loretta Weaver of The Mowa Band of Choctaw Indians, Director of Indian Education in Washington County, a teacher in The McIntosh School system, leader of The Mowa Dance Team, and wife of Chief Gallasneed Weaver the Chairman of The Alabama Commission of Indian Affairs to come and explain Tribal Dances that might be done as part of The Celebration of The Busk.

In the Third Day, the emphasis is on a time of being together, visiting, sharing fellowship, etc. We now turn to Chief Joseph Stewart of The Echota Cherokees to come and tell us The Cherokee Legend of Creation. And now we ask Chief Travis Staggs of The Northeast Alabama Cherokee to come and explain Stick Ball, a beloved athletic interest or sport of The American Indian and with the help of several youth to demonstrate it.

In the Fourth Day, we reach the real high point, the most sacred time of The Busk—The Lighting of The Sacred Fire and of worship and of communion with The Great Spirit. The Beloved Man will come forth into The Ceremonial Plaza and light The Sacred Fire and then sing a beloved hymn in his native Cherokee language. Loretta Weaver will sing a beloved hymn in the Choctaw language.

The Beloved Man comes forth into The Ceremonial Plaza for one of the most sacred moments in the Indian world—The Calumet Offering unto The Great Spirit.

Tom Queen will sing The Lord's Prayer as Loretta Weaver does it symbolically in Indian Sign Language.

The Beloved Man comes forth into The Ceremonial Plaza to talk with The People about Forgiving those who have offended us, and Being Forgiven, about living together in harmony and Peace as Brothers.

The Annual Council meets around The Great Council Fire as The Annual Busk comes to an end.

GREAT PRINCIPLES OF THE INDIAN

Intensely Spiritual Cultures—Religion Permeates All.
Live in Harmony with All Things.
In His Natural State, He Was a Very Good Neighbor.
Regarded the Earth as Beloved Mother Earth.
Great Love of Freedom.
Widely Practiced the Basics of Pure Democracy.
A Disciplined People—A Society of Law, By the People.
He Made Use of What Was Available to Meet His Needs.

VI

ENCOUNTER—WHITE MAN—DESOTO EXPEDITION

In 1540 few Indians in the area, destined to become the State of Alabama, had ever seen a white man or 'paleface'. An exception to this would be the limited expedition in the Mobile area of Narvaez. In July 1540, the Cherokee Indians of Northeast Alabama (some contend they entered Alabama along the Tennessee River, others say along the Coosa River.) witnessed a strange sight, an army of some 600-1,000 palefaces wearing glittering armor, many on horseback, with a large number of Indians carrying burdens and driving a large herd of hogs along. This was the Hernando DeSoto Expedition from Spain whose purpose was to find Indian treasures and take them, as Spanish Conquistors had previously done in South America, to return to Spain to sustain a standard of living that the Spanish could not, or would not sustain for themselves.[1]

Such exploits, unfortunately was not apart from any relation to, or with, the church. The Church, possibly out of fear for its survival, participated in, or at least consented to such as the basis for 'progress sake'. The presence of the Church was in the DeSoto Expedition and doubtlessly related their interests in, and prayers for the success of the same, as being the desire to sustain the church and through such expeditions expose pagans and savages to the gospel. It is difficult, for me impossible, to see how such could evolve, or could ever be thought to appear to these so called savages as 'Good News'.

The priests no doubt justified the stealing, pillaging, enslaving and even murdering done by the DeSoto Expedition as necessary means to a supposed noble end.

In this same light Anson West justifies the driving out the Indians that the whites might use the land to high and noble purpose. West in History of Methodism says, "Alabama is no longer menaced and down trodden by savages. It was a joyous day, and the consummation of a glorious achievement was reached when this lovely land was redeemed from the dominion of savages. It is a matter of profound regret that this goodly land was allowed to remain so long under the blight and waste of savage cruelty and superstition.[2]

There are various views about the size of the DeSoto Expedition and their point of entry into Alabama. W. G. Brown says there were 600 men under the command of DeSoto.[3] On the other hand, Albert James Pickett says there were some 1,000 soldiers under DeSoto's command. Pickett contends the Expedition entered Alabama along the Coosa River from the area of present day Rome, Georgia.[4,5] Whereas others contend, among whom is the DeSoto Commission Report, that the Expedition entered Alabama area from Tennessee into the Tennessee River area. (Part of the problem in this is centered around the village of Chiaha and a custom of the Indians to move villages about, in particular as the land was worked out by their farming, and carry the old name to the new location. There are various sites held to be Chiaha and all may be right.)

DeSoto was looking for gold and there was 'gold in them thar hills' through which, or near which his expedition travelled. And there still is, though DeSoto didn't get any of it! Legend has it there were Indian

This picture of the historical marker about Coosa Village that was located on the bank of the Coosa River in the edge of presentday Childersburg, Alabama. These Cooshatta Indians were closely related to the Alibamos Indians who were mainly in the area of Montgomery. They became part of the Creek Confederacy.

Mural of DeSoto group entering Coosa Village in 1540 (on wall in Childersburg, Al)

runners who went ahead of this expedition warning the villages about DeSoto and the purposes of his expedition among them. And that thus warned the villages hid their valuables, especially any gold. He did take whatever treasure of the Indian he found, the most valuable being the river pearls the Indian had found and used as jewelry or ornamentation. Though the most significant Indian treasure DeSoto took was food. I am sure it is reasonable to assume that many of the villages through which the DeSoto Expedition passed suffered the loss of most of their food supplies, and even worse, many members of the tribe or village were taken as slaves and hostages. The hostages were village or tribe leaders or chiefs who were taken to assure safe passage of the DeSoto Expedition through their areas. They generally were released when hostages from the next village or chiefdom were taken.

For various reasons, such as the need for rest and recuperation of both men and animals, DeSoto decided to stay about a month in Coosa Village, which is nearby presentday Childersburg, Alabama. The village was along the east bank of the Coosa River and along the mouth of the creek. From the writings of DeSoto's Chronicler it seems this village had fine fields of maize and other food crops probably including peas, beans, squash and melons. According to the view of Wilcomb E. Washburn in *The Indian in America* about half of the Indians were farmers when the first whites came among them. The others still lived in the old ancestral ways of foraging, hunting, and fishing.[6]

The Gentleman of Elvas says, "The Cacique (Chief of the Coosa Village) came out to receive him (DeSoto) at the distance of two crossbow shots from the towns, borne in a litter on the shoulders of his principal

This picture is of DeSoto encountering the Chief of The Cherokee Nation in his trek through their country of North Georgia, Tennessee, and North Alabama. This scene is from the outdoor drama, "Unto These Hills". (Courtesy of The Cherokee Historical Society, Cherokee, North Carolina.)

men, seated on a cushion, and covered with a mantle of marten skins, of the size and shape of a woman's shawl: on his head he wore a diadem of plumes, and he was surrounded by many attendants playing upon flutes and singing. Coming to where the governor (DeSoto) was, he made his obeisance, and followed it by these words; 'Powerful lord, superior to every other of the earth: although I come but now to meet you, it is a long time since I have received you in my heart. That was done the first day I heard of you, with so great desire to serve, please and give you contentment.'"[7]

David H. Corkran in *The Creek Frontier* says, "After 25 days in Coosa, in which the Spaniards consumed all the town's old and new corn, they moved southward."[8]

It was in the Coosa Village that DeSoto's men first enjoyed a treat of corn bread cooked in nut oil (like that which was destined to become a much sought after item with fine cooks of the day, and an important item in the developing trade of the Indians with the white men.) and with hickory nut meats in it. I would certainly think those who ate some liked it much! It must have greatly impressed these Spaniards that these people live about as well as the people of Europe. Certainly one of the most common tools to be found in Indian village sites all over the area is 'nutting stones'. I have found many of them, which certainly underlines the widespread and very significant use of hickory nuts, pecans, chestnuts, walnuts, etc. as a part of the Indian's food supply.[9]

This long stay of DeSoto probably means they drew heavily on the produce in the fields and the village storehouses of the Coosa Indians. It would take vast amounts of food to feed some 1,000 men, soldiers, slaves, etc. daily for about a month. I suppose as DeSoto prepared to leave, he took whatever other available food there was and hostages and left.

Soon after leaving the Village of Coosa, DeSoto's Expedition entered the Province or Chiefdom of Maubila, of Chief Tuscaloosa. According to Cyrus Thomas in *History of North America* these Maubilian Indians of the Chiefdom of Tuscaloosa were of the Choctaw linage.[10]

This picture is of two nutting stones, which were very important tools in the Indian village. They were also very important in the trade that developed between the whites and the Indians, as the nut oil was a trade item. These nutting stones usually have an indenture on both sides of the stones and some of them have several on the same side.

This picture taken by the author, of the mural in the Rotunda at The State Capital in Montgomery, Alabama. It is of Chief Tuscaloosa confronting DeSoto.

Chief Tuscaloosa was well informed, by his runners, of the movement, activities, and purpose of the DeSoto Expedition. He doubtlessly knew of DeSoto's search for Indian treasures, of his treatment of the Indians, and of his extensive use of slaves and hostages. Tuscaloosa most likely also knew of the Narvaez Expedition, and he probably had personal reasons for bitterness about such expeditions among his people. All of this probably was part of the reason Tuscaloosa laid a plan to encounter DeSoto in battle in his fortified Village of Maubila. He no doubt longed for revenge on these intruding 'pale faces' and to rid his people of such a menace.

In a show of peace and friendship, Chief Tuscaloosa, in royal fashion, was brought on a litter some distance to meet and greet DeSoto and return with him to Maubila.[11] He greeted DeSoto with, "Mighty Chief, I bid you welcome. I greet you as I would my brother. It is needless to talk long. What I have to say can be said in few words. You shall know how willing I am to serve you. I am thankful for the things which you have sent me, chiefly because they were yours. I am now ready to comply with your desires."[12]

In October, 1540 the DeSoto Expedition accompanied by Chief Tuscaloosa entered the Village of Maubila. According to Albert James Pickett in *History of Alabama* there were some 80 fine and large houses in Maubila, each of which could accomodate 1,000 men. These houses fronted a large public square and were surrounded by a high wall of large logs set in the ground and having towers on it at about 50 paces apart. A fierce battle broke out between DeSoto's forces and the forces of Chief Tuscaloosa. After several hours the Village of Tuscaloosa had been burned and utterly destroyed and most of Tuscaloosa's people were killed. The overwhelming victory of DeSoto's forces over the forces of Tuscaloosa, for the most part was due to the superior 'Iron Age' equipment—iron armor, etc.—of DeSoto's forces versus the 'Stone Age' equipment of Tuscaloosa's forces. The fires set by DeSoto's men no doubt trapped many of Tuscaloosa's warriors possibly including Chief Tuscaloosa himself, and caused a state of panic among those who could engage in battle. There are various estimates of the loss suffered by Maubila which run from some 2,500 to some 11,000. There is disagreement as to what happened to the noble and powerful Chief Tuscaloosa, he may have been burned to death in one of the buildings of Maubila. After about a month of recuperation at this place, the much weakened DeSoto Expedition moved up the Tombigbee River and into present day Mississippi. With him he carried almost nothing of the treasures he had taken from the Indians of Alabama.[13] We can only speculate about the suffering of the Indian Villages because of DeSoto's plundering of their food supplies.

These fine artifacts are from my son, Danny Ross Phillips' collection, with whom I have shared many happy hours looking for artifacts.

VII

SIX SIGNIFICANT INDIAN NATIONS IN ALABAMA AND THE SOUTHEAST

Across the eons of Indian life and culture, in the area that became Alabama, there have doubtlessly been many powerful and significant chiefdom developments in the area. In the closing era, the historical period of Indian domination of the area, there were at least six significant groups, tribes, or nations that shared in this history. The period of which we speak is the sixteenth, seventeenth, and eighteenth centuries; or the period from the Narvaez and DeSoto Expedition to the great influx of white settlers about 1800. Most of these tribes or nations were not entirely or exclusively in the area that became the State of Alabama, for they were spread out in an area that became part of several different states. Such as the Cherokee Nation, that in its zenith was spread into parts of what is today Alabama, Tennessee, North Carolina, South Carolina, and Georgia. (And some enlarge that to include part of Kentucky and West Virginia.)[1]

In the period of the DeSoto Expedition there were at least two very significant chiefdoms in Alabama. The Coosa Village (site of the present-day city of Childersburg), seems to have been the dominant village or influence in the Coosa or Cooshatta Chiefdom. This chiefdom covered much of the area of Alabama through which DeSoto's Expedition passed. This chiefdom seems to have covered most of the Coosa valley from the area of present-day Rome, Georgia and Guntersville, Alabama down to about Selma, Alabama.[2] (From the notes of DeSoto's chronicler, which represent the oldest, most significant historical data on the Coosa Chiefdom of Alabama.) In the Selma area DeSoto entered the Maubilian Chiefdom of Chief Tuscaloosa. This chiefdom seems to have covered most of the southwest area of Alabama. This probably included the river valley areas of the Alabama River, the Tombigbee River, the lower Warrior River basin, the Cahaba River, and the Mobile River. This chiefdom may have evolved from the Moundville Chiefdom.

When the French opened the Mobile area to trading and settlements these Maubilians were still significant, though probably not nearly so much so as under Chief Tuscaloosa. We wonder if the widespread use of the Maubilian Trade Language at this time doesn't indicate the Maubilian Chiefdom was very much involved in the trading business. It may well mean the Maubilians were the most ancient, and most significant influence in the development of trade among the Indian tribes and nations of the Southeast. This may be one of the reasons why Iberville and Bienville chose the Mobile area to establish strong trading interest for France. Considering the Indian's natural esteem for traders and the Maubilian's involvement in trade, this would certainly be a wise move, and would give them a better chance of getting established in the area.[3]

Prior to the coming of the Creek, the Alibamos Indians were in villages from the Cahaba River confluence with the Alabama, up the Alabama River to, or just beyond the confluence of Coosa and Tallapoosa Rivers. It seems the principal village of this chiefdom was near the site of Fort Toulouse. Based on the location of their forts-trading posts it seems the French found the Maubilians, the Choctaw, and the Alibamons more receptive and hospitable than the Creeks and Chickasaws with whom they also had trade relations. These Alibamons, who had been overrun by the Creeks, of their own choice had stayed in the area and had become part of the very formidable Creek Confederacy.[4]

Anson West in *History of Methodism in Alabama* says of the evolvement of the Creek Confederacy, "The Muscogees, a migratory and aggressive tribe, emigrated from point to point, first from Mexico to Red River (Oklahoma, Texas, and Arkansas area); and finally, in the course of their rambling and usurpation, they supplant the Alabamas and take possession of the country on the Alabama River and on farther west. The Alabamas were allowed by the Muscogees to return to their homes and towns on the Alabama River, but in a state of subordination. From the Ohio River came the Tookabatcha, and obtained a settlement on the Tallapoosa River. The Tuskegees reached and obtained a habitation between the Coosa and Tallapoosa Rivers, immediately above the junction. The Ozeailles settled the plains through which runs the magnificent Hatchee Chubbee Creek, a few miles above the grounds of the Tuskegee. A remnant of the Natchez Tribe, which escaped from the city of Natchez, on the Mississippi River, settled on the Coosa River about the Talledega Creek. The Uchees settled on the creeks which bear their name today, and which empty into the Chattahoochee River. The Alabama, the Tookabatcha, the Tuskegees, the Ozeailles, the Natchez, and the Uchees were all dominated by the Muscogees, confederated in their government, and subordinated to their laws and interests. These tribes, thus allied, were called by the general name of Creeks."[5]

The Seminole Tribe, formed in part by a rebel element of the Upper

Creeks, had part of their history in Alabama. From their first formation following the Yamasee War between the Creeks and South Carolina, the Seminole were participants in the Creek Confederacy. It seems that Chief Alexander McGillivray was the principal chief of the Seminole also. In some treaties with the United States the Seminole were included with the Creek Confederacy. This relation continued into the 1830's when the issue of Removal was so very heated.

The Choctaw Nation was, in part, in southwest Alabama, along the Tombigbee, lower Warrior and Cahaba, and Alabama, and the Mobile Rivers. The larger part of the Choctaw Nation was across the southern part of Mississippi. The Maubilians became part of this nation.

Angie Debo in *The Rise and Fall of The Choctaws* tells of various legends of the development of the Choctaw Nation in this area. One of these held that the Choctaws and Chickasaws were once one tribe led by two brothers, Chahtah and Chikasah, who became founders of their respective tribes. The Choctaw, Chickasaws, Creeks, and Seminole were all of the Muskogean linguistic stock (Some hold these are related to the ancient Iroquois, based on the similarity of many root words in the two

This picture of the historical marker of The Chickasaw Old Fields. This is evidence of how from time to time the boundaries of Indian Nations changed.

groups.) In the passage of time these tribes had evolved many differences in language, ceremonies, and customs.[5a]

The Chickasaw Nation covered northeastern Alabama, northern Mississippi, and part of Western Tennessee (mostly that west of the Tennessee River). At times the Chickasaws Nation extended to the area of Alabama where present-day Whitesburg Drive crossed the Tennessee River. This area was known as the Chickasaw Old Fields.

The boundaries between the various Indian Nations or Confederacies were often disputed and also was changed from time to time by war or other mediums of agreement.

The Cherokee Nation was in part in the northeastern section of Alabama, in part of Tennessee, North Carolina, South Carolina, and Georgia. As white settlers encroached on the northeast border of the Cherokee Nation, the Cherokee gradually pushed farther and farther into Alabama, until they controlled most of the area from about Piedmont, Gadsden, Cullman, and to the Tennessee River in the area of the Quad-Cities.

The Cherokee, Choctaw, Chickasaw, Creek, and Seminole, all of which were at times, in part, in the Alabama area, became known as 'The Five Civilized Tribes'. Of this Alvin M. Josephy, Jr. in *The Heritage of America* comments, "A name applied to them in the nineteenth century because of their adoption—more rapidly than other tribes—of much of the white man's civilization. Many of them raised stock, tilled large farms, built European-style homes (an excellent example of this is John Ross, The Principal Chief of The Cherokee Nation.), and even owned Negro slaves like their white neighbors. They dressed like white men, learned the white's methods, skills, and arts, started small industries, and became Christians. In 1821, Sequoyah, a remarkable Cherokee, invented a syllabary for his people. The Cherokees published a newspaper, adopted a formal constitution and legislature for their nation and, like most of the other Five Tribes, put their own law codes in writing."[6]

Chief Sequoyah with the Cherokee sylabary he invented.

VIII

THE 'TOMEBECBE' COUNTRY

France set her sights on establishing her power in the Gulf of Mexico, up the Mississippi River and across the colonial frontier to her stronghold of The Great Lakes region. The Primary goal being to establish France's economic interests and contain the English between the Applachian and the Atlantic. To achieve this required good relations with the various Indian Tribes.

Pierre LeMoyne, Sieur de Iberville and his brother, Jean Baptiste LeMoyne, Sieur de Bienville led this expedition into the Mobile area to establish France's claims. They first settled on Dauphin Island in early 1699 and set out from there to explore the area with the aid of some Mobiliens as guides or scouts to find a site to establish a fort and settlement.[1] (seems the French made considerable use of these Mobilien or Maubilian guides, probably in part because of the significance of the Maubilian Trade Language.) Iberville, with an exploring party, went up the Mobile River to the village of Maubilians. According to Pierre Jay Higginbotham in *The Mobile Indians* the Maubilians desired to sing the Calumet of Peace with Iberville, but he requested it be later.[2]

The Indian used tobacco mainly for a time of meditation or communion with God. The Calumet had great religious significance for it was an effort to create community or brotherhood. Surely we Christians agree with the Indian that a high result of worship of God is 'Peace-Goodwill among men!' The probable intent of the Maubilian in

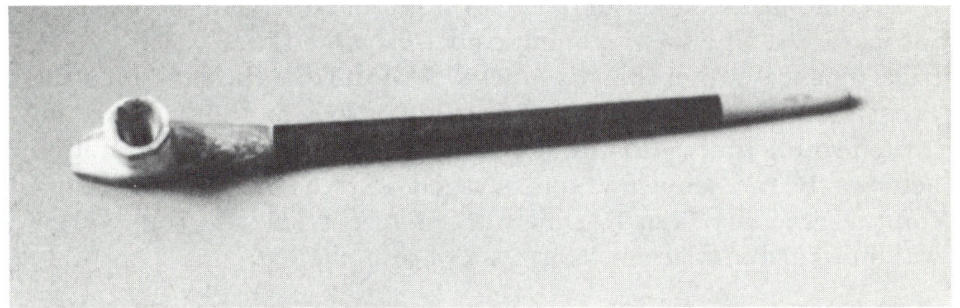

Calumet

inviting the French under Bienville to sing the Calumet was to seal an agreement to be friends and good neighbors—Brethren dwelling together in peace!

Bienville Diplomacy

Iberville discussed with the chief the building of a fort and seemingly they agreed on a site some 6 leagues from the village of the Maubilians back toward the Mobile Bay. In 1701 Iberville directed his group to establish Fort Louis de La Mobile on the Mobile River a short way above the Mobile Bay.[4] The name chosen was no doubt to honor the Maubilian Chief who helped pick the site and agreed to the fort being built there. There was much wise diplomacy involved in all of this. About a month after Fort Mobile was built the chiefs of the Mobiliens, Tomez, and the Gens des Fourches came together to Fort Mobile and sang the Calumet of Peace, and afterward they went home quite satisfied.[3,5]

Prieur Jay Higginbotham makes the observation that the fact that Fort Louis de La Mobile was not fortified with walls is a strong indication of the friendly disposition of the Maubilians of the area toward the French. Does this possibly indicate the Maubilian, remembering their tragic encounter with the DeSoto Expedition, wanted to do all possible now to establish friendly relations with these newcomers? They may well have thought this would be far better for all concerned than what had happened in the encounter with the DeSoto Expedition. They also may have noted some basic differences of attitude and purpose between the Spanish and the French. The Spanish came seeking their wealth, the French came to settle and trade with them and be neighbors.

In *The World of The American Indian* the author says,

> "If the French left a less sanguinary record in their occupation of the New World, the reasons stemmed from a different logic of self-interest. Colonization was never strongly promoted; a string of settlements and posts could maintain the lucrative fur trade, and the wilderness be kept for its riches. The same economic goal prompted the French to seek tribal alliances rather than conquests. Almost from the beginning the French sent young men to spend a season or so in an Indian camp and invited young Indians to winter with the French. Thus communication between the two peoples was encouraged—a rare thing in days of early contact. And the French gained access to fur lands in the interior without tribal displacement or wars of annihilation."[7]

From the beginning of this colonial venture of the French, one of the

Site of Fort Louis

most outstanding parts of it was the work of Bienville. Though only eighteen years of age, he did make great achievements in developing friendly relations with the Indians of the area, especially the Maubilians. I would be inclined to believe this was, by far, the most singular of their achievements for their efforts at establishing a thriving and profitable colony at Biloxi had failed, their mining ventures were not worth mentioning, and the same was true of their efforts at farming. But Bienville's work to make friends among the Indians of the area helped to open the vast area to trade and to the influx of white settlers. Bienville's work was made easier no doubt by the common use all over the area, and even far beyond it, of the Maubilian Trade Language.

The authors of Alabama Heritage say "With patience and wisdom Bienville for many years served the city (Mobile) he had founded. He was a colonizer rather than a seeker of New World silver or gold. He foresaw the productive potential of the new province and was responsible for initiating the plantation idea that later flourished. Bienville introduced the first cattle, hogs, and chickens. He grew and shipped the first cotton and tobacco, and he experimented with the raising of indigo and silk. He gave Mobile its first camelias and azaleas imported from France."[7a]

The most significant of the contributing factors to Bienville's success among the Indians of the area was no doubt the generally peaceful relations among the various Indian groups. The French, coming from a world of great and constant conflict, struggle, and bloodshed—The Hundred Years War—must have been impressed greatly by these various, different, independent groups of Indians living in such close proximity with an amazingly low level of hostility and conflict. This is no doubt one of the reasons the French moved rather freely and seemingly courageously among them.

In *Sun Circles and Human Hands* the authors say, "Some authorities seem to believe that those who engaged in barter-commerce were given free passage among the tribes, possibly even in times of war. Several artists depict the trader being warmly received and fed. This speaks of the great significance, attached by the Indian, to the place or role of the traders among them. It also says something of the ease with which the Indians generally were able to move among each other, especially the traders.[8]

There are several factors that seem to contribute to the French being able to move into the area and settle the area. First, there seemed to be little interest among the Indian of the area about the area the French were interested in. It seemingly posed no threat to the domain of the Maubilian or the Alibamos, partly because of the distance from them. It probably was also related to their interest in the trade possibilities.

In 1709, following a flood on the Mobile River, the little colony or settlement of Fort Louis de La Mobile was moved to the present day site of Mobile. This became the first lasting and significant settlement of whites in Alabama. These settlers, and especially the work and influence of Bienville among the Indians encouraged and influenced an influx of traders among the Indians. This influx of traders with the economic significance of their trade resulted in the establishment of forts where the trade centers were developing or showing promise of developing. The traders had gone into the principal villages of the Maubilians up the Mobile River, the Choctaw of the 'Tombecbe' area, the Alibamos of the area around the confluence of the Coosa River and Tallapoosa River. These traders were quite well received by the Indian villages because the Indians were very much interested in the trinkets, colorful beads, and colorful cloth, etc., the traders offered them in exchange for furs.

The Impact of Trading

The trading business in the interiors of the area of Alabama so flourished as to encourage two very significant developments. The first was the development of the French system of forts to protect the trading

This picture is of a house in the Ocnaluftee Living Indian Village in Cherokee, North Carolina. It represents one like the Indians might have been living in when the white men first came to the area. It is probably typical of the dwellings of the Cherokee families the first missionaries related to about 1822.

interests. Secondly, the forts provided a security, or at least a sense of security that encouraged many families to venture into these areas which were in close proximity to large Indian villages, to settle and establish homes, farms and businesses.

The French built a fort at Mobile in 1702 to encourage the development of a settlement, to protect their subjects in that development, and to protect their economic interests and colonial aspirations in the area. In 1711 they built Fort Conde.

By 1714 Bienville had so developed a friendly relationship with the Alibamons as to secure their approval to build a fort among their villages. Penicaut in *Fleur De Lys and Calumet* says, "The Grand Chief of all the savages in the direction of Carolina, whom all those savages called their Emperor, came accompanied by all the other chiefs of those nations, seeking M. de la Mothe at Mobile; and they sang their Calumet of Peace to him.

The Grand Chief of the Alibamons with his other chiefs was also with him there. He begged M. de la Mothe to grant peace. They proposed to have a fort built in their village at their expense, the kind that would be suitable for French people. M. de la Mothe took him at his word and dispatched M. de la Tour, a captain, with two lieutenants and one hundred men. When M. de la Tour got there, he chose a very high place on the bank of their river, at a distance of two musket shots from their village; and here he had them build a fort about fifty toises square, with quarters for officers and soldiers and a large magazine for munitions and food supplies."[9] The expedition of Bienville enroute up the Mobile and the Alabamo River to build the fort encountered the Indian villages of Atagi, Nawoti, Ikon Ichati, Coosawda, Tasheigi, Tukabatchi, according to author W. G. Brown in *History of Alabama.*[10] Probably another evidence of the wise leadership of Bienville was the fact that he had a religious ceremony conducted with many of the Indians of the area present, before the work of building the fort was begun. This seems to have made the presence of the fort and the 'white show of strength' more acceptable to them. This fort was named Fort Toulouse. Probably the establishment of this fort was tied very closely with the continuation of the trade with the Tribe or village of The Alibamos of the area. Generally, the Tribes and Villages were so interested in getting the trade goods as to be willing to make many concessions to assure the continuing presence of the French traders in their area. The traders went and lived in the villages among the Indians which probably was a plus in the building of goodwill. The marriage of many of the traders to Indian maidens was also of significance in developing goodwill, all of which would help open the door to the influx of more whites, especially the kinsmen and friends of these traders. Thus, goodwill or at least tolerance for the whites was developing among these Indians. Had the traders exhibited the arrogance, greed, and anti-Indian attitude of many of the whites of this period, I am sure these Indians would have never allowed or tolerated the

This scene depicting an early settlement in the 'Tombecbee Country' of Alabama was done for me by a dear friend, Joe B. Vann, who is a member of the congregation at The First United Methodist Church of Trussville, Alabama. Joe is also distinguished by being a decendant of the Vann family line of the famous 'Vann House' of Georgia, seen elsewhere in this book.

first white settlers into the area. The Indian's desire for such things as colorful glass beads and other such trade items, and their concept that most whites would be like these traders they had come to know, caused them to tolerate the increasing influx of white traders and other whites who were pursuing other interests, especially farming. This encroachment was gradual and was in areas not of intense interest or use to the predominant tribes or groups of the Indians. It was also so very closely tied or related to the trade centers that the Indians did not resist it. The French built Fort Tombigbee in 1735 and soon a settlement that became known as Jones Bluff, was developing in the area. By the end of the 1700's some 100 years of white presence in the area opened by the French, their settlements in the area of Mobile, the Tensaw, Fort Toulouse, and 'Tombecbee' were quite entrenched.[11]

Trading with the Indian, especially for furs, was most important in helping the white's become entrenched in the area. A most significant development of this era, related to this trade, was the diplomacy between the Indians and the State of Georgia, The United States, Britain, France and Spain. Each of these governments sought to use the Indian Nations of the Alabama area to buffer or counter the other's colonization efforts or economic interests. The primary method of this was to find Indian Chiefs who could be used by gifts or bribes. Little of this was based upon mutual interest or sound principles, and much of it was dependent upon secrecy.

The fur trade had a profound affect on the Indians. In order to get the trade items he desired he became especially involved in hunting. This caused the neglect of other skills. The Indian became dependent on steel axes, knives and iron pots, etc. And in order to get more skins he turned to the use of white man's guns. In time he became so efficient that the game grew scarce. This is turn created tension between competing groups of hunters resulting in many wars and conflicts.[12]

Indian Diplomacy—Alexander McGillivray

All this was made to order for a person like Alexander McGillivray, who is often called The Talleyrand of Alabama. He was born at Little Tallassee on the bank of the Coosa River near present day city of Wetumpka. His father, Lachlan McGillivray, was a Scotch trader, and his mother was Sehoy Marchand, whose father was the French Commander of Fort Toulouse and mother was of a most influential Creek family of the Wind Clan.[13] Lachlan first sent Alexander to the local school begun by John Pierce, this was the first American type school in Alabama. He then sent Alexander to school in Savannah, Georgia and then to Charleston, South Carolina.

He was an excellent student of Greek, and Latin, and history. He had particular interest in reading and studying of diplomacy.[14]

After receiving the finest of educational opportunities, Lachlan hoped Alexander would work in the business world in a possible relation with his friend William Panton of Pensacola, Florida, or that he might remain in Charleston and become a great lawyer.[15] But Alexander came home, choosing to cast his lot in life with his Indian side of the house. He soon became a prominent leader in the Creek Nation. With keen insight, due probably to both native ability and the fine educational training he had received, he saw ways to take advantage of, and to manipulate, the surge and resurgence of the colonial and economic interests of the various powers.[16]

The colonial powers were looking for just such persons as Alexander McGillivray to use them for advantage, and he was looking for them. And he would be dealing with all of them-at the same time-and on strong terms! Alexander's first evidence of great diplomatic and chieftan leadership was in the struggle of the Creek Nation with the State of Georgia over disputed land. The Creek National Council met in 1776 in the village of Coweta, which is on the west bank of the Chattahoochee River at the site of present day Phoenix City, Alabama. The dispute with Georgia seems to have been the primary concern, and through it Alexander had emerged as Chief of the Creek Confederacy.[17]

The British sent Colonel Tait to secure the agreement of McGillivray to help them get the alliance of the Creek Confederacy against the State of Georgia. Pledging his support for the cause, McGillivray received from Colonel Tait the commission and pay as a British Colonel. Colonel McGillivray was able to persuade the Creeks to provide many warriors to harass the Georgians to the satisfaction of the British.

Through McGillivray's relation, both business and personal, with Scotchman William Panton, and Panton's influence with the Spanish Government, he received the rank and pay of Colonel.[18] The Spanish used Colonel McGillivray to help them thwart the British interests in the Creek Confederacy area. With the defeat of the British in the Revolutionary War, the Creek lost their primary ally and source of trade and supplies. In desperation Chief McGillivray turned to his long time friend William Panton for help. And Panton was able to secure an enlarged trade relation with the Spanish.

With the backing of Spain, McGillivray now rallied the Creek again to confront the Georgians about the conflict over the contested land in Georgia, called the Augusta Cession. In order to avoid war with the Creek Confederacy, Governor Troup assured the Creek that Georgia would not take over the contested land. But for the next several years there were many conflicts and skirmishes between Creeks and Georgians over this matter. In an effort to resolve this conflict to the satisfaction of his people, Chief McGillivray sought to establish a union with the Iroquois, Hurons, and Shawnees.[19]

Long before Tecumseh made the effort, for which he is famed, to unite the Indian tribes against white encroachment Chief McGillivray had conceived of the policy of 'Strength through Union'. He called for a Council of all the southern tribes to meet with him at Pensacola, Florida to discuss the merits and possibilities of such a union.[20]

As I sit writing on this, on the 7th floor balcony of the Everett and Wynelle Chambliss[21] condominium home, overlooking the beautiful Santa Rosa Island, I wonder if I can see the area of Pensacola where McGillivray intended this Great Council Fire. Moreso, I wonder how very different the history of our area might have been had he been able to fulfill that noble dream of the unity of his people. Such a union of this magnitude had been achieved by the Six Nations of the Iroquois of the Great Lakes region. Though Chief McGillivray had great leadership and oratorical ability, he evidently lacked the ability to persuade the various tribes to unite. He may have lacked the right concept—one seen as open and having mutual benefits. Whatever the case, he failed in this mission.[22]

The Spanish now fearing they might get drawn into a war between the Creek Confederacy and the State of Georgia, or even worse with The United States withdrew their support of the Creeks.[23]

Thus in grave concern over the developments in the situation, Chief McGillivray wrote to James White, Superintendent of Indian Affairs for the United States, "There are chiefs of two towns in this nation, who, during the late war, were friendly to the State of Georgia, and had gone, at different times, among those people, and once, after the general peace, to Augusta. They there demanded of them a grant of lands, belonging to and enjoyed as hunting grounds by the Indians of this nation in common, on the east of the Oconee River. The Chiefs rejected the demand, on the plea that these lands were the hunting grounds of the nation, and could not be granted by two individuals; but, after a few days, a promise was extorted from them, that, on their return to our country, they would use their influence to get a grant confirmed. Upon their return, a general convention was held at Tookabatcha, when these two chiefs were severely censured, and the chiefs of ninety-eight towns agreed upon a talk, to be sent to Savannah, disapproving, in the strongest manner, of the demand made upon their nation, and denying the right of any two of their country to make cession of land, which could only be valid by the unanimous voice of the whole, as joint proprietors in common. Yet these two chiefs, regardless of the voice of this nation, continued to go to Augusta, and other places within that State. They received presents and made promises; but our customs did not permit us to punish them for the crime. We warned the Georgians of the dangerous consequence, that would certainly attend the settling of the lands in question. Our just remonstrances were treated with contempt, and these lands were soon filled with settlers. The nation, justly alarmed at the encroachments, resolved to use force to maintain their rights; yet, being averse to the shedding of the blood of a people whom we would rather consider as friends, we made another effort to awaken in them a sense of justice and equity. But we found, from experience, that entreaty could not prevail, and parties of warriors were sent, to drive off the intruders, but were instructed to shed blood only where self-preservation made it necessary.

This was in May, 1786. In October following we were invited by commissioners of the State of Georgia, to meet them in conference, at the Oconee, professing a sincere desire for an amicable adjustment of our dispute, and pledging their sacred honors for the safety and good treatment of all those that should attend and meet them. It not being convenient for many of us to go to the proposed conference, a few, from the motives of curiosity, attended. They were surprised to find an armed body of men, prepared for and professing hostile intentions. Apprehension for personal safety induced those chiefs to subscribe to every demand that was asked by the army and its commissioners. Lands were again demanded, and the lives of some of our chiefs were required, as well as those of some innocent traders, as a sacrifice to appease their anger. Assassins have been employed to effect some part of their atrocious purposes. If I fall by the hand of such, I shall fall the victim of the noblest of causes, that of maintaining the just rights of my country. I aspire to the honest ambition of meriting the appellation of the preserver of my country, equally with the Chiefs among you, whom, from acting on such principles, you have exalted to the highest pitch of glory. And if, after every peaceable mode of obtaining a reddress of grievances proved fruitless, a recourse to arms to obtain it be a mark of savage, and not of the soldier, what savage must the Americans be, and how much undeserved applause have your Cincinnatus, your Fabius, obtained. If a war name has been necessary to distinguish that Chief, in such a case, the Man-Killer, the Great Destroyer, would have been the proper appellation.

I had appointed the Cussetas, for all the Chiefs of the Lower Creeks to meet in convention. I shall be down in a few days, when from your timely arrival, you will meet the chiefs, and learn their sentiments, and I sincerely hope that the propositions which you shall offer us will be such as we can safely accede to. The talks of the former commissioners, at Galphinton, were much approved of, and your coming from the White

Town (The Seat of Congress) has raised great expectations that you will remove the principal and almost only cause of our dispute, that is by securing to us our hunting grounds and possessions, free from all encroachment. When we meet, we shall talk these matters over, meantime,

I remain with regards
Your obedient servant,"
Alexander McGillivray[24]

The Superintendent did nothing to resolve the situation, thus the tensions continued between the Creeks and the Georgians. There were sporatic outburst of hostilities and bloodshed. President Washington fearing the tensions were going to lead to war, intervened and invited Chief McGillivray to New York to discuss the possibilities of a peaceful settlement. Chief McGillivray and twenty-six Creek chiefs went to New York to meet with President Washington. Enroute President Washington had planned a parade type response to the McGillivray party as they passed through the City of Philadelphia, but especially as they were marched down Wall Street in New York with flags and banners, music and great pomp and ceremony. It was doubtlessly pleasing to McGillivray and the other chiefs.[25]

Chief McGillivray took full advantage of this opportunity to impress both the United States Government leaders and the Spanish leaders who were in New York at the same time.[26]

After some time President Washington and Chief McGillivray agreed to terms of peace. Pitt Lamar Matthews in *History Stories of Alabama* says, "A treaty was signed by Chief McGillivray and President Washington which promised that peace would be kept forever between the Indians and the Americans."[27] The terms of the agreement included $1500 a year annuity for the Creek Nation, scholarships for four Creek youth annually, and in a secret part of the agreement McGillivray was made a Brigadier General of the United States Army with the pay of $1200 a year.[28]

At last all the intrigues of Chief of the Creek Confederacy, Colonel of the British, Colonel of the Spanish, and Brigadier General of the United States, Alexander McGillivray became known and the various parties withdrew their titles and pay. McGillivray decided to go to Pensacola, Florida to visit his long time friend and business associate, William Panton. And while there he became very ill and died on February 17, 1793. William Panton had him buried in his garden in Pensacola with Masonic honors.[29]

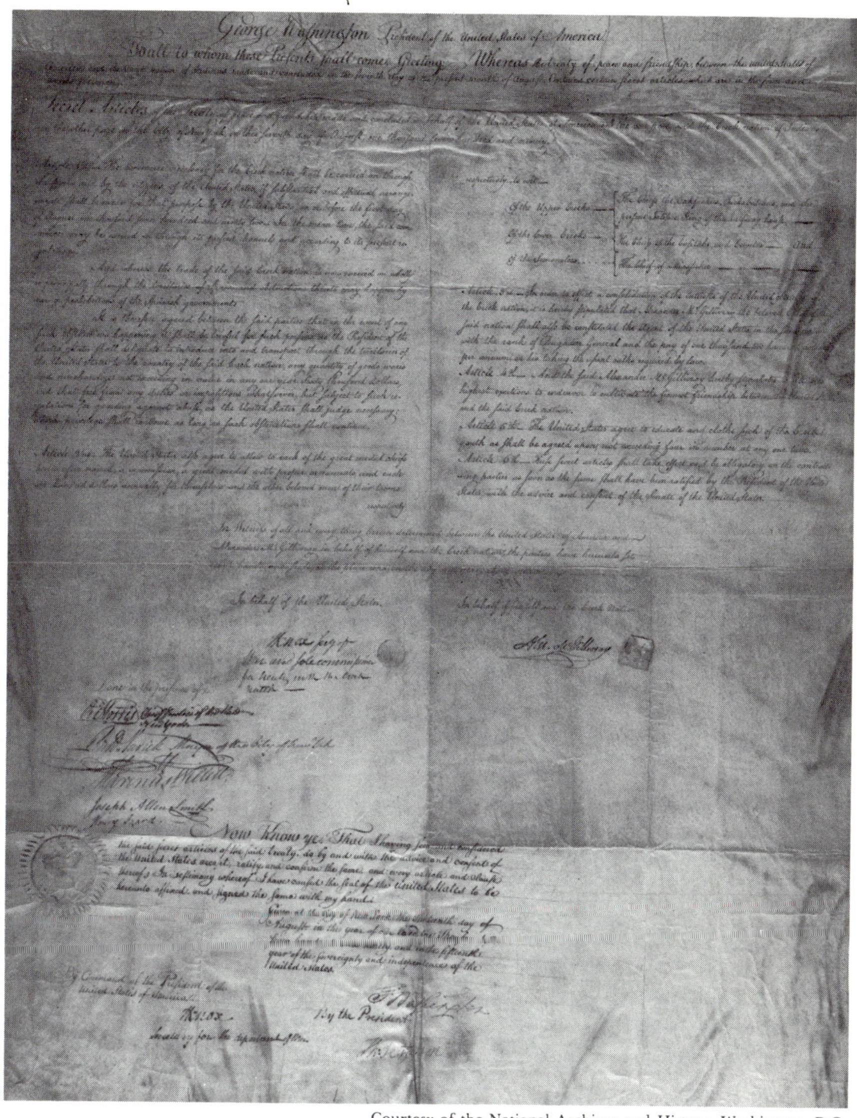

George Washington President of the United States of America

To all to whom these Presents shall come Greeting

Courtesy of the National Archives and History, Washington, D.C.

The United States Factory System

There was considerable vying for the Indian's trade between the English, Spanish, and the Americans after the French left the area. The United States Government felt more effort should be made to secure the Indian friendship and trade. Thus in 1795 The United States Factory

System was begun.[30] One of the significant Indian traders was Abram Mordecai, who began the first cotton gin in the Wetumpka area, near Weatherford's race track, and a short distance below Fort Toulouse. He bought cotton from the Indian and ginned it. He also did much trading with the Indians for pink root, hickory nut oil, and skins or furs. The hickory nut oil was a luxury item with the French and Spanish epicures.

Albert Pickett says the hickory nut oil, "was manufactured by the Indians in a simple manner—by boiling the cracked nuts in water, and skimming off the oil as it floated on the surface."[31] These trading opportunities were seen as a means to keep an eye on the Indian in order to know their activities and movements. It was also seen as a way to help the government keep control of them.[32]

There were those who promoted this system who believed the Indian could be helped through these 'factories,' and encouraged to become more like the white man. The authors of Alabama Heritage says, "The Indians were trying hard to become 'civilized', and had it not been for conflicting ideas about land ownership it is possible that the Indians and the white settlers could have found a peaceful co-existence."[33] Albert Pickett in *History of Alabama* says the St. Stephens factory, or trading-house pleased the Choctaws and helped create goodwill with them toward the United States Government. It also helped entice them away from the Spanish influence.[34]

There were also those in Government positions who saw the Factory System as a means of getting the Indian into debt, and when he could not pay these debts demand land cessions to satisfy them. Thomas Jefferson felt this was a way to appease the land greedy whites and also to force the Indian onto agriculture reservations where they would learn to farm and become as their white neighbors.[37]

President Washington initiated the United States Government Indian Policy. The Government would deal with the Indian on the basis of, and legally by treaties. President Washington promised the Indians that these treaties they agreed to would be 'As strong as the hills, and lasting as the rivers.'[36] Tragically the Indian soon learned they were generally not worth the paper, or in some cases the sheep skins, they were written on!

IX

THE PRESSURE OF WHITE COLONIZATION

The Nineteenth Century began with a rapid increase of whites moving into the area, and with a growing awareness of it by the Indians. Though there had been conflicts between them all along, for the entirety of the some 100 years of the presence of white settlers, it now moves into a far more serious and intense stage. By now there is an almost universal consciousness, among the Indian, of the white's greed for the Indian's land, and of their arrogant manner of encroachment.

The British Proclamation of October, 1763, assured the Indians of the area of Alabama that they would discourage and resist the expansion of the colonial states, especially Georgia, into their area. The Georgians did not agree with this position of the British. Thus, there continued to be conflict over the Georgians trying to get Creek and Cherokee land for use of the white settlers. During the Revolutionary War the Creeks and Cherokee were openly pro-British. After the United States had defeated the British, they took advantage of the situation, and demanded land cessions from the Creek and Cherokee as punishment for their support of the British. White settlers moved into these areas immediately. But to make matters even worse, these land greedy whites moved into other areas as well as those ceded. The Indians were outraged and tensions grew. President Washington expressed concern over the unjust treatment of the Indians, but neither The United States Government or the State of Georgia would make the encroachers move out. Thus there was a growing alarm among the Indians about 'White encroachment pressure on them'.

Tecumseh Challenge

This general concern or alarm among the Indian set the stage for the rise of a strong and universal cry from the Indian all across the colonial frontier to unify. The most significant leader of this movement was Tecumseh, a war chief of the Shawnee of the area of the Great Lakes. Tecumseh is thought by some to have been born in Alabama. At least his mother had been born in Alabama, as part of a Shawnee group, who had been part of the Creek Confederacy.[1] He went from his home in the area of Detroit, Michigan to the various tribes along the frontier edge of Colonial America, seeking to stir them to unite to resist further encroachment and drive the whites from their ancestral lands. He urged a show of force tempered with humaness that would gain the respect and even the support of the whites.

The British, who had regathered their forces and strength after their defeat in the American Revolutionary War, responded to Chief Tecumseh and his following and agreed to an alliance against the Americans. Chief Tecumseh seemed to see in the possibility of the British going to war on the Americans an opportunity to get the Indian Tribes and Nations to create a Confederacy over the entire colonial frontier, from the Great Lakes to the Gulf of Mexico.

In the summer of 1811 Chief Tecumseh came into the Alabama area to attempt to stir the Choctaw, Chickasaw, and Creeks to join him in war on the Americans. Let us imagine a Great Council Fire and hundreds, and hundreds of warriors silently marching in and sitting down in a great circle. When at last the great throng has gathered, from all over the Choctaw Nation, Chief Tecumseh rose and said, "Brush from your eyelids, the sleep of slavery, and strike for vengeance and your country! The red men have fallen as the leaves now fall. I hear their voices in those aged pines. Their tears drop from the weeping skies. Their bones bleach on the hills of Georgia. Will no son of those brave men strike the pale face and quiet those complaining ghosts! Let the white race perish! They seize your land; they corrupt your women; they trample on the bones of your dead! Burn their dwellings—destroy their stock—slay their wives and children that the very breed may perish! War now! War always! War on the living! War on the dead! Dig their very corpses from their graves. The red man's land must give no shelter to a white man's bones. This is the will of The Great Spirit spoken in the ear of my brother the mighty Prophet of the Lakes. He sends me to you."[2] When he finished his talk, he cast his ballot or vote—war club—on the side of the Council fire for war on the whites.

Pushmataha Responds

Then Chief Pushmataha rose and strongly rebuked Tecumseh. "Attention, my good red warriors! Hear ye my brief remarks. The great Shawnee orator has portrayed in vivid picture the wrongs inflicted on his and other tribes by the ravages of the paleface. The candor and fervor of his eloquent appeal breathe the conviction of truth and sincerity, and, as

(This picture provided courtesy of The Smithsonian Institute, Washington, D. C.)

kindred tribes naturally we sympathize with the misfortunes of his people. I do not come before you in any disputation either for or against these charges. It is not my purpose to contradict any of these allegations against the white man, but neither am I here to indulge in any indiscreet denunciation of him which might bring down upon my people unnecessary difficulty and embarrassment.

"The distinguished Shawnee sums up his eloquent appeal to us with this direct question. 'Will you sit idly by, supinely awaiting complete and abject submission, or will you die fighting beside your brethren, the Shawnee, rather than submit to such ignominy?'

"These are plain words and it is well they have been spoken, but they bring the issue squarely before us. Mistake not, this language means war. And war with whom, pray? War with some band of marauders who have committed these depredations against the Shawnees? War with some alien host seeking the destruction of the Choctaws and Chickasaws? Nay, my fellow tribesmen. None of these are the enemy we will be called on to meet. If we take up arms against the Americans we must of necessity meet in deadly combat our daily neighbors and associates in this part of the country near our homes.

"If Tecumseh's words be true, and we doubt them not, then the Shawnee's experience with the whites has not been the same as that of the Choctaws. These white Americans buy our skins, our corn, our cotton, our surplus game, our baskets, and other wares, and they give us in fair exchange their cloth, their guns and tools, implements and other things which the Choctaws need but do not make. It is true we have befriended them, but who will deny that these acts of friendship have been abundantly reciprocated? They have given us cotton gins, which simplify the spinning and sale of our cotton; they have encouraged and helped us in the production of our crops; they have taken many of our wives into their homes to teach them useful things, and pay them for their work while learning; they are teaching our children to read and write from their books. You all remember well the dreadful epidemic visited upon us last winter. During the darkest hours these neighbors whom we are now urged to attack responded generously to our needs. They doctored our sick; they clothed our suffering; they fed our hungry; and where is the Chocktaw or Chickasaw delegation who has ever gone to St. Stephens with a worthy cause and been sent away empty handed? So in marked contrast with the experience of the Shawnees, it will be seen that the whites and Indians in this section are living on friendly and mutually beneficial terms.

"Forget not, O Choctaws and Chickasaws, that we are bound in peace to the Great White Father at Washington by a sacred treaty and The Great

Spirit will punish those who break their word. The Great White Father has never violated that treaty and the Choctaws have never yet been driven to the necessity of taking up the tomahawk against him or his children. Therefore, the question before us tonight is not the avenging of any wrongs perpetrated against us by the whites, for the Choctaws and Chickasaws have no such cause, either real or imaginary, but rather it is a question of carrying on that record of fidelity and justice for which our forefathers ever proudly stood, and doing that which is best calculated to promote the welfare of our own people. Yea, my fellow tribesmen, we are a just people. We do not take up the warpath without a just cause and honest purpose. Have we that just cause against our white neighbors, who have taken nothing from us except by fair bargain and exchange? Is this a just recompense for their assistance to us in our agricultural and other pursuits? Is this to be their gracious reward for teaching our children from their books? Shall this be considered the Choctaw's compensation for feeding our hungry, clothing our needy, and administering to our sick? Have we, O Choctaws and Chickasaws, descended to the low estate of ruthlessly breaking the faith of a sacred treaty? Shall our forefathers look back from the happy hunting grounds only to see their unbroken record for justice, gratitude, and fidelity thus rudely repudiated and abruptly abandoned by an unworthy offspring?

"We Choctaws and Chickasaws are a peaceful people, making our subsistence by honest toil; but mistake not, my Shawnee brethren we are not afraid of war. Neither are we strangers to war, as those who have undertaken to encroach upon our rights in the past may abundantly testify. We are thoroughly familiar with war in all its details and we know full well all its horrible consequences. It is unnecesary for me to remind you, O Choctaws and Chickasaws, veteran braves of many fierce conflicts in the past, that war is an awful thing. If we go into this war against the Americans, we must be prepared to accept its inevitable results. Not only will it foretoken deadly conflict with neighbors and death to warriors, but it will mean suffering for our women, hunger and starvation for our children, grief for our loved ones, and devastation of our beloved homes. Notwithstanding these difficulties, if the cause be just, we should not hesitate to defend our rights to the last man, but before that fatal step is irrevocably taken, it is well that we fully understand and seriously consider the full portent and consequences of the act.

"Hear me, O Choctaws and Chickasaws, for I speak truly for your welfare. It is not the province of your chiefs to settle these important questions. As a people, it is your prerogative to love either peace or war, and as one of your chiefs, it is mine simply to counsel and advise. Therefore, let me admonish you that this critical period is no time to cast aside your wits and blind impulse sway; be not driven like dumb brutes by the frenzied harangue of this wonderful Shawnee orator; let your good judgment ruse and ponder seriously before breaking bonds that have served you well and ere you change conditions which have brought peace and happiness to your wives, your sisters, and your children. I would not undertake to dictate the course of one single Choctaw warrior. Permit me to speak for the moment, not as your chief, but as a Choctaw warrior, weighing this question beside you. As such I shall exercise my calm, deliberate judgment in behalf of those most dear to me and dependent on me, and I shall not suffer my reason to be swept away by this eloquent recital of alleged wrongs which I know nought of. I deplore this war, I earnestly hope it may be averted, but if it be forced upon us I shall take my stand with those who have stood by my people in the past and will be found fighting beside our good friends of St. Stephens and surrounding country. I have finished. I call on all Choctaws and Chickasaws endorsing my sentiments to cast their tomahawks on this side of the council fire with me."[2]

When the voting was done the vast majority of the Choctaws and Chickasaws had joined Pushmataha in supporting 'Peace with their white neighbors! One of the great things about this event is that it shows something of Indian style of government—Democracy! The decisions were not made by the chiefs, sometimes called and viewed as micco or king or monarch. Marie Owen reports Pushmataha speaking to this issue and saying, "The chieftains, (of the Choctaws and Chickasaws) do not undertake the master of their people, but rather are they the people's servants elected to serve the will of the majority—the majority has spoken—and Pushmataha will see that the will of the majority so expressed is rigidly carried out to the letter.[3]

Tuckabatcha Council

Pushmataha assigned a group of his warriors to escort Chief Tecumseh and his party safely to the border of the Choctaw Nation. In time, Tecumseh is at the meeting of The Creek National Council at Tookobatche (presently Tallasee, Al.) where he sought to stir the Creek to join him and his cause against the whites. The Creeks had had much more of the same kind of bitter experiences Tecumseh and the Shawnees knew than had the Choctaws and Chickasaws. They were much more prepared, through white encroachment and harassment, to respond to Tecumseh. And there was a small element of the Creek that did respond to him and began to talk war. But it took a direction Tecumseh did not suggest or want, for it hurt his cause. These rebels took issue with the primary

Tooka-batcha, The Village of The Chief (usually) was the principal city or village at the time of The War of The Creek Indian with The United States. This was the site of The Great National Council Fire, just prior to the outbreak of the Creek-U.S. War. It was here that the Creek warriors heard the firey talk of Chief Tecumseh and a rebel element, The Red Sticks" began to talk war.

leadership of the Creek Nation over adopting ways of the white man. Their position was—return to the old traditional ways of the Indian and reject the white man's ways. There are those who believe the basis of the rebellion was more against the Government's Civilization Program led by Indian Agent Hawkins, rather than the influence of Tecumseh's war talk.

Probably Tecumseh did stir deep feelings and cause them to really begin an intensive look at what is happening to them, and to give expression to their dissatisfactions. Thus, in that sense the firey, anti-white speech of Tecumseh is an important influence in the development of the rebellion. Had this been the only contributing factor it would soon have fisseled out. But the power or steam that kept the rebellious movement alive and caused it to become a serious civil strife between the factions of the Creek Confederacy was the deep resentments against that element of Creek National leadership who were so supportive of Hawkins' Civilization Program.

Three of the rebel Creek leaders, Minewa, William Weatherford or 'Red Eagle' and Josiah Francis were probably influenced by Tecumseh. Anyway, following this time they began seeking support for their opposition movement.

Concerning this movement Alexander Cornells, interpreter among the Upper Creeks sent a report on June 22, 1813 to Colonel Benjamin Hawkins. In part, he said, "We now believe the public talk was to deceive the old chiefs, always opposed to war, and that the talk of Tecumseh was the plan for the prophets. It was well known the Creeks were a settled people, and their chiefs occupied in peaceful pursuits; of course, the chiefs were enemies to war. Hence, a determination to keep the whole plan secret from them, and let it mature itself among the opposers of civilization and the young people. From the confidence with which the prophets speak of their power, and the source of it, their ability to punish all who reveal their secret, which they have ways of knowing, prevents the young people from even communicating anything to their own families. The prophets are, for the present, confined to the Alabamos, who, although of the Creek Confederacy, are not Creeks. The towns of the Creeks who are said to have taken their talks, have not done it actively; their people are dancing their dances, but no man has moved to assist them. The prophets are enemies to the plan of civilization, and advocates for the wild Indian mode of living. It appears they are first to put to death every chief and warrior who aided to execute the murderers, then the old chiefs, friends to peace, who had taken the talks of Col. Hawkins, from whom the orders for punishing the murderers came, then Mr. Cornells, because he was the interpreter, and if they could, at the same time, to put Col. Hawkins to death. But having killed all the others, if he escaped, it would be of no consequence, as then none would be left alive to receive and communicate his talks; and the nation could fix their affairs their own way. After this they would be ready for the white people who could do them no injury, if they came among them, as the prophets would draw circles around their abode, and render the earth quazzy and impassable. If any Indian town refused their aid to the prophets, they should be sunk with earthquakes, or hills should be turned over them. They had also the aid of the lightening whenever they wanted.

The chiefs sent a guard with me from Tuckabatchie, being apprehensive for my personal safety; and ordered me to travel by night, till I saw and reported to you. Since they have begun to murder, they give out, Tecumseh is to be here this fall. Having done what I was ordered to do, your judgment will direct for the future. I have directed runners to be sent after us, to let us know what is doing. As I came on, receiving information from you that General Wilkinson was on the road, with a guard, coming through, I sent after the Little Prince, to send notice to him immediately, if he heard of any hostility against white people on the road. I have done the same to the Cussetahs.[4]

With friendly chiefs and towns being greatly threatened by the rebel element a runner from Tuckaubatchie was sent with the following message to Colonel Hawkins on July 5, 1813.

"The chiefs have sent me to state to you that their difficulties continue to increase. Their opponents have killed, in all, nine of their people; one of them a woman. Fooscehaijo, of Auttosse, is missing; supposed to be murdered, as blood was seen in one of his houses. He was a good man, and opposed to mischief-makers. The chiefs sent two of their great men, Tuskeenohen, of Cussetah, and Atchou Havjo, of Coweta to Hoboheilthle Micco, of Tallassee, to induce him to have the war sticks and projects thrown aside, and repeated their message. But the old man rejected every thing, declared his determination to persevere until he destroyed all who aided and assisted to put the murderers to death. He looked on them as people of the United States. He would march from Tuckaubatchee to Coweta, destroy all of them, and move on for the white people, and would not stop till he had marched to Ogeechee. There he would pause and rest, then put off for the sea coast. All north of this line of march would be destroyed by the British. He had been plotting this secretly for some time, and now having brought it to bear, he was determined not to stop. He had his bows, his arrows, and war clubs, and, with the magic powers he possessed, aided by the British and Shawanese, who were now coming from the northwest, and were now more then half way to him, he was able to crush the Americans, and would do it.

"The chiefs say they have brought themselves into their present embarrassments by their fidelity to their treaty stipulations with Washington. In giving satisfaction for the murders on the post road, on Duck and Ohio, which it was the duty of their nation to do, they are placed in a war attitude by their opponents. By doing justice to the white people, they are to be punished with death. They have about thirty fit for war, but badly armed, and without ammunition. They fear not death, although they are in a dangerous situation, and may expect it. The Prophet's party have burnt the village of Hatchechubbau and several detached settlements, and destroyed cattle, hogs, horses, and corn. All who are friends to the United States are doomed to destruction. This is our true situation; we ask for aid from the white people. If you, Colonel Hawkins, cannot afford it from the troops of the United States, who we hear are towards the sea coast, ask the Governor of Georgia to aid us. If they could send from six hundred to eight hundred mounted men in two divisions, one on the old, the other on the new post road, to unite near the bridges, on Ucher Creek, and then along the mail road, we would join them with two hundred horsemen, point out and attack our enemies. A number of well-disposed Indians would join. We know, when this is done, we shall conquer them. We are willing the lands on Alabama should go to pay our white friends, who, although in aiding us, will effectually aid themselves. We have sent to the Cherokees for aid, but know not the success. If we are destroyed before you aid us, you will have the work to do yourselves, which will be bloody, and attended with difficulties, as you do not know as well as us the swamps and hiding places of those people. We cannot find that the Spaniards have had any hand in this, but can clearly trace it to the British on the Lakes."

Written as interpreted by Alexander Cornells, Public Interpreter.[5]

The rebels of some 350 warriors, made up of Tallases, Autauges, and Alabamas and led by Peter McQueen, High-Head Jim, and Josiah Francis were become more active and vocal for war. Colonel Hawkins, who kept in constant contact with the situation was making effort possible to defuse this very dangerous development. He sent a demand to the fanatical chiefs and their associates, for an explanation of their conduct.

Colonel Hawkins, agent for Indian Affairs, to Hoboheilthle Micco, Peter McQueen, the chiefs of Tallassee, Auttossee, Foosee Hatchee, and all other chiefs who have taken the talks of the prophets: "I hear you are preparing yourselves for war; I hear you have taken part with the prophets. The prophets have taken part with the prophets. The prophets have put to death nine people, because they helped the chiefs to save their country, by putting the murderers of our white friends to death, which they were bound to do by their treaty with Washington. I hear you have begun the war dance, made your war clubs, and are for war with the white people. What is this for? What injury have the white people done you? You know who I am; I have been long among you. My talks have been always for peace, and they have been the saving of your country. Are you going to divide your nation, and destroy it? Do you not know the prophet's talk will be the destruction of the Creeks, and give joy to your enemies? You have threatened the life of my interpreter, and to destroy his property. What had he done? Delivered you my friendly talks. If you do him any injury, you do it to me and all the people of the United States. I never will forgive the murderers of white people, or red people friendly to them. You threaten Kialijee, Tuckaubatchee, and Coweta. What is this for?

"Speak plain to me. I have ordered four great chiefs of Cussetah to carry this talk, and bring your answer. We can settle things much better now than when you see me with an army. I am now your friend; I shall then be your enemy. You may frighten one another with the power of your prophets to make thunder, earthquakes, and to sink the earth. These things cannot frighten the American soldiers. The American soldiers are now your friends, and I hope will always be so. Take care how you make them your enemy. The thunder of their cannon, their rifles, and their swords, will be more terrible than the works of your prophets. If you are friendly, you have nothing to fear. If the white man is safe in your land, you are safe. If the white man is in danger in your land, you are in danger; and war with the white people will be your ruin.[6]

The rebels did not respond to Colonel Hawkins but rather set out for Pensacola, Florida to receive ammunition, arms, and other supplies to carry on their threatened hostilities. The scattered white villages were greatly threatened by the movement of this group. They watched them very closely. A group of State Militia gathered to attack the rebels on their return from Pensacola. The militia was led by Colonel James Coller and Captain Dixon Bailey, a half-breed Creek who had been educated in Philadelphia under the terms of the Creek-U.S. Treaty of 1790. They attacked the Indians at Burnt Corn Creek. Following this battle the fear and alarm of the area spread, and in response General Ferdinand Leigh Claiborne was ordered to take command of the militia at Fort Stoddart for the defence of Mobile. He so distributed his troops over the area as to provide the most possible protection for the settlers.[7]

In concern for the development of these hostilities, Big Warrior and Tustunnuggee Hopoie sent the following communication to Colonel Hawkins, August 4, 1813.

"Colonel Hawkins, you have requested to know the number of towns that are friendly. There are sixteen towns down Chatahoochee, from Coweta, are friendly; there are sixteen towns have met here—there are a few small villages, which are not come in; when they go out from the meeting we will know their whole strength. The number of men we cannot give any certainty for the present—a great many are sick, which we cannot account for. We have made the broken days to go on an expedition against the hostile Indians. In twelve days from today, we are in hopes you will be able to join us here at this place. We have a great many villages down this river and Flint river; and, in that time, we expect to have them all collected. We told you at your house that we were in haste; we now send you the appointed time to go on this expedition. We told you to be in readiness, and we hope you are, to accompany your soldiers, as you are appointed to have the care of the Indians; we hope you will be with us; we wish you to be expeditious. Let your heavy baggage come along, as you have a public road to come in our nation. We are scarce in arms and ammunition; we hope you will bring that along to furnish our people with it; we have told you our distresses and our grievance. We hope you will make all the haste you can to come to our assistance. The war party has nearly destroyed all our cattle; we will not trouble you with a long talk; we talked the whole over at your house; only come as soon as possible. We cannot give you a true account of the strength of the warring Indians; we suppose it to be at least two thousand five hundred, or thereabouts. There are, in the whole, twenty-nine towns and villages of the Upper Creeks has joined the war party; there are but five towns of the Upper Creeks that are for peace."

Big Warrior, his X mark
Speaker of the Nation

Tustunnuggee Hopoie, his X mark
of Coweta, and head Chief of
the Lower Creeks[8]

On the same day, August 4, 1813, that Colonel Hawkins received Big Warrior's request for help, Big Warrior sent him additional information. Big Warrior sent the following letter to Colonel Hawkins from the home of Chief William McIntosh, a principal Chief of the Lower Creeks:

"After our meeting this day, we received information from Hardy Read's wife, which is a red woman of Hoithlewaulee; she is straight from that town, who gives the following information—she saw two white men's scalps; they were brought there shortly before she left that town. Peter McQueen went to Pensacola to obtain ammunition; as he passed James Cornell's house, he took James Cornell's wife prisoner off to Pensacola; at the same time there was a white man at Cornell's house; McQueen and his party did beat him almost to death, and also a Negro at Cornell's, and went on their journey to Pensacola: now, on their return, they were met by James Cornell and David Tate,[9] and a small party of white people, where the old furrow path turned off to Pensacola; an engagement took place; there were five Indians and one Negro of McQueen's party killed, and a great many wounded: of Mr. Cornell's company there were two white men killed, and several wounded; the battle lasted nearly three hours. McQueen's party kept the ground; his force was three hundred and fifty strong. Cornell's party is not ascertained to be but a small number. It is supposed that James Cornell and Tate are wounded. McQueen got Tate's horse. They scalped the two white men and brought them to Hoithlewaulee. Hardy Read's wife saw the two scalps with her own eyes. She says that Peter McQueen had one hundred horse loads of ammunition, which he received at Pensacola from the Spaniards.

"After we had made the broken days, this day this information came on.

It is our sincere wish for you to come on to our assistance in three or four days, if it is only two hundred men, and let the rest of the army follow as fast as they can. This is the day appointed for the war party to make an attack on us here at this place. We are all under arms, and expect every moment to be all attacked by the warring Indians.

Big Warrior, his X mark[10]

It may be that had Colonel Hawkins been able to respond immediately to the urgent plea of Big Warrior and William McIntosh for an army to help them put down the rebel or warring group the grave situations that soon follow might not have happened. I am sure it was the desire of Chiefs Big Warrior and McIntosh to put this element down in the best interest of the Creek Confederacy and out of their friendship with the whites. But such help is not forthcoming, and on August 30, the hostiles under the lead of 'Red Eagle' fell on Fort Mims in a terrible and bloody battle. There is evidence that 'Red Eagle' tried to control the Indians and keep the

This picture of The Massacre of Fort Mims, 1813 from an original painting by Chappel is provided courtesy of the Alabama Department of Archives and History, Montgomery, Alabama.

women and children from being brutally slaughtered, to no avail. And that failing such, he withdrew and left the scene." This action of the rebel or hostiles was a retaliation for the white's attack on them at 'Burnt Corn Creek', and probably the Creeks would now return to their internal struggle.

The Massacre at Fort Mims

Colonel Benjamin Hawkins sent the following report to Secretary of War apprising him of the dire situation:

"An express mail has arrived from Mobile, in which you have, I hope, a detail of the melancholy occurrence at Mimm's Fort, on the 30th ultimo. I have by Mr. Cornell's express, from the Chiefs low down Chattahoochee.

"Notwithstanding the loss the Prophets have sustained, they express confidence in the successful issue of their plan. Several of their party have lately been down on Chattahoochee, encouraging the Indians, within and without our limits, to join them; and urge an immediate junction of all their forces, for an attack on Coweta, which was determined on by the Prophets, and to take place on Friday next. They are determined, if they can, to destroy Coweta, and Tuckaubatchee in terrorism. After that, they should go towards Savannah river, and were determined to give Colonel Hawkins a chase and take him, unless he was on a fleet horse, before he got there. Whilst they came this way, the British were to attack New Orleans, and Mobile, and probably Savannah; they boasted much, and declared the inability of the white people to fight them in the field, or from their forts; boasted of the immense slaughter they made at Mimm's fort, and quantity of property taken in that expedition; if the red people would unite, nothing could withstand them: and those who would not join, were to be put to death, and this was the last warning they were to have. The chiefs of Eufaulau, having made this discovery, gave notice to Coweta, they should be with them with their warriors, and those of four other towns; and if they could get ammunition, would make common cause with them and their white brethren. They directed that Mr. Cornell should be sent off immediately to Colonel Hawkins with this information; and added, if our white friends can come soon, the Indians on both sides of our line of limits will join them, and if delayed, they, from their fears, will be compelled to join the 'Red Clubs".

"I have apprised General Floyd of similar information received, direct from the hostile Indians, and of the necessity to arm a detachment to Coweta. He informed me he had sent to the Governor of Georgia for orders, and as soon as a movement can be made with a part of the troops,

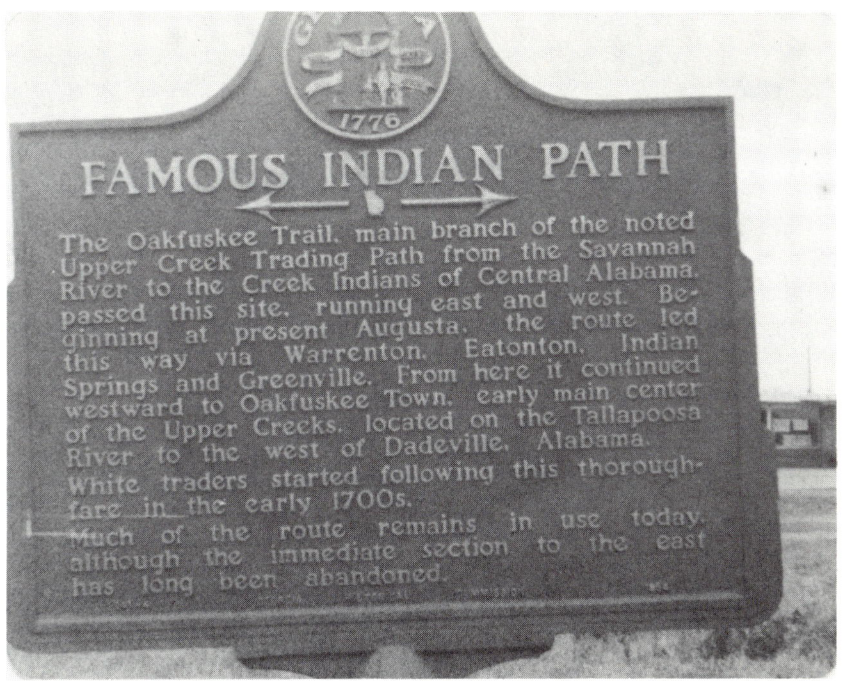

This picture is of an Indian Trail Crossing in the Creek area of Alabama.

he shall send them to a situation between the agency and the enemy. The information I received today goes also by express to him."

I am, respectfully, dear sir, your obedient servant,

Benjamin Hawkins[12]

In the state of general alarm there were leaders like George S. Gaines who were reaching out, seeking to gather help in the event of further attacks. He met with Chief Pushmataha and ask the help of the Choctaw Nation, and sent an urgent message to Governor Willie Blount of Tennessee and General Andrew Jackson asking the aid of the Tennessee Volunteers. And Colonel McKee asked the aid of the Chickasaws.

X

THE UNITED STATES GOES TO WAR ON THE CREEKS

The 'Massacre of Fort Mims' became the rallying cry and from many places the response was beyond expectation. It is fitting to note that Colonel Hawkins was a friend of both white and Indian and was a man of integrity and no doubt had made an effort to apprise the various parties concerned of the growing seriousness of the conflict between the Indians and whites, hoping to head off war, but to no avail. But now with this emotional rallying point (it would be well to note the beginning of the war could be put on the white's attack of the Indians at Burnt Corn Creek) the cry for help brought a fine response.

The appeal of George S. Gaines to Chief Pushmataha was warmly received for he was a proven friend of the whites of the Tombigbee area. Chief Pushmataha asked the Choctaw warriors to join him in support of the whites in opposing the hostile Creeks and many hundreds responded. The call of Colonel McKee to the Chickasaws also brought forth a response of support. The call of Colonel Hawkins and others brought a response from General Floyd and the Georgia Militia. And the Tennessee Volunteers under command of General Jackson responded. In a real sense help was on the way from every direction.

The 'Red Sticks'[1] were now in a state of war with The United States. They were called such by their habit of getting dye type rock from 'Red Mountain', (in present-day Birmingham), to crush and use to paint their war clubs and as war paint on themselves.[2]

The 'Red Sticks' were led primarily by Peter McQueen, William 'Red Eagle' Weatherford, Josiah Francis, Menowa and Highhead Jim. The 'Red Sticks' led by 'Red Eagle' were gathered at 'Holy Ground', where the Prophets had declared the white man could not defeat them. General Claiborne with his army from the Mississippi Territory, assisted by Chief Pushmataha and the Choctaw Warriors engaged these 'Red Sticks' at 'Holy Ground and thoroughly defeated them. It was here that tradition has it that the brave Chief Weatherford, 'Red Eagle',[3] leaped his horse Arrow from a high bluff into the Tallapoosa River and escaped.[4]

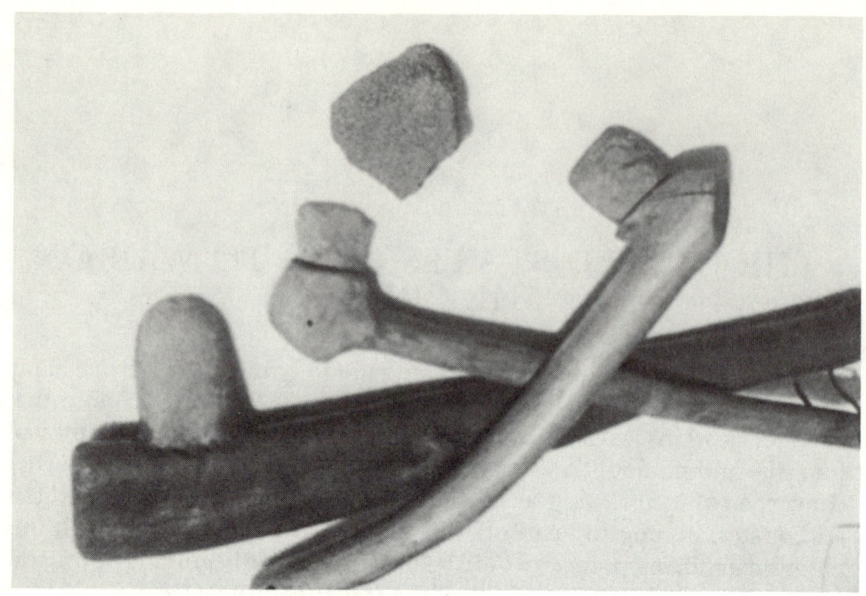

Red Sticks—War Clubs & 'Red Mountain rock'

About this time one other of the colorful participants in the Alabama Drama, David Crockett joined others like 'Red Eagle', William McIntosh, and Alexander McGillivrary. David Crockett tells of being part of the Tennessee Volunteers, under the command of General Coffee, taking part in the invasion of the Creek Nation, and taking the corn and dried beans of the Creek village (at present-day Tuscaloosa) called Black Warrior's Town, and burning the town as the Indian had fled before the army got there. He tells of killing hogs and cows for the soldiers to eat and giving the Indians an order to collect pay for them from Uncle Sam.

In the battle of Tallushatchee, Davy says he saw some 46 warriors run into a house. When an Indian woman shot and killed one of the soldiers, they opened fire and killed her and then burned the house. He says, "I recollect seeing a boy who was shot down near the house. His arm and thigh was broken, and he was so near the burning house that the grease was stewing out of him. In this situation he was still trying to crawl along; but not a murmur escaped him, though he was only 12 years old. So sullen is the Indian, when his dander is up, that he had sooner die than make a noise, or ask for quarters."[5]

Davy Crockett tells of an Indian runner bringing word to General Andrew Jackson at Fort Strother (just below the H. Neeley Henry Dam on the Coosa River). On December 7, 1813, General Jackson led his army

Write nothing above this line.

August 16, 1915.

Respectfully returned to

Mrs. Jean P. Day, President,
Oklahoma Division,
U. S. Daughters of 1812,
506 E. Seminole Street,
McAlester, Oklahoma.

The records of this office show that one Pushmattahaw served in the War of 1812 as a captain in a company of Choctaw Indians under command of Uriah Blue, from Sept. 21, 1814, to Jan. 27, 1815. Nothing further relative to this officer has been found of record.

The Adjutant General.

I wrote the National Archives concerning whether Chief Pushmataha was commissioned a General of The United States Army as I frequently ran across reference to him as Gen. Pushmataha. This letter was sent me from the Records of the Adjutant General's Office, 1780-1917, courtesy of The National Archives and History, Washington. D. C.

against Talladega. When the battle was over and the hostile Indians defeated Davy said all the Volunteers, whose 60 days of service was completed, informed General Jackson they were going home. He ordered the regular troops to stop them, but they would not open fire and Davy and the other volunteers walked out. Davy returned to his home in Tennessee, got a fresh horse, more clothes, and returned to rejoin Jackson's forces. When he got back to Fort Strother, Jackson had already left to further engage the hostile Creeks, and Davy caught up with them at Fort Williams.

In the battle of Enitachopeo, Davy says he thought there was an Indian behind every tree. He felt they would have been defeated had it not been for the bravery and leadership of Governor Carroll.[6]

Chief Minewa's Red Sticks fortify at Horseshoe Bend

Chief Menowa gathered all the forces possible of the 'Red Sticks' and fortified themselves at the 'Horseshoe Bend' on the Tallapoosa River. Menowa had some 1000 warriors primarily from Hillabee, Ocfuske, Ockehoie, Eufaulahatche, New-Yauca, Hickory Grounds, and Fish Ponds Towns. They erected a very formidable breastworks of logs across the narrow peninsula of land between the two points of the river. They doubtlessly felt it a very defensible stronghold, and so far as the cannon effect on it, it was so. But with the various elements of Jackson's forces fairly well surrounding them, the main force stormed the breastworks

This historical marker about Menawa Creek War Chief of The Battle of Horseshoe Bend, is located near Horseshoe Bend National Park near Dadeville, Alabama.

and after a few very bloody hours of hand to hand combat the 'Red Sticks' were defeated. And not only were these hostiles defeated, but the power and resistance of The Creek Nation was crushed.

Menowa and some 200 of his 1000 warriors survived the awful, and bloody battle of Cholocco Litsbixee-The Horseshoe. Albert Pickett says, "Menowa, one of the bravest Chiefs that ever lived, was literally shot to pieces. "Menowa told Pickett he escaped by jumping into the river where it was shallow lying underwater and breathing through a short cane. After dark he left the area through the forest.[7]

A short time after the battle of The Horseshoe, Jackson had built a fort at the site of old Fort Toulouse and named it Fort Jackson. Now many of the 'Red Sticks' began to come in and surrender to General Jackson.

One of the most picturesque and courageous scenes of the whole war took place here in the appearance and surrender of Chief 'Red Eagle', who had led the battle of Fort Mims, Calebee, and Holy Ground. 'Red Eagle' had come alone, accompanied by neither warriors or soldiers. I am sure General Jackson was greatly surprised. According to Pickett, General Jackson upon seeing 'Red Eagle' ran from his marque and exclaimed, "How dare you, sir, to ride up to my tent, after having murdered the women and children at Fort Mims?"

Weatherford replied, "General Jackson, I am not afraid of you. I fear no man, for I am a Creek Warrior. I have nothing to request in behalf of myself; you can kill me, if you desire. But I come to beg you to send for the women and children of the war party, who are now starving in the woods. Their fields and cribs have been destroyed by your people, who have driven them to the woods without an ear of corn. I hope that you will send out parties, who will safely conduct them here, in order that they may be fed. I exerted myself in vain to prevent the massacre of the women and children at Fort Mims. I am now done fighting. The 'Red Sticks' are nearly all killed. If I could fight you any longer, I would most heartily do so. Send for the women and children. They never did you any harm. But kill me, if the white people want it done."

At this point, many persons present cried out, "Kill Him! Kill Him! Kill Him! But General Jackson commanded silence, and in an emphatic manner, said, "Any man who would kill as brave a man as this would rob the dead!" Thus his life was spared and Chief 'Red Eagle' took no more part in the war except to encourage his warriors to surrender. He became a resident of Monroe County where he operated a farm and gained the respect of his neighbors.[8]

Pickett reports that some 5000 of the Indian women and children for whom 'Red Eagle' pled for were fed at the various American Posts.[9,10]

From Fort Jackson, Major General Andrew Jackson, Commanding

Officer, sent the following report to The President of The United States in April, 1814, (written by General Pickney)

Headquarters, Sixth and Seventh Districts
Camp, Confluence of the Coosa & Tallapoosa
23 of April, 1814

Sir:

"The complete success with which it has pleased the Almighty to bless the arms of the United States, in the present war with the hostile Creek Indians, having amply retaliated upon these infatuated people the loss of blood sustained by the citizens of the United States, and by that part of the nation who remained faithful to them; and their insolence, ingratitude, and perfidy, having been severely chastised; the Government of the United States, willing to spare the dispersed remnant of the miserable people, who may be sincerely disposed to atone for their former misdeeds, by their future good conduct; you will be pleased to communicate to them the following terms, upon which peace will be granted to them.

"The United States will retain so much of the conquered territory as may appear to the Government thereof to be a just indemnity for the expenses of the war, and as a restitution for the injuries sustained by its citizens, and the friendly Creek Indians. The United States will retain the right to establish military posts and trading houses, and to make and use such roads as they may think necessary, and freely to navigate all the rivers and water courses in the Creek territory. The enemy must, on their part, surrender their prophets, and such other instigators of the war, as may be designated by the Government of the United States; and they must agree to such restrictions upon their trade with foreign nations, as shall be established by the Government of the United States. You will please, sir, to communicate these terms to the friendly Indians, and to enjoin them in the prosecution of the war against such as may continue hostile, to abstain carefully from injuring those who may be returning, with the intention of making their submission. You may likewise inform them, that the United States will not forget their fidelity, but, in the arrangements which may be made of the lands to be retained as indemnity, their claims will be respected; and such of their chiefs as have distinguished themselves, by their exertion and valor in the common cause, will also receive a remuneration in the ceded lands, and in such manner as the Government may direct. You will please, sir, to take such measures as you may think expedient to communicate the above terms to the hostile party, and to point out the roads whereby they may approach the parts of the United States to surrender themselves, which roads you will also please to designate to the friendly party. The calamities of the war having reduced many of the women and children of the nation to the utmost distress, for want of subsistence, the United States will furnish provisions for them at the posts to which it can be most conveniently conveyed.

"I have the honor to be, very respectfully, sir, your most obediently servant,

Thomas Pinckney[11]

Peace Treaty at Fort Jackson

In July, 1814, General Jackson and Colonel Hawkins, now empowered by The United States Government to make a treaty with the Creeks, met with the chiefs of The Creek Confederacy and concluded a Treaty of Peace.[12]

In a report to the Secretary of War, General Armstrong, the following was written by Colonel Benjamin Hawkins:

"General Jackson terminated his negotiations with the Creeks on the 9th and left there on the 11th, with all the regular troops, going by water down the Alabama. The line of limits is Coosa river, with a reserve of two miles square for Fort Williams, to the falls of the river, seven miles above Fort Jackson; thence, eastwardly to a point, two miles north of Oakfuskee, (a large creek, six miles below Fort Decatur) thence, across Tallapoosa, to the mouth of the creek, and, up the same, ten miles in a direct line; thence, to Chattahoochee, and across it, at the first creek, two and a half miles below Oketoyocenne (about sixty-eight miles north of the confluence of Chattahoochee and Flint;) thence, east to Georgia, with an eventual reservation to accomodate the Kinnards. The details you will receive by the General's secretary.

We continue to receive daily rumors of hostile appearances at Apalachicola and Pensacola. The British armed vessels off that coast, have maneuvered dexterously, by landing and re-embarking their crews, to deceive the Indians in that neighborhood. They have, unquestionably, furnished a considerable supply of the munitions of war, and some clothing, and are training the Indians and some Negroes, for purposes hostile to us. The Indian training is to fire a swivel, sound the war whoop, fire three or four rounds of small arms, send the war whoop to every village, who repeat it, and are ready to march with the shortest notice; some have recently been to the frontiers of Georgia, and done mischief. The British officers have applied to the

The "treaties", which preceded the expulsion of some 125,000 Indians from the area of colonial America to West of the Mississippi River by the use of military force, were masterpieces of intimidation, bribery, threats, misrepresentation, force, and fraud. (There were 94 of these treaties made during Jackson's time.) Virgil J. Vogel, *This Country was Ours* (New York, Evanston, San Francisco, London: Harper & Row, Publishers, 1972 pp 285 "The Indian in American History; 1968" by Virgil J. Vogel pp 284-299.

stock-holders, in that quarter, to supply beef to the Indians, and they will pay for it. They have informed me they are apprehensive they shall not be paid.

"I have communicated, in detail, to Generals Pinckney and Jackson, who must soon take orders to crush the mischief batching in that quarter; or as soon as our new line of limits for the Creeks is known, it will rouse up and combine their whole force, in that quarter, against us. We should have ready our friendly warriors, of the Four Nations, to aid our troops in crossing them, without delay, which could readily be done.

"We have, from a creditable Indian source, the following, from a British Naval officer to the hostile chiefs: "The British and other Powers had conquered France. Seven Powers were now united against America. A little before white frost you will hear of smoke all round the United States, in the seaports, and the burning of powder. The war is just beginning; there will be several armies landing in different places. His King, George, said the seven Powers would be able and were determined to conquer America, and the British would be masters of it. They need not expect to be deceived; the British would fulfill their promise, and never leave this land again."

"I am, very respectfully, your obedient servant,

Benjamin Hawkins[13]

In the first quarter of the nineteenth century, The United States, by various methods, extracted the following cessions from the Indians:

Treaties with the Choctaws:

1802—The Choctaws ceded part of present day Mobile and Washington Counties.

1805—The Choctaw ceded part of Washington, Clarke, and Choctaw Counties.

1816—The Choctaw ceded part of Perry, Bibb, Shelby, and most or all of Marengo, Hale, Greene, Pickens and Tuscaloosa Counties.

1830—The Choctaw ceded part of Choctaw and most or all of Sumter Counties. This was all their remaining land in Alabama.

Treaties with the Chickasaws:

1816—The Chickasaws ceded part of Franklin, Marion, Fayette, and most or all of Lamar Counties.

1830—The Chickasaws ceded part of Marion, Franklin, and Colbert Counties. This was all their remaining land in Alabama.

Treaties with the Cherokees:

1806—The Cherokees ceded part of Madison, Lauderdale, and Limestone Counties.

1816—The Cherokee ceded part of Colbert, Franklin, Winston, Cullman, Morgan, Blount, St. Clair, and most or all of Lawrence County.

1817—The Cherokees ceded part of Limestone and Lauderdale Counties.

1819—The Cherokees ceded part of Madison, Marshall and most of Jackson County.

1835—The Cherokees ceded part of Morgan, Blount, Marshall, Etowah and most or all of Cherokee, and DeKalb Counties. This was all their remaining land in Alabama.

Treaties with the Creeks:

1814—The Creeks by the Creek Indian War Treaty of Fort Jackson ceded part of Winston, Cullman, Blount, St. Clair, Talledega, Elmore, Bullock, Barbour, Henry, Baldwin, Clarke, Perry, Bibb, and most or all of Walker, Jefferson, Shelby, Chilton, Autauga, Montgomery, Pike, Dale, Houston, Geneva, Coffee, Crenshaw, Lowndes, Butler, Covington, Conecuh, Escambia, Monroe, Wilcox, and Dallas Counties.

1832—The Creeks ceded part of Henry, Barbour, Elmore, Talledega, and most or all of Macon, Russell, Lee, Coosa, Tallapoosa, Chambers, Randolph, Clay, Cleburne, and Calhoun Counties. This was all their remaining land in Alabama.[14]

glass-looking quartz points found in Alabama and Georgia by the author.

XI

POLICIES OF CO-EXISTENCE OR PARTICIPATION OR • • •

Many factors enter into efforts toward co-existence and participation or absorption, 'the melting pot'.

The Indian and whites had intermingled and intermarried from the very beginning of their contacts. And many of the Indian tribes, nations, and confederacies were at times led or greatly influenced by the 'half-breeds', such as John Ross, Alexander McGillivrary, William McIntosh, William 'Red Eagle' Weatherford, and the Colberts. And no doubt this element among the Indian helped cause them to incline toward co-existing or even close cooperation, and to be responsive to such overtures from the whites.

There were Indian leaders, who though their natural inclination was not such, saw the handwriting on the wall. By the time of and immediately following the Revolution War, they came to believe the Indian must develop close relations with the whites or be forever threatened and pushed back. There were some among this element that came to believe that by learning and adopting white man's ways of dressing, of farming and husbandry, of speaking, and even their governments, the whites would be more inclined to accept them, and allow them to co-exist with them.

Another factor involved in this was the concern of many Government leaders that the Indian be pulled away from his relationship with the Spanish, French, and British and tied to the United States. This concern had three specific goals, to help break the power and influence of these other countries, to avoid or remove the potential causes of conflicts of war, and to secure for the United States the rich opportunities for trade.

Indian Civilization Act

The efforts of Government leaders such as Colonel Benjamin Hawkins was toward such goals. I believe this man was widely known among the Creek as their friend and that he had considerable success in his work among them. It may be that such men as he influenced the development of the idea that resulted in the Indian Civilization Act passed by The United States Congress in March, 1819. Certainly a very significant area for it to be applied was the emerging or developing southern Gulf area states, particularly Alabama and Mississippi.

In the development of the Government Factory System, the trading posts, efforts would be made to break up the Indian relationship with the Spanish, French, and British, and to gain all these trading opportunities and advantages for the United States. To be sure, such was vital to the development of the economy of the United States, to the strength and growth of the Government, and to the developments like Port Mobile and Port Charles Town Landing, etc.

Though there were accomplishments made by the Government Factory System, most of which was for the United States, by the early 1800's there was a growing feeling of the need for other programs.[1] Thus on March 3, 1819, (at the same time Alabama is struggling for statehood, (and I feel this Act was to aid that), the Congress of The United States passed the following Act, an Act making provisions for the civilization of the Indian tribes adjoining the frontier settlements.

"Be it enacted by the Senate and House of Representatives of The United States of America, in Congress assembled, that for the purpose of providing against the further decline and final extinction of the Indian tribes, adjoining the frontier settlements of the United States, and for introducing among them the habits and acts of civilization, the President of the United States shall be, and he is hereby authorized, in every case where he shall judge improvement in the habits and condition of such Indians practicable, and that the means of instruction can be introduced with their own consent, to employ capable persons of good moral character, to instruct them in the mode of agriculture suited to their situation; and for teaching their children in reading, writing, and arithmetic, and performing such other duties as may be enjoined, according to such instructions and rules as the President may give and prescribe for the regulation of their conduct, in the discharge of their duties.

Section 2: And be it further enacted, That the annual sum of ten thousand dollars be, and the same is hereby appropriated, for the purpose of carrying into effect the provisions of this act; and an account of the expenditure of the money, and proceedings in execution of the forgoing provisions, shall be laid annually before Congress.

Approved March 3, 1819.[2]

Mission Boards Established

A part of the general or grass roots support that enabled or encouraged the passage of this Indian Civilization Act was Church support of such. For in the same period the Church had been becoming involved in a Missionary Program to the Indians. In part, through the influence of John Stewart, a Negro, who as a missionary, made a great impact on the Delaware Indians. This mission success story stirred much interest across the area, and in 1819, The Ohio Conference of The Methodist Church adopted the work of John Stewart and other missionaries were sent among the Indians.[3] Then in 1820 The General Conference of The Methodist Church adopted the Missionary and Bible Society.[4]

This picture is of the historic log church at McIntosh Bluff, the first significant area in the Tombecbee Country where The Methodist Church was able to begin work. This area is again of great significance because of the struggle of the Mowa Band of Choctaw Indians, led by Gallasneed Weaver the Principal of Reed's Chapel School of McIntosh, Alabama. I feel this heroic struggle is to be recognized as Indians and as Americans, and granted the right of 'Self-Determination' and the opportunity of employment. (I am confident that such opportunities will result in the Indian youth of the area staying in school preparing themselves for a better life and greater usefulness).
(similar Churches were begun by Rev. Alexander Talley in Montgomery and Wetumpka (which the Indians called, "Tumbling Waters")

At this same time Bishop Francis Asbury assigned Rev. Alexander Talley to the 'Tombecbee' Country to work in the same area that Matthew Parham Sturdivant had been sent in 1808. In 1819 Rev Talley organized the Alabama Circuit.[5] Rev. Talley soon began to work among the Indians of the area. It seems reasonable to assume that he would have sought to relate to the Alabamo, the Coushatta, the Mobilian, and the Creek of the area as well as the Choctaw. But we have no records, I know of, that would indicate any success among any except the Choctaw. In 1821 the South Carolina Conference of The Methodist Church established the Mission to the Creeks and the Asbury School, led by Rev. Isaac Smith, was begun near Fort Mitchell. In 1822, Richard Neely, who had been sent into the north part of Alabama by the Tennessee Conference met a Cherokee named Richard Riley and was invited to preach in his home. This was the beginning of the Cherokee Mission in Jackson County, Alabama.

Rev. Talley is reported to have visited extensively among the Choctaw and that he came to know every Chief of the Nation.[6] Holland N. McTyeire in *A History of Methodism* says Chief Greenwood Leflore was Rev. Talley's interpreter, 'and a more fluent and eloquent one, according to accounts, a missionary never had.'[7]

Alexander Talley took a delegation of Indian converts to the Mississippi Annual Conference which met at Tuscaloosa in 1828. The Conference requested one of the Indians give an account of the work of Grace and the prospects of the Choctaw Nation. Captain Washington, a Chief of the Choctaw, responded through the interpreter and the Conference was powerfully moved. Bishop Soule rose from the chair, shook the hand of the Chief, and welcomed him and his people to the church, and exclaimed "Brethren, the Choctaw Nation is Jesus Christ's!

The Impact of Missionaries

I believe the first and most singular impact of the Christian Faith on the Indians of Alabama was through the person and work of Rev. Dr. Alexander Talley, (he was also a medical doctor in the area). Building on the goodwill toward whites, especially with Chief Pushmataha and Chief Greenwood Leflore, he began to reach out to the Indians of the area. Rev. Talley, had served the Alabama Circuit in the Tombecbee area, the Pensacola, Mobile, and Blakely Circuit, as District Superintendent in the Louisiana Conference, and practiced medicine several years in the Vernon and Dutch's Bend area, but his crowning, most singular work was that among the Choctaw Indians. Rev. Talley established such a relation of trust with the people of the Choctaw Nation that he was asked by them to help them in their removal to Oklahoma. Rev. Talley believed it was in the best interest of the Choctaw to remove to Oklahoma, and he worked at persuading them to do so. But this was out of his own conviction of such being best for the Indian, not as an agent of white interest and greed, (too often the missionary is an arm or agent of imperialism.). He worked with Chief Pushmataha[8] in the writing of an agreement of removal that Pushmataha took to Washington and tried to get approved. The Congress of the United States rejected this proposal of removal as being much too much in favor of the Choctaw Indians. Rev. Talley not only helped them prepare for the very difficult experience of leaving their beloved ancestral homeland and the long, hard journey to the new territory of the Indian Nation in Oklahoma, but we went with them! In 1827 Rev. Talley had been assigned as the Superintendent of the Choctaw Mission by the Mississippi Conference of The Methodist Church. He continued in that responsibility and work in Oklahoma until 1834. He then came to Vicksburg, Mississippi, where in the summer of 1835 he died of Cholera.[9]

Holland N. McTyeire in *A History of Methodism* holds the view that under the leadership of Rev. Alexander Talley, assisted by Rev. R. D. Smith and Rev. Moses Perry, over 3,000 Choctaws and Chickasaws had become members of the Methodist Church prior to their removal to the West.[10]

Schools—US Govt. Support

Under the direction of Government Agents The Indian Civilization Act was to promote 'White man' arts of civilization. The Missionary Societies of the various denominations, some of which had been organized about the time this Act was passed, were invited by the Government to participate in this work. The Federal Government would tolerate religious instructions if an adequate amount of mission attention was given to instructing the Indian Youth in secular subjects, agriculture, and domestic and mechanical arts. For their work among the Indians, the Missionary Societies received an annual federal grant as reimbursement for Indian tuition costs. Congress had appropriated $10,000 to be used annually for this work.[11]

This Government backing and financial support probably did influence the thrust of Missionary work among the Choctaw, the Creek, the Cherokee, and the Chickasaw Indians by the Baptist, the Methodist, and the Presbyterian.

In 1822 the Cumberland Presbyterian Association had 28 pupils in Charity Hall School near Cotton Gin Port on the Tombigbee River. By 1834 this school had closed because of the disenchantment caused by removal pressure. The South Carolina-Georgia Synod also established

Monroe School in 1820. This school was on the Natchez Trace near McIntoshville. The Chickasaw Council was so impressed with the Monroe School that they appropriated $5,000 from tribal funds to establish other schools. The Synod established three other schools, one Caney School was in Alabama. The administration of these Chickasaw schools was spread among the missionaries, the tribal council, and the Chickasaw agent.[12]

In 1821, Rev. Isaac Smith began the Asbury School for the Creek. This school was near Fort Mitchell and was named in honor of Bishop Francis Asbury who had appointed Rev. Smith to the mission. Colonel John Crowell, the United States Agent of Indian Affairs, opposed Smith's work among the Creek, but the work continued.[13]

By 1825, Rev. Smith had so favorably impressed the Creeks with his work that he was invited to preach to an assembly of some 50 chiefs of the Creek Nation, 'Little Prince', the Chief of The Creek Nation. After which 'Little Prince' signed his X in agreement to a letter that read, "I, Tustinuggee Hopoie, or 'Little Prince', head man of the Creek Nation, certify that I reside in the immediate neighborhood of the Asbury Missionary School in this Nation, and so far as I am informed the conduct of those who have charge of the institution has been perfectly satisfactory, and I have no cause to complaint. The children seem to be satisfied, and say that they are kindly treated.

'Little Prince, his X mark.[14]

One of the interesting experiences of Rev. Isaac Smith during his work at Asbury School was the privilege of joining with some 50 Creek Warriors in welcoming one of the most distinguished visitors ever to visit the State of Alabama. The State Legislature had extended an invitation to General LaFayette to visit Alabama, and he came. Isaac Smith had served with General LaFayette under General George Washington during the American Revolutionary War. These two noble men embraced on the banks of the Chattahoochee near Fort Mitchell, evidencing their deep felt affection for each other, and the joyous privilege of seeing each other again after the lapse of so many years.[15]

In 1829, Rev. Smith reported 71 members of The Methodist Church and 50 school students at Asbury. Of these Creek students, one of them, Samuel Checote, became Chief of The Creek Nation in Indian Territory in 1867, and was twice reelected. He served The Indian Missionary Conference, of which he was a leading member, as a presiding elder.[16] He also was a delegate to the Ecumenical Conference held in London, England in 1881.[17]

In 1822, Richard Neely began the Mission to the Cherokee and within a year there were about 100 members of The Methodist Church. In five

This picture of a likeness of General LaFayette and a plaque noting the visit of LaFayette to Alabama and to 'Goat Hill' later to be Capital Hill in Montgomery. It is located between The Capital and The Archives and History Building.

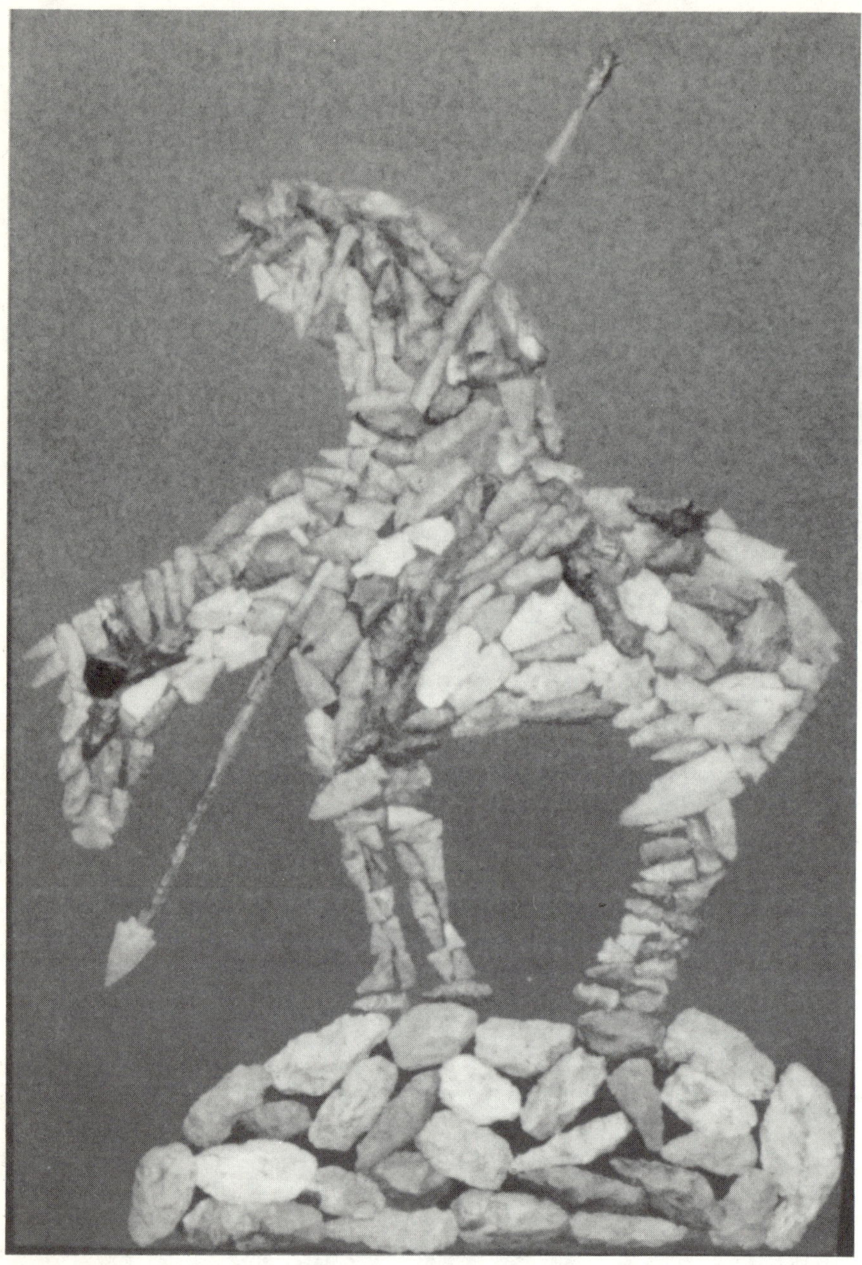

This picture is a copy of a famous one, 'End of The Trail' and is made of Indian artifacts. It was given me by Don Osborne, Principal of The Owens Jr. High School, Athens, Alabama, It is made with arrows, spear points or projectile points, drills, scrapers etc.

years there were upwards of 700 Cherokee who had been baptized into the Christian Faith and had become members of The Methodist Church. Most significant among them was Turtle Fields, an imminent Chief, who became a Methodist preacher. This Cherokee Chief, who had served as a soldier under General Andrew Jackson in the war against the 'Red Sticks', was admitted into membership of the Tennessee Annual Conference in its session at Tuscumbia, Alabama in 1827. By 1830 there were five mission schools being conducted by The Methodist Church among the Cherokee.[18]

Two of the greatest fruits of Methodist Missionary work among the Indian was the winning as a convert of Chief John Ross, who was for some 40 years a most influential leader of the Cherokee. The other was the Indian alphabet (syllabary) invented by Chief Sequoyah of the Cherokee Tribe. It was a very simple arrangement and could be easily mastered by students. Through this means the Scriptures were made available, hymns translated, and a literature prepared. Thus, education and Christianity were promoted.[19]

There was evidence in all these Indian Nations that coexisting with the white settlements was possible, but there were also those who were determined such would not be and instigated conflicts. Thus, by the late 1820's there was a developing ground swell for 'Removal'.

XII

REMOVAL

The idea of removal developed slowly. At first the whites were able to get the land they needed or desired by barter or encroachment. In some cases of open conflict the whites defeated Indian villages or tribes and then drove them from the area, thus taking the land by conquest. This was an acceptable national policy used all across the colonial period and especially heavily by General Jackson against the defeated Creek Nation. Through the application of this policy the United States acquired millions of acres of Alabama territory from the Creeks. In the signing of the Peace Treaty at Fort Jackson ending the Creek Indian War was Captain Isaac a chief of the Coushatta, and thereby they lost most of their land in Alabama.[1]

Virgil J. Vogel, in *This Country Was Ours,* says "Expediency alone determined the formula that was used to acquire Indian land, and a variety of arguments have been used to justify expropriation of the Indians. These have included the right of discovery, the right of conquest, purchase, the doctrine of the primacy of civilized over uncivilized men, and the principle that unused or underused land may be appropriated by those who will cultivate it. Usually the Indians right of occupancy only of such land as they required *to* survive was grudgingly conceded; but even this ideas was abandoned by some in favor of a belief in the extermination of the aboriginal inhabitants."[2]

H. H. Breckenridge says, "I am so far from thinking the Indians have a right to the soil, that not having a better use of it for many hundreds of years, I conceive they have forfeited all pretence to claim, and ought to be driven from it."[4]

In the development of Removal, as a national policy, many factors or ideas were contributors. To be sure, some of these were based on humanitarian concern for the future well being of the Indians. In the early years of the colonial period many whites shared Rosseau's view of the Indian as a 'Noble Savage' much of which was probably influenced by the help the Indians gave the new settlers. But as the Indians resisted the land greedy encroachment of the whites this attitude shifted to that shared by John Adams, in a view he expressed in 1790, "I am not of Rosseau's opinion. His notions of the purity of morals in savage nations and the earliest ages of civilized nations are mere chimeras."[6]

The decadence of greed creeps into even Christian groups, or maybe I should say it creeps into groups influenced to some degree by Christian ideas and principles. It seems strange to me that seemingly from the church circles or groups came the idea that God willed the whites replace the Indian in order that the land be properly used. (I would like for those who expounded that theory, and even more those who practiced it, to tell me how they explain how those same whites could in a very few years virtually destroy the land by their greedy over emphasis of producing cotton and tobacco, etc. in a mad rush to gain wealth and power.) This idea became quite widespread. It was evidenced by the Puritans when they lashed out at Indian resistance to their encroachment and killed some 500 Indians of the Pequot Village. The Puritan evangelist Cotton Mather was grateful to the Lord that "on this day we have sent six hundred heathen souls to hell."[7]

Peter Farb reports that the Puritans failed miserably in their dealings with the Indian because of their attitude toward the Indian. Part of which was their demand that the Indian express faith as they did.[8]

Peter Farb further reports that the whites coined phrases such as expressed by Senator Thomas Hart Benton of Missouri, "The Whites must supplant Indians because the whites used the land, 'according to the intentions of the Creator', to justify encroachment and the taking of the Indian's land by whatever means it took. Even the enlightened Benjamin Franklin observed that rum should be regarded as an agent of Providence, 'to extirpate these savages in order to make room for the cultivators of the earth."[9]

Thomas Jefferson, prior to January, 1803, seems to have felt the best solution to the Indian problem of the United States was the amalgamation of Indians and whites or the 'melting pot' idea.[10] When Jefferson saw the possibility of buying the Louisiana Territory he began to see that land acquisition as a possible solution. The Indian groups could be persuaded to trade their land in the various states for land west of the Mississippi River, thus separating the Indians from the whites.[11]

In the Louisiana Territorial Act of 1804 the President was empowered to effect Indian emigration. "The President of the United States is hereby authorized to stipulate with any Indian tribes owning land on the east side of the Mississippi and residing thereon, for an exchange of lands, the property of The United States, on the west side of the Mississippi, in case the said tribes shall remove and settle thereon: but in such stipulation, the said tribes shall acknowledge themselves to be under the protection of

The United States, and shall agree that they will not hold any treaty with any foreign power, individual state, or with the individuals of any state or power; and that they will not sell or dispose of said lands, or any part thereof, to any sovereign power, except The United States, nor to be subjects or citizens of any other sovereign power, not to the citizens of The United States.[12]

From this time on, the idea of 'Removal' began to spread across the United States, and to take firm root. In 1802 the Georgia Compact was passed, in which the United States agreed to extinguish, at its own expense, Indian title within the reserved limits of Georgia, (this contention was concerning most of the land of the Alabama and Mississippi Territory) as soon as it could be done peaceably and on reasonable terms. Evidently President Jefferson felt these conditions could be met in the securing of the Louisiana Territory.[13]

Annie Heloise Abel in her Ph D Dissertation, 'The History of Events Resulting in Indian Consolidation West of The Mississippi River' says President Jefferson was trying to use this purchase to two ends. (1) He was trying to secure a monoply on the valuable fur trade of the far west and northwest. (2) And he felt the removal of the Indian would stop white encroachment on Indian land that caused conflict and war between them and thereby put a serious drain on the Federal Treasury.[14]

Another approach of 'Removal' initiated by President Jefferson was the Government Factory System. The plan of this was to get the Indians in debt beyond his ability to pay and then pressure them to settle the debt by giving up land. Jefferson did this as a means of satisfying whites's demand for more land. In 1803 the United States acquired some 853,700 acres of Choctaw land in the Treaty of Hoe Buckintoops in exchange for cancelled debts and a modest amount of additional goods.[15]

Ironically, the Indian, in the late 18th century and early 19th century, had come to believe that they could coexist with the whites by adopting the white man's ways. The Chickasaws, The Cherokees, The Choctaws, The Creeks, and The Seminoles had become known as 'The five Civilized Tribes'. Charles M. Hudson in Four Centuries of Southern Indians, says, "they were not called civilized because of aboriginal achievements, but because they successfully adopted many of the cultural patterns and social institutions of the white man."[16]

The Creek National Council voted in 1829 to stay and submit to the laws of the State of Alabama.[17]

Though there was much pro-white feeling and desire among the Indian to co-exist with the white, there were many Indian leaders who felt 'Removal'—the trading of their lands for new homes west of the Mississippi River—was in the best interest of the Indian. Most of these felt

Historical Marker in Dahlonega, Georgia. This marker bears the phrase "Thar's gold in them thar hills" that became famous for the area and tragically stirred the base greed of the whites of Georgia to pass an act of legislation to the disenfranchising of the Cherokee Indians of the area.

the whites were a corrupting force on the Indian, and they desired to retain their ancient, tribal customs and traditions.

But there seemingly was no way to turn back the tide—flood tide—of political pressure to move the Indian out of the way of an ever increasing white need and demand for more of the Indian's land (and there was a legitimate need for more land to provide for an evergrowing number of whites.) And the whites's discovery of gold at Dalonega, Georgia, in 1820, added fuel to the fire. Following this growing clamor of the whites for this land, the State of Georgia passed a law forbidding the Indians to mine gold or trade in gold, and prepared to survey the land and sell it to whites.[18]

The Indian Tribes, who had roots in the soil of Alabama and the Southeast, who would have to face and deal with the bitter and tragic experience of removal are many in number. The primary ones are the so called, 'Five Civilized Tribes', the Cherokee, The Creek, The Choctaw, The Chickasaw, and The Seminole. Many smaller groups or tribes, or

Fine points from the author's collection.

parts of tribes who were participants in these larger tribes or confederacies also experienced removal.

After two missionaries among the Cherokee were arrested and jailed by Georgia officials, Chief John Ross employed counsel and carried the matter before the Supreme Court of The United States. The decision of the court stated, "The Cherokee Nation, then, is a distinct community, occupying its own territory, with boundaries accurately, and while the citizens of Georgia have no right to enter, but with the assent of the Cherokees themselves, or in conformity with treaties and the acts of Congress. The whole intercourse between the United States and this nation is, by our constitution and laws, vested in the government of The United States. And the law under which Worcester was convicted is consequently void and the judgment a nullity.[19]

It is reported that President Jackson upon hearing this decision of the Supreme Court of The United States retorted, "John Marshall has made his decision, now let him enforce it." President Jackson ignored the ruling and advised officials of the State of Georgia to continue their pressure and harrassment of the Indians.[20, 21, 22]

In 1830 with the passage of the 'Removal Act' it became the official National Policy. The most powerful and influential proponent of this National Policy was President Andrew Jackson, whose attitude toward the Indian certainly contributed to his rise to the presidency. The spirit of the frontier—'clear the Indian out'—was an important factor in elevating General Andrew Jackson of 'Horseshoe Bend' fame to the presidency. The Treaty of Fort Jackson by which Jackson extracted millions of acres of Alabama from the Creeks certainly helped him achieve the presidency.

Following the passage of the Indian Removal Act in 1830 the Indian began to realize they had little hope of being able to continue to live in this ancestral homeland.[23]

At this time the Southeastern Tribes were a settled people, who had complex institutions, and who were developing constitutional governments, establishing schools, and churches, and farming by American frontier standards.[24]

After the Federal Government passed the Indian Removal Act, the next step was to seek the agreement of the Indian to follow through on it. Grant Foreman in *Indian Removal* says, "The Indians were called into councils and gorged with pork and beef and plied with whiskey; chiefs, warriors, and other influential men of the tribes by argument, persuasion, cojolory, threats, or bribes, the means depending on the exigencies of the occasion, were induced to agree to terms set down on paper called treaties."[25]

It was a very painful experience for the Indians to consider leaving their beloved ancestral homeland. Speaking concerning this, Grant Foreman says, "They loved their streams and valleys, their hills, and forests, their fields, and herds, their homes and firesides, families and friends. They cherished a passionate attachment for the earth that held the bones of their ancestors and relatives. The trees that shaded their homes, the cooling spring that ministered to every family, friendly watercourses, familiar trails and prospects, bush grounds, and council houses were their property and their friends; these possessions filled their lives and their loss of them was cataclysmic. Grief and desolation overwhelmed the Indians as they were compelled to leave all these behind forever and begin the long journey toward the setting sun which they called the 'Trail of Tears'."[26]

Some groups began to face up to what they now felt inevitable and prepared to move west. And some of these were soon on their way. This only encouraged the whites to put more pressure on those who yet resisted such removal. This pressure took many forms such as groups of whites moving in and claiming the land and property being vacated, other whites came among the remaining Indians using liquor, etc. in widespread efforts to defraud the Indians of their property, and the state imposed offensive laws upon them to further pressure them to leave. The Indians protested such treatment and were told President Andrew Jackson and the United States Government were powerless to help them.

They were told it was therefore best for them to remove to the west. To be sure there would have been grave problems, even a civil war, from rugged individualists and strong, adamant states righters' had the government sought to ensure fair treatment for the Indians. But the major reason the Indian experienced such treatment was that so many influential leaders of The United States Government, like President Jackson, were supportive of it or even advocates of it.

There were many factors contributing to the development of Removal. The factionalism within the Indian communities and nations was certainly one of the significant factors. To be sure, part of this, maybe, even the most of it, was planned and promoted by whites. Yet, the facts remains, part of it was rivalry of leadership and differences of opinion. Some of the Indians felt it was to the advantage of the Indian to adopt some of the white man's ways, while others strongly opposed such and urged the Indians to keep old ways and traditions, rejecting all ways of the white man. Some Indians felt it was best for the Indian to move beyond the Mississippi, because of conflict with whites when they lived in close proximity, as was now inevitable in the East. Others felt the Indian must hold on to their ancestral homelands, and continue to live in them.

This factionalism was greatly influenced and used by devious methods of whites, especially the Georgians. Sometimes this was an attack on the integrity of tribal leaders. Often it was to deal or treat with the majority or rebel factions, knowing that to be valid Treaties had to be approved by National Councils. This was to divide and conquer.[27]

By the fall of 1833, the tensions between the Indians and whites were such that the situation was deemed grave. In October, President Jackson sent Francis Scott Key, the author of our national anthem, "The Star Spangled Banner", to Alabama to seek to reconcile the conflicting parties of Indians and whites. He felt these tensions would not have developed had the Federal Government kept the whites from encroaching on land belonging to the Indians. He sought, with some success, to persuade leaders of the State of Alabama to help enforce the Federal laws preventing land speculators from harassing or defrauding the Indians.[28]

Though there were many whites who treated the Indian unjustly, there were also whites who were friends of the Indian and who objected to the inhumane treatment of Indians. There was such a group of whites in Macon County who met in the home of James Abercrombie and adopted a resolution as follows:

". . . great fraud has been recently committed in obtaining title to lands, belonging to Indians without their knowledge or consent in any way whatever; the person committing such frauds or rather stealing the lands of the Indians has some other Indian who he has drilled with the description of locations and other matters in relation to the land; the Indian when thus drilled and a new song put into his mouth goes before the certifying agent and passes his land by certificate as being the real Indian owning that tract of land to the stealer or white man, who immediately sends such certificate to Washington City for the approval of the President; the Indians who are the rightful owners of the lands knowing nothing of this foul and dishonest transaction until nearly all their lands have been swept from under them", and they ask the President to re-examine all such transactions to prevent such gross mistreatment of the Indian.[29]

CHOCTAW REMOVAL

As early as 1818 efforts were being made by The United States Government to get the Choctaw Nation to agree to Removal to the west. At first Chief Pushmataha was opposed to the idea, but in time his close friend and adviser, Rev. Alexander Talley, a Methodist Missionary to the Choctaw people, persuaded him to try to work out an agreement. Rev. Talley prepared the text of a treaty proposal and Chief Pushmataha took it to Washington, D. C. where he argued for it with government leaders. The United States Congress rejected the proposal because, as they said, it was too much in favor of the Choctaw Indians. Sick and deeply disappointed at his failure in behalf of his people, Chief Pushmataha died and was buried in the Old Congressional Cemetery in Washington, D. C. (He was probably buried in the Old Congressional Cemetery because of his commission as an officer to lead the Choctaw and Chickasaw Warriors who joined the United States Army under General Andrew Jackson, against the Creek Red Sticks, and the British in the War of 1812.) The body of Chief Pushmataha was later removed from The Old Congressional Cemetery and brought back to his beloved homeland and buried.

In the fall of 1830, President Andrew Jackson sent Secretary of War John Eaton and General John Coffee to negotiate a removal agreement with the Choctaw Nation at Dancing Rabbit Creek. The method of bribery of Indian leaders played a large part in the final extraction of the agreement.[30]

The Choctaws requested the government to secure their long-time friend of The Government Factory System of Fort St. Stephens Association, Colonel George Strother Gaines of Demopolis, Alabama, to be placed in charge of their removal. Some of those were moved a large part of the way by steamboat, others were moved by large wagon trains, others went essentially by foot in order to drive their cattle and horses to their new home in the west. One of these groups, at the Choctaw's request, was led by Rev. Alexander Talley, the Methodist Missionary to the Choctaw. Arthur H. DeRosier, Jr. in The Removal of The Choctaw Indians says, "Talley was informed in a letter from Major David W. Haley in the Choctaw Nation that he would be followed by several hundred Indians who would arrive by the first of January, 1831. Haley also notified Talley of the government's generous position on voluntary removal: "The president has the five hundred thousand dollars at his disposal, and he never will let the Choctaw suffer that emigrate. Do not be timid in providing for the poor Choctaws, on your arrival on Red River."[34]

Evidently Rev. Talley thought this was official and it was alright for him to see to it that the most basic needs of the emigrating Choctaws would be taken care of as required. It is reported that in great concern for the unnecessary suffering of the Choctaw, and the poor manner in which the Government agents made provisions for them, he spent all his money for rations for the Choctaws.[31] In footnote 26 on page 40 of *Indian Removal,*[32] Grant Foreman says, "In 1836 General J. F. H. Clairborne wrote the Secretary of War, 'I have the honor to transmit to you the papers and acts of the late Alexander Talley precisely in the situation in which I received them. He died suddenly while preparing to present this claim and it is now offered for the benefit of his infant heirs.' " (Claiborne to Cass, Jan 25, 1836, OIA, "Choctaw Emigration")[35]

Three months later the Secretary of War reported to the Senate against Talley's claim on the ground that his employment and disbursements to purchase food for his starving Indians had not previously been authorized by the government. (U. S. Senate Files, Twenty-fourth Congress, first session, Report of The Secretary of War.)[36]

After several groups removed, the Government terminated its efforts at further Choctaw removal leaving some 6,000 still in the area. Still later, between 1844-1847, the Government responded to white pressure and removed about 3,000 more of the Choctaw.[37] (Of those allowed to remain there are an estimated 6,000 of the decendants in Mobile and Washington Counties of Alabama today.) W. David Baird in *The Choctaw People* says, "From the point of view of the government the Choctaw removal was wholly successful. To be sure the cost was more than anticipated, altogether exceeding five million dollars if the value of the scrip issued in the 1840's, the expense of surveying the tribal domain, and the amount of the temporary annuities paid the tribe are included. Nevertheless, the United States had made a handsome profit. In 1859 it estimated that when finally sold the land obtained from the Choctaws would gross over eight million dollars, leaving three million dollars as the net proceeds of the transactions."[38]

Much of the suffering the Choctaws experienced would not have been,

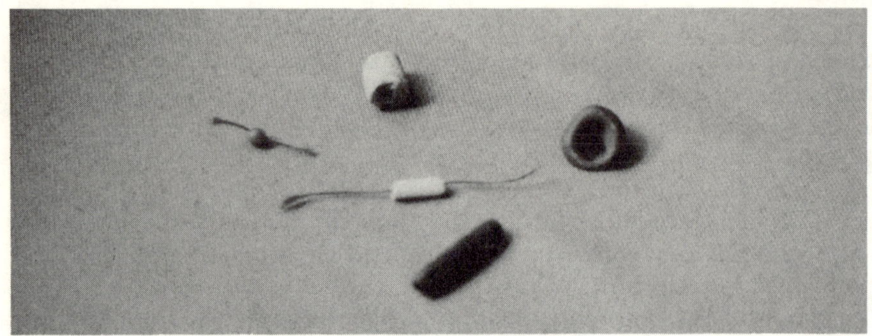

beads from the author's collection.

had the request for a doctor to be assigned to each group and adequate rations provided along the way, had been fulfilled by the United States Agents. (These requests seems to have been the work and influence of Rev. Dr. Alexander Talley, a Methodist Missionary to the Choctaw. He was also a doctor. He went with one of the Choctaw groups to Oklahoma.)

Grant Foreman in *Indian Removal* says much of the provisions provided the Choctaw were barrels of meat the soldiers had refused because of its foul or rotting condition.[39]

CHICKASAW REMOVAL

In 1826 leaders of the Chickasaw Nation met with the United States Commissioners to discuss a Treaty of Removal. The Chickasaws rejected the proposed terms. With the success of President Jackson in getting the passage of The Indian Removal Act of 1830, they began to consider removal inevitable. About this time Alabama and Mississippi both passed laws abolishing the tribal governments within their states and declared all Indian subjects to the laws of the state. Thus in order for them to be, and remain a separate nation they must remove. Therefore, at Franklin, Tennessee in August, 1830, the leaders of the Chickasaws agreed to cede their homeland for one in the West. But when the Chickasaws heard the report of Chief Levi Colbert on the proposed home in the West they again rejected the Treaty.

Following an agreement, the United States Government worked out for part of the Choctaw area of the West, the Chickasaw Tribal Council met with The United States Government Commissioners at Pontotoc Creek in 1837 and agreed to Removal terms.[40]

In July, 1837, the Chickasaw Removal under Agent A. M. M. Upshaw got underway. The Chickasaws, known as The Bear Creek Indians,

Stockade as might have been built by Troops of General Scott to retain Indians being rounded up for Removal to the West. Courtesy of Joe B. Vann and Bruce Gragg of Trussville.

probably the only part of the Chickasaws still remaining in Alabama at the time of Removal, were removed in the charge of Lt. Phillips.[41]

Grant Foreman in *Indian Removal* holds the view that the Chickasaw Removal was a comparatively tranquil affair.[42] In comparison to the Removal of the Creek and Cherokee and Seminole it probably was. Certainly from the standpoint of the efforts and expense of the Government, it was far less than these. But to those Chickasaws who were being torn from their beloved, ancestral homeland it was anything but tranquil.

CREEK REMOVAL

In 1829, the Creek National Council voted to stay in their ancestral homeland and submit to the laws of The State of Alabama. There were several leaders of the Creeks like William 'Red Eagle' Weatherford and Chief Menowa who would have helped to create goodwill among their people had the State of Alabama discouraged land greedy whites from further mistreatment of the Indians. William Brandon in *The Last Americans* says, "In 1821 and 1823, some years before the push for removal, William MacIntosh of the Creeks had made treaties with citizens of Georgia ceding 15,000,000 acres of Creek land. He had been supported in these treaties by twelve other Creek chiefs under his control, but opposed by thirty-six chiefs representing ninetenths of the Creek nation. MacIntosh was in the pay of the Georgia commissioners, and in 1825, said emoluments being fattened, MacIntosh and his followers signed a treaty ceding the remaining Creek land—10,000,000 acres—to Georgia. These treaties were not only in violation of Creek custom—"Among the Creeks there is no such thing as selling or ceding of lands. *'It is for me, for thee, and for all'*. . . . " but the MacIntosh treaties were also in violation of a specific Creek law that provided the death penalty for any Creek who sold land without the consent of the entire nation in council. Formal sentence was passed on MacIntosh after the signing of the 1825 treaty, and on the morning of May Day, 1825, a party of Creek warriors went to his house and shot him to death, and his son-in-law as well for good measure. The appointed executioner who killed William McIntosh was Menewa, the ex-Red Stick commander.

The illegal treaty of 1825 was annulled, and the following year Menewa went to Washington and signed a new treaty, supposedly securing the Creeks in the possession of their remaining territory, and promising his loyalty henceforth to the United States."[44]

Chief Menowa, famed leader of The Red Sticks at Horseshoe Bend, had become a steadfast American Ally.

Angie Debo speaking of the harrassment of the Indian during this period says, "These lands grabbers used misrepresentation, the Indian not knowing what he was signing, the use of intoxicants, the misuse of notary seals on blank instruments to be filled in at the swindler's convenience, outright forgery, the bribing of some subservient Indians to impersonate the owner and sign in his place, and rigged probate procedure in the state courts corrupted by the general dishonesty to get title to Indian land."[45]

By 1835, there was rebellion among the Creek, protesting the injustice they were experiencing at the hands of whites of the area. This condition was disturbing to some leaders in Alabama. General Gilbert Shearer, head of The Militia of The State of Alabama, said, "Many persons are interested in producing an alarm and provoking hostilities, with the hope of diverting a scrutiny into their own fraudulent transactions with the Indian."[46]

It was such fraud by whites upon the Indians that had deprived them of homes and food, and reduced them to such wandering, hunger, and desperate conditions as to result in their hostilities. These hostilities created a state of alarm and in May, 1836, The United States Secretary of War, Cass, ordered General Thomas S. Jesup into Alabama to subdue the hostile Indians. His orders was not just remove all hostile Indians from the state, but remove all the Creeks from Alabama. This included those who had supported The United States efforts against the hostile Red Sticks, and those who had been assured by the Treaty of Removal that those who wished could receive a tract of land and remain in the State of Alabama.

In June, Chief Eneah Emathlo and some 1,000 of his hostile followers were captured and put in a stockade at Fort Mitchell. In July, some 1,600 Creek, guarded by 3 Companies of armed soldiers, left Fort Mitchell for the West. Near Tuskegee some more prisoners, including Jim Henry, were added to this number. (In later years Jim Henry, one of the leaders of The Red Sticks in the Creek Indian War, was converted, joined the Methodist Church, and became a Methodist preacher. For many years he was an influential religious leader.) These Indians were handcuffed and manacled and marched 90 miles to Montgomery. In Montgomery, they were put on steamboats for Oklahoma.

In August, 1836, Chief Opothleyehalo led some 2,700 Creeks from Tallasee for the West. This group went through Tuscaloosa for Memphis.[46] A. B. Moore tells of Chief Eufaula being allowed to address the Legislature of The State of Alabama in session in Tuscaloosa. He said, "I come, brothers to see the great house of Alabama and the men that make the laws, and say farewell in brotherly kindness before I go to the far West where my people are now going. We leave behind our goodwill to the people of Alabama, who build the great houses, and to the men who make the laws. This is all I have to say. I came to say farewell to the wise men who make the laws, and to wish them peace and happiness in the country which my forefathers owned, and which I now leave to go to other homes in the West. I leave the graves of my fathers, but the Indian are going out, almost clean gone, and new fires are lighting there for us."[47] In Memphis, this party was loaded on steamboats for Arkansas.

Lieutenant R. B. Screws led a group of some 3,022 Creeks from Wetumpka in August. He delivered some 2,000 at Fort Gibson, for many starving groups had stopped along the way to search for food.

When the Creek Removal was finished and they were enumerated in Oklahoma it was determined they had lost about 45 percent of their members. A few stragglers were probably left in Alabama, (This is probably the ones from whom decend many of the members of The Creek Nation East of The Mississippi, headquartered at Poarch near Atmore, Alabama.)[48] There were many others unaccounted for that probably fled to Florida to join the Seminole Tribe. But the tragic fact remains that many thousands had died or were killed through all the bitter experiences of Removal. William Brandon says, "The terms of the

Stockade built by troops of General Scott to hold Indians rounded up for Removal to the West. Courtesy of Joe B. Vann, member of 1st United Methodist Church of Trussville, Al.

Creek treaty permitted individual Creeks to elect to stay in their native land (if they were willing to brave continued persecution by the States) and quite a few meant to do so. However, these provisions were abrogated by the government, and all the Creeks were forced to leave, including Menewa, who had received a personal promise from high authority to the contrary. On the night before he left he went back to his town of Okfuskee and spent the night alone. He said to an old white friend the next morning, "Last evening I saw the sun set for the last time, and its light shine upon the tree tops, and the land, and the water, that I am never to look upon again." Then he walked away. He was an old man, and had been many times wounded. But those who believe that Indians don't cry haven't looked over the official reports of the Great Removal."[49]

SEMINOLE REMOVAL

The Seminole Tribe was made up largely of rebel elements from The Creek Confederacy—Muscogee, Hitchiti, Yamassee, Yuchi, etc.—that fled from Georgia after the Yamassee War, and from Alabama after the Creek Indian War, and also from Alabama during the Removal of The Creek.

Chief Osceola, realizing the Creek Nation was being crushed by General Jackson's forces, led some 1,000 'Red Sticks' to Florida to become part of The Seminole Tribe. There as a part of the Seminoles, this group became the neuculeus of the strong defiance of the Seminoles, to the efforts of The United States Government to remove them.

Following The Second Seminole War a large part of The Seminole Tribe was removed to the West. After the expenditures of many lives, much suffering, an estimated $20,000,000 (some records indicate as much as $40,000,000 and about 1,500 soldier's lives) the United States Government called a halt to its efforts to totally remove the Seminole from Florida. And a remnant of the Seminoles have remained a part of Florida.

Hand holder & press for the top of an 'arrow like' drill, from the author's collection.

This picture is of a scene from the outdoor drama, "Unto These Hills" and is of Elias Boudinot invoking The Great Spirit in concern for his people about to be driven from their ancestral homeland to Oklahoma. Courtesy of The Cherokee Historical Society, Cherokee, North Carolina.

Courtesy of The Cherokee Historical Association

CHEROKEE REMOVAL

Chief John Ross was strongly opposed to the idea of the removal of the Cherokee from their homeland. He was supported by many leaders of the Cherokee Nation. Chief Ross led many efforts to unify the Cherokee against removal, and to frustrate the work of The United States Government in their effort to convince the Indians to agree to remove. His efforts were in vain, for in 1838 Major General Winfield Scott was ordered into the Cherokee Nation to remove them by force of arms.

General Scott moved the Army, under his command, into the area and set up his headquarters at Calhoun, Tennessee. He assured Chief Ross and The Cherokee that every effort would be put forth to accomplish their removal without bloodshed. In General Order Number 25, he so directed the troops in his command.

Stockade or Concentration Camp

Scott's troops set immediately to the task of getting stockades or 'concentation camps' built at various points in The Cherokee Nation. One of these Stockades was at Barry Springs in Cherokee County, Alabama.[51]

Colonel Robert N. Mann in *The Cherokee County Heritage,* volume III of The Cherokee County Historical Society, Inc., says, "After much national debate and negotiations with the Indians May 23, 1838 was set as the date for their removal to Indian Territory west of the Mississippi River in what is now the northeastern section of Oklahoma. Before removal the Indians had to be gathered at control points by U.S. Government Army and State Militia troops. One of these points or stockades was at Barry Springs, where there was an ample supply of fresh water. The stockade consisted of a large circular chestnut log enclosure—the split logs about 20 feet in length were set end wise in the ground. The stockade was located a few hundred yards north of the spring and was large enough to permit the approximately 400 to 500 families to set up their tepees for shelter and cook their meals, the food being furnished by the U. S. Government, under the supervision of the soldiers. Many of the Indians died while thus imprisoned.

'The Trail of Tears'

Barry Springs thereby became one of the points from which 'The Trail of Tears' began. The Cherokee suffered indescribable hardships from which 4,000 of the 13,000 forced emigrants died.

Barry Springs is located in the extreme northeastern part of Cherokee County on State Route 99. The rather large spring runs into Mills Creek some 100 feet east of the spring, which in turn runs into the Chattooga River. Local residents say the spring has no bottom and believe it to be the mouth of an underground cavern."[52]

Then, General Scott ordered the troops to round up all the Cherokees and put them in these stockades in preparation for forced removal. These squads of troops with rifle and bayonett were to search out every family, arrest them and bring them to the stockades. A Georgia volunteer, afterward a Colonel in The Confederate Service, said, "I fought through the Civil War and have seen men shot to pieces and slaughtered by

BARRY SPRINGS INDIAN STOCKADE
ONE HUNDRED FEET EAST WAS ONE SITE WHERE "THE TRAIL OF
TEARS" BEGAN. ON MAY 23, 1838 THE INDIANS OF THIS GENERAL
AREA, WHO HAD BEEN HELD IN A CHESTNUT LOG STOCKADE AFTER BEING
GATHERED BY THE U.S. ARMY, BEGAN THEIR LONG TREK TO OKLAHOMA.
THE SPRING, WHICH WAS THE SOURCE OF WATER FOR THE INDIANS
IS BELIEVED TO BE THE MOUTH OF AN UNDERGROUND CAVERN.
ELI O. ALEXANDER AND WIFE MARGARET (BARRY) ALLISON AND
RICHARD BARRY SETTLED IN THIS AREA ABOUT 1838.
THE RICHARD BARRY LOG HOUSE C. 100 YARDS WEST OF THE
SPRING WAS RECENTLY (C. 1970) DESTROYED BY FIRE.
CHEROKEE COUNTY HISTORICAL SOCIETY

thousands, but the Cherokee Removal was the cruelest work I ever knew."[52]

The soldiers were ordered to take the Indians by surprise to prevent any escaping. Gary C. Moulton tells of one old patriarch, when thus surprised, calmly called his children and grandchildren around him, and kneeling down, bid them pray with him in their own language, while the astonished soldiers looked on in silence. Then rising he led the way into exile.

Chief John Ross, out of great concern for his people, moved into the Cherokee Agency at Calhoun, Tennessee to oversee the details of each group being removed to the West.[53]

Gary E. Moulton says, "No accurate figures exist for the number who died as a result of this tragic trek, and present generations have but slight sense of the suffering involved. Some put the death toll at 1,600. When added to that number those who fell victim to the harsh encampments before removal and the many who succumbed to the debilitating circumstances after arrival, nearly four thousand Cherokees or a quarter of the tribe, were lost in process. (But) dismal and deadly as removal became, it was certainly less harsh, than it would have been had it been executed under the heavy hand of martial law."[54]

Many of us in seeing the splendid television production of 'Holocaust' about the Nazi Regime or Third Reich treatment of the Jews was reminded of our own forcible uprooting and removal of some 60,000 American Indians. The tragic experiences of the 'Trail of Tears' is woven into the rich and colorful fabric of our national history. But it need not be the final word or chapter. The 'teardrops' fell, and for almost a hundred years it seemed they fell in vain—hopeless—hopelessness, but wait----! HOPE. . . "a new day is dawning for the American Indian," so says Chief George Pierre.[55]

THE TRAIL OF TEARS: This picture done by artist Robert Lindneux and is provided for this book by The Woolaroc Museum, Bartlesville, Oklahoma. This scene could have been of the Cherokee who had been gathered in the stockade at Barry Springs and now were being driven out of their homeland to exile in the area to become Oklahoma, or it might have been the Creek being driven out of East-central Alabama, etc.

XIII

OUR NATIONAL HERITAGE FROM THE INDIAN

All who share in the present day life and culture of America are benefactors of the American Indian. Though it is quite complex, there are many noteworthy aspects of this great heritage. In remembering, like the Apostle Paul speaks of himself, that we are debtors to the American Indian because we have from them so bountifully received will surely cause us to be moved with gratitude. And gratitude is one of the greatest, most important graces of human life.

In a day when much of our world emphasis and concern is on the problem or grave crisis of 'Hunger', it is certainly worthy that we take note of the American Indian's great achievements and contributions of products that are usuable as food. It seems those who began the colonies at Jamestown and Plymouth Rock would not have survived had it not been for the great neighborliness of the Indians who lived nearby. Captain John Smith tells of the importance of the food the Indians shared with the folk at Jamestown.[1] And these Indians shared their seed for them to be able to plant gardens for their future needs. They also taught them how to fish in the bay and make use of the bountiful fish supply so close at hand. The writer of Better Homes and Gardens Heritage Cookbook tells of Squanto, an Indian neighbor, teaching the Pilgrims how to plant and grow corn and about other edible plants to be found in the area. He taught them how to use fish scraps as fertilizer for their gardens.[2, 3]

The contribution of the American Indian to the development of food products is a truly amazing feat or achievement. In *Better Homes and Gardens Heritage Cookbook* the authors says, "American Indians were excellent farmers and were the first to cultivate what today comprises almost 50 percent of the world's plant foods, maize (Indian corn), beans, peanuts, potatoes, manioc (also known as cassava), tapioca, squashes, pumpkins, papayas, guaves, avocados, pineapples, tomatoes, chili peppers, cocoa (for chocolate), chicle (for chewing gum), and many other vegetables and fruits."[4] It is truly an amazing achievement that in the field of food the American Indian would accomplish about the same as all the

'Old Charles Town Port' was built largely through the influence and significance of trade with the Indians. Jesse Burt and Robert B. Ferguson in *Indians of the Southeast Then and Now* report that a million and a quarter deer skins were shipped to England from Charleston, South Carolina between 1739 and 1759. p. 116 (Nashville, & New York: Abingdon Press, 1973.)
(This picture provided me for this book courtesy of The Chamber of Commerce of Charleston, South Carolina.)

rest of the human family combined. The sad part of that story is some parts of the human family contributed very little, and part of the reason is, like the DeSoto Expedition, too many were always looking for an opportunity to ride on the back of someone else. In other words, they were ever looking for an opportunity to take what someone else had accomplished.

The economy of The United States was built on trade, and its first real impact was the trade with the Indians for skins. Many of the Europeans were, above all else, traders and saw, in the Indian's use of skins, particularly doe and buck skins, for their clothing, a splendid opportunity to develop a trading enterprise. In a very short time the Indian style deer skin coat was a very popular item of clothing all across Europe, as well as the Colonial Frontier.[5] (These dear-skin Indian style coats and moccasins are still important in our total economy). I can imagine seeing an old Indian countryman with his mule or horse pack train, maybe 75 or 100 of

Courtesy of The Charleston Museum

these pack animals loaded down, winding their way from the area of Fort Toulouse along the Indian trail toward the port of Old Charles Town Landing (presentday Charleston, South Carolina). And within a few years literally tons of deerskins are being brought to the trading posts across this land to be offered for colorful beads, cloth, guns and ammunition, and other trade items. Though there were other items of significance in this trade, such as corn and tobacco, skins were, by far, the most important in volume and value. (Tobacco caught on quickly among the Enlgish at Jamestown and tobacco became the most important medium of exchange in Virginia.)[6] I am of the opinion that this skin trade gave birth to the vast and world-wide United States economy. I also believe the financial returns of this trade was vital in the development of the colonies and indeed the very life blood of the birth of this great nation! To be sure, this trade was vital to the very survival of the colonies. The first business enterprise established by the early colonists was a glass business at Jamestown, Virginia, and much of its products, like the colorful beads, were probably involved in this skin trade with the Indians. And in terms of value for value, I am of the opinion the Indian was really 'being skinned.' There is evidence of another angle of the significance of this trade with the Indian to be found at Jamestown. There is evidence from archeological research of the area, that virtually every man and woman in Jamestown had a pipe and was smoking the 'Indian tobacco.'[7, 8]

This trade with the Indian was of great significance, first, in terms of building a trade economy. But it was also of great significance in that it provided much of the food so very vital to the colonies. Many of the colonists were not accustomed to, nor willing to do the hard manual work of clearing new grounds and tilling the land that was necessary in order to produce the food they needed. Others were slow in learning the necessary skills required and in acquiring the seeds and the tillable land that was needed to grow food crops in sufficient quantity to meet their needs. Thus, these people found in the Indian villages the opportunity to trade for the food they needed or wanted. The food received from the Indian, either as gifts in gestures of friendliness or neighborliness, or through their trading, was essential in the very survival of the colonies. One of the famous stories in the development of Colonial America is of the Indian bringing gifts of food to the Pilgrims—it is part of the tradition of Thanksgiving in America!

In the story of the development of the American economy, in the trade with the Indians, there are two stories that are truly fascinating and significant. One is of the impact of maize or corn on the markets of the world. Maize was readily an universally favorite food—'corn on the cob', hot buttered corn bread (yum, yum!)—and it was good for both man and beast! Corn was easily kept over long periods of time, as in its harvest stage, dry in the shuck it could be stored indefinitely in cribs or barns, in trading posts, or in ships. And certainly of economic importance (though greatly debatable in character development), corn could be turned into liquid and stored in bottles as beverages. And in our day it has become even more significant, in the development of gasohol, as a part of the solution of our energy crisis. Corn had many usages in Colonial America, such as feeding stock, chickens, etc., or for table use as grits, hominy, corn on the cob, and corn bread, etc. And it was adaptable for growth all over the world. It is an amazing story how this plant, which was domesticated and called 'maize' by the Indians, and was used exclusively by them for several thousand years, in a few centuries through the influence of white traders had become one of the most significant grains on earth. The other such story is that of tobacco which the Indian had domesticated and used for eons and which he gave as a gift to Columbus—and thusly, to the world. In a century or two, tobacco had made a very significant impact on a major part of the world market.[9] An interesting symbol of this impact on world trade is the wooden Indian that often marked or identified 'The Tobacco Shoppe'. This is probably the most nearly universal or international symbol of a shoppe to be found all over the world. One such symbol well known in Alabama, is 'Ole Kowliga', the old wooden Indian at Kowliga Beach on Lake Martin (that one was probably made to mark a famous 'Tobacco Shoppe', too.)

In our generation leisure and sports events have been most significant in our economy—and part of that—popcorn, peanuts, and cracker-jacks–are all gifts of the Indian.[10]

The Indian language has added much to our present day language. Sidney Lanier speaks of the softness and beauty of the Indian language. The names of rivers, streams, mountains, communities, cities, counties, and even the name of our state have come to us from Indian heritage. The Tennessee, Flint, Coosa, Tallapoosa, Tombigbee, Sipsee, Warrior, Buttahatchie, Cahaba, Alabama, Chattahoochie, and the Mobile Rivers all derive their present day name from the Indian. The name of our state—Alabama—derives from the Alibamos Tribe, who lived in the area of present day Montgomery. And the name means, 'Thicket Clears', probably noting their changing forest or thicket land into farmland. I feel it is fitting that our state name pay tribute to those noble working folk who many, many centuries ago brought forth abundant harvest through their toil. As we travel the roads and interstate highways of this great and beautiful land we see names of states, counties, cities, communities, streams, and rivers, etc., that derive from the Indian. But along these roads we also see the influence of the Indians on our signs—the use of

These tools of the Shaman, American Indian Medicine Man, and genseng roots remind us of the great achievements of The Indian in the field of medicine.

Great Moments in Medicine courtesy of Park Davis Drug Co. A division of Warner-Lambert Co. and Druid City Hospital Tus—Ala.

arrows in giving directions. And surely it is fitting that the role and great contribution of the Indian Scout in the development of America be memorialized. These Indian Scouts guided the early explorers of this nation, assisted and counseled the surveyors, served as scouts and trained Scouts for her first state or colony militia and her Continental Army."[11] I am sure General George Washington relied heavily on this resource. Indian style of warfare was significant in the Revolutionary War.[12] Boy Scout Movement *too!* In summer camps all across this country Boy Scouts and Girl Guides learn Indian lore and woodcraft. Charles Eastman, a Sioux Indian, was a founder of the Boy Scout Movement in America.[13]

The Indian made a significant contribution to the development of modern medicine in America. There are many roots, barks, leaves, herbs, and concoctions the Indian used, that through his sharing with white men, we use today. Michael A. Weiner in *Earth Medicine-Earth Food*[14] says, "Many early settlers asked the Indian to show them which plants were useful for curing sickness. Since the Indians were, at first, friendly to the newcomers, they showed them some of their healing plants. Soon many Indian medicine men were treating both whites and natives." He also said, "Our grandfather's physicians learned about the medicinal uses of many plants from the Indian. Indian remedies came to us from the writings of travelers, missionaries, soldiers, anthropologists, and botantists."[15]

C. Fayne Porter in *Our Indian Heritage,*[16] speaking of the Indian's contribution to the development of modern medicine, reports that "So skillful were the Indians in the knowledge of natural remedies that 'in the four hundred years that the European physicians and botanists have been analyzing and examining the flora of America, they have not yet discovered a medicinal herb not known to the Indian.' "[15]

In the hallway of the laboratory section of The Lanier Memorial Hospital in Langdale, Alabama, there is a gallery of pictures that tell something of the story of the development of modern medicine. Among those pictures is one of an Indian dragging his canoe ashore on Mackinac Island for bringing medicine for the 'white doctor' on the island. I have walked along that shoreline and through that little hospital shack where part of this great drama unfolded. But I am impressed it happened similarly many times over all across colonial America often unrecorded or remembered. As I ponder the first doctor of the Alabama area, Dr. Alexander Talley, who was also a great missionary to the Choctaw, I wonder how many times as he visited the different Indian villages the shamans or medicine men shared their insights and their medicines to help him in his work. I feel he received from these Indians, as well as, so bountifully gave of his life and ministry to them.

I believe the Indian offers to all Americans an example of

Across the years, in doing research on the American Indian I had hoped to meet an Indian Shaman. While visiting at The United Methodist Church at Cherokee, North Carolina I had asked about some Indian who gathered bark, leaves, roots, and herbs to sell to pharmaceutical companies. One of the ladies told me of Dinah Welsh, a Cherokee woman whose father had been a medicine man. Dinah had learned from her father and for years had practiced medicine. It was my privilege to visit with her at her home in Big Cove near Cherokee. She told me about gathering bark, roots, and herbs and using them for medicine. In the picture she is showing me genseng roots which she said was good medicine. I asked her about buying the genseng and she told me, "Indian not sell medicine. Medicine is a gift from The Great Spirit. Indian share medicine."

attitude—Faith—that is worthy of all acceptation. His faith in God expressed itself in attitude toward other human beings, and animals-in fact, all living things, and the earth as his Mother. We would do well to take a long hard look at the Indian's love for the earth, especially in view of the importance of ecology and conservation in our day! Surely, Chief Sealth of the Duwamish Tribe speaks with great wisdom when he says, "All things are connected. Whatever befalls the earth befalls the sons of the earth."[16]

Chief Sealth speaking of faith says, "One thing we know, which the white man may one day discover. Our God is the same God. You may think now that you own Him as you wish to own our land. But you cannot. He is the Body of man. And His compassion is equal for the redman and the white. This earth is precious to Him and to harm the earth is to heap contempt on its creator."[17]

Surely, we would be remiss, if we did not note the great contribution of the Indian in basic integrity, 'his word is his bond.' One of the great scandals of this country is to compare the word of Indian vs White man particularly in the treaties they made. The Indian kept them scrupulously and the white man flagrantly violated virtually every one he made. One glowing, and noble example does stand out—and that is the word of William Penn. Speaking of the Indian's integrity, George Catlin said, "I love a people who have always made me welcome to the best they had, who are honest without laws, who have no jails and no poorhouses, who never take the name of God in vain—who worship God without a Bible, and I believe God loves them also—who are free from religious animosities—who never fought a battle with white men except on their own ground—and oh!! how I love a people who don't live for the love of money."[17]

I believe The United States and The State of Alabama became realities only because the American Indian allowed the whites to settle these areas. The American Indian was naturally inclined to friendliness and hospitality. They obviously welcomed the newly arrived colonists at Jamestown, and Olde James Towne Landing, and Mobile, etc, and graciously allowed them to establish their villages. Had they chosen to at that point, they could easily have exterminated them. Therefore, I believe it can rightly be said that The United States of America was born at Jamestown and Alabama was born at Mobile.

I believe the greatest contribution of the Indian to us, of present day America, is Democracy. The freedom loving attitude, self-determination, and democratic form of government of the Indian that many of the early colonists were in contact with, doubtlessly influenced their thinking. It also influenced the thinking of some of the most influential philosophers of the day. In turn their pamphlets and writings, and speaking would greatly influence the colonists. I feel sure, this was one of the most significant influences in the development of the movement for independence.

I am sure ideas from various 'Old World' countries influenced the framing of our Constitution and our form of government. But, I am of the opinion, that Thomas Jefferson, Benjamin Franklin, George Washington and many others were much more influenced by the governments of the Indian Nations, such as The Iroquois Nation or League and The Creek Confederacy, which they observed, dealt with, or encountered. Many of the Indian communities and nations were quite democratic, that is there was opportunity for widespread individual participation in the decisions that affected their lives, community, and nation. Most community and national concerns seemed to have been discussed and the course of actions or action determined by all the men, of good standing in the community or nation, in Council. Many of the things done, in the decision making process, was the equivalent of a vote. One famous example of this was in the matter of the challenge of Chief Tecumseh for the Choctaw to go to war on the whites of the 'Tombecbee Country'. When he finished his firey speech he cast his ballot or vote—war club—on the side designated for war. Then Chief Pushmataha, noble Chief of The Choctaw Nation or Tribe, rose and rebutted Chief Tecumseh, and cast his vote on the side of The Great Council Fire designated for Peace! Had it ended there it would have been essentially as such matters were normally decided in the countries of 'The Old World'. But that was not the norm for The World of The American Indian, for all the men and often the women had a share in such decisions. Chief Pushmataha then challenged all the warriors of The Choctaw and Chickasaw Tribes to rise and cast their vote—war club—for war or peace. When the voting was finished the vast majority had voted for peace with their white neighbors.[18] Now that seemed to be the normal way the decisions were made in the village Council House, or around the Great National Council Fires. And I ask where else on earth, prior to the establishment of The United States of America, did the common man, the grass roots help make the decisions?

Benjamin Franklin proposed a scheme of 'lobbyist' to go among the various colonies and promote the idea of a union of the colonies. We can, I believe, assume that Mr. Franklin had been influenced in reading Caldwallader Colden's, History of the Five Indian Nations.[19]

In League of The Ho-de-no-san-nea or Iroquois, the author Lewis Henry Morgan says the Iroquois commended to our forefathers a union of the colonies similar to their own as early as 1755. They saw in the common interests and common speech of the several colonies the elements of a confederation.[20]

C. Fayne Porter in *Our Indian Heritage* says, "By the time the colonists (1607) came, the Iroquois were a tightly organized social and political unit, with rules and regulations governing relations with each other as well as with outside groups and with a complex, democratic form of constitution symbolized in the great wampum belts of the Confederacy. For a century and a half the colonist would live side by side with a people

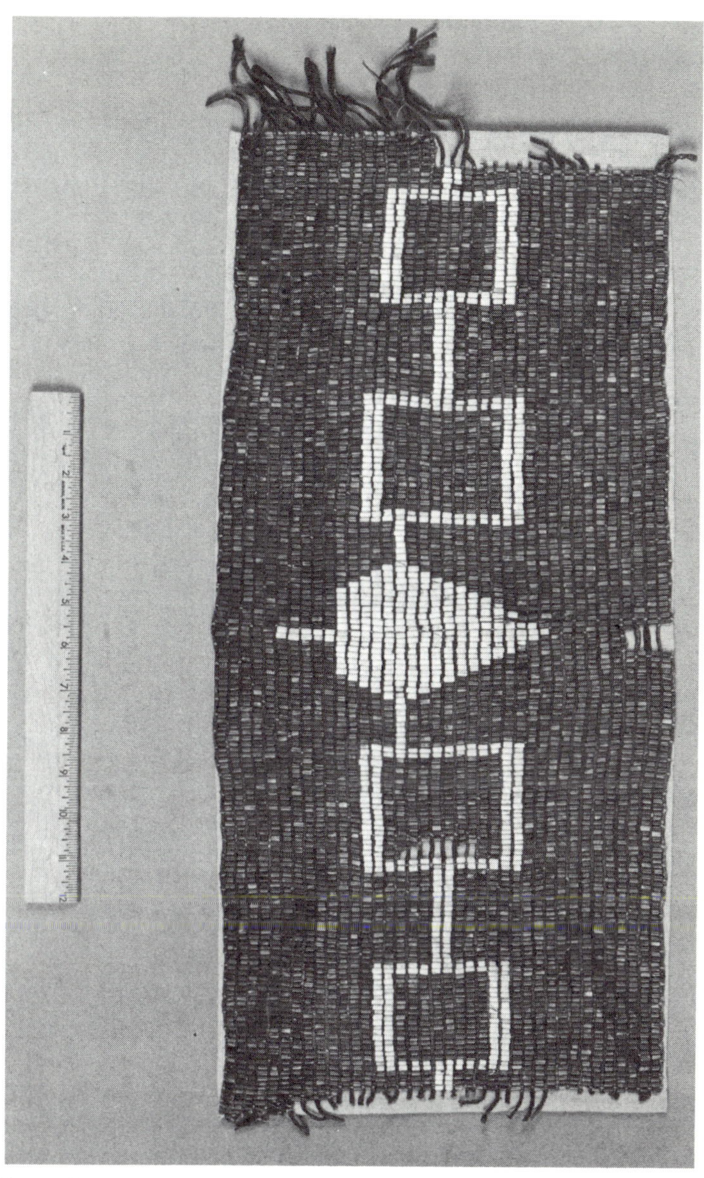

This picture of The Hiawatha Wampum belt is of The Iroquois League or Confederacy. The first league was composed of five states or nations of Iroquois, but the sixth joined later. Henry R. Schoolcraft in *History of The Indian Tribes of The United States* in speaking of the Legend of Hiawatha says, "Hiawatha, in a meeting with the five Iroquois Tribes in Council to discuss the northern enemy tribes, recommended the Union or Confederacy of The Iroquois. The Council considered it and adopted it." p. 314 of volume 3. (*Picture Courtesy of The New York State Museum.)*

governed by a strict constitution; when it came time for them to make up a set of procedures of their own, where more logically could they look than to the Ho-de-no-san-nee?"[21]

In 1744 a Council was held between the representatives of the Six Nations of Iroquois and the colonies of Pennsylvania and Connecticut to seek some solution to the problems or conflicts between them. In that Council an Oneida Sachem suggested to the representatives of the colonies that they might consider an organization or union like theirs as a possible solution to the problems of the colonies.[22]

When Thomas Jefferson and Benjamin Franklin and others began to talk the possibility of a union or confederation they were met on every hand by those who were saying, "it can't be done". Benjamin Franklin responded to this pessimism, with, "It would be a strange thing if Six Nations of ignorant savages should be capable of forming a scheme for such a union and be able to execute it in such a manner, as that it has subsisted for ages, and appears indissoluble; and yet that a like union should be impracticable for ten or a dozen English colonies, to whom it is more necessary and must be more advantageous, and whom cannot be supposed to want an equal understanding of their interest."[23]

Alvin M. Josephy, Jr. in *The Indian Heritage of America* says, "The Way in which Congressional Senate and House conferees work out bills in compromise sessions is very similar to ways of the Iroquois League."[24]

Thus the Indian not only provided the basic model, but probably more important the climate or environment, the attitude of Self-Determination of the Indian, that was so contagious and was the root from which the giant oak, the institution of The United States of America grew!

This picture depicting the Eagle Dance, a scene from the Drama Unto These Hills, was provided me for use in this book courtesy of The Cherokee Historical Association.

XIV

REMNANTS REMAIN ACROSS THE SOUTHEAST

THE CREEK INDIAN REMNANT

There is a legend that says Chief Lynn McGhee saved the life of General Andrew Jackson during the American-Creek War of 1812-1814 period. This legend was shared with me by Mrs. John W. Bradshaw of Ensley, Alabama, who, under the direction of The Episcopal Bishop of Alabama, had worked as a missionary for some five years with the Creek Indians of the Atmore area.

In 1836 Chief Lynn McGhee and two other friendly Creeks were given a tract of land each. Some hold this was done because Chief McGhee had saved the life of General Jackson. Others hold the view that this land grant was made because the three were guides or Indian scouts for Jackson's Forces. The primary basis of this claim was the Treaty between The United States and The Creek Nation of Indians of February 16, 1815 granting Samuel Smith, Lynn McGhee, and Semoice each a reservation of 640 acres of land in the area.

THE PRIVATE STATUTES AT LARGE OF THE UNITED STATES OF AMERICA,

CHAP. CCCXXXIII.—*An Act for the relief of Samuel Smith, Lynn MacGhee, and Semoice, friendly Creek Indians.*

Be it enacted, &c., That Samuel Smith, Lynn MacGhee, and Semoice, friendly Creek Indians, who were entitled, under the treaty with the Creek nation of Indians, ratified on the sixteenth of February, eighteen hundred and fifteen, to reservations of six hundred and forty acres of land each, including their improvements, which lands have been sold by the United States, be, and they are hereby, authorized to enter, without payment, with the register and receiver of the land office for the land district in which the same may lie, in Alabama, one entire section each of land subject to entry at private sale; to be held by them on the same terms and conditions as the reservations given by said treaty.

Approved, July 2, 1836.

Statute I.
July 2, 1836.

Authorized to enter a tract of land.
Act of March 2, 1837, ch. 29.

3 G 2

Chap. XXIX.—*An Act to amend an act approved the second of July, eighteen hundred and thirty-six, for the relief of Samuel Smith, Linn McGhee, and Semoice, Creek Indians; and, also, an act passed the second July, eighteen hundred and thirty-six, for the relief of Susan Marlow.*

Be it enacted, &c., That so much of the acts for the relief of Samuel Smith, Linn McGhee, Semoice, and Susan Marlow, as restrict them to the entry of one entire section of land, be, and the same is hereby repealed; and the said Samuel Smith, Linn McGhee, Semoice, and Susan Marlow, are hereby authorized to enter, without payment, and by legal subdivisions, a quantity of land not exceeding six hundred and forty acres each, which is subject to entry at private sale.

Approved, March 2, 1837.

Statute II.
March 2, 1837.

1836, ch. 333.
1836, ch. 334

So much of acts as restricts them to one section, repealed.
Authorized to enter, &c.

It is further contended that when the Creeks were driven out of the Southeast for the Indian Nation west of the Mississippi River, Chief Lynn McGhee and his family and close associates were allowed to remain in their homeland.

Another of the well known Creek leaders of the Jackson Era, Chief William 'Red Eagle' Weatherford was allowed to remain. By the Creek Removal time Chief Red Eagle had become a respected farmer and neighbor in Monroe County. He was also given a land grant and spent the remainder of his lifetime in the area. There is today a monument erected in the area to his honor.

THE ETERNAL FLAME
THIS FIRE WILL BURN FOREVER AS A SYMBOL OF FRIENDSHIP ETERNAL BETWEEN THE WHITE MAN AND THE RED MAN. IT WAS KINDLED WITH A FLAME FROM A CHEROKEE INDIAN COUNCIL FIRE THAT HAS BEEN BURNING IN OKLAHOMA SINCE 1839. THE ORIGINAL FIRE WAS TAKEN TO OKLAHOMA WHEN ALL BUT A REMNANT OF THE PROUD CHEROKEE NATION WAS REMOVED WEST OVER THE INFAMOUS "TRAIL OF TEARS". IN MAY 1951 FOUR TRIBAL LEADERS FROM THE QUALLA BOUNDARY, CHEROKEE INDIAN RESERVATION, RETRACED THAT TRAIL OF HEARTBREAK TAKEN BY THEIR ANCESTORS AND BROUGHT LIVE COALS FROM THE OKLAHOMA FIRE. THE ETERNAL FLAME HERE AT THE MOUNTAINSIDE THEATRE WAS KINDLED FROM THE CENTURY OLD OKLAHOMA FIRE ON JUNE 23, 1951.
PSALM 121 1:2 IN THE CHEROKEE SYLLABARY:
I WILL LIFT UP MINE EYES UNTO THE HILLS, FROM WHENCE COMETH MY HELP. MY HELP COMETH FROM THE LORD, WHICH MADE HEAVEN AND EARTH.

Today there are some 500 Creeks in the Poarch area. They have organized as an Indian Tribe or Band. They have established an Agency in the Poarch Community and call it The Creek Nation East of The Mississippi River.

In 1950 The State of Alabama recognized this group. And on October 19, 1950 The Creek Nation East of The Mississippi was formally recognized and established. They elected a twelve man Council of the Perdido Band of Friendly Creek Indians of Alabama and Northwest Florida with Calvin McGhee as Chairman of The Council. Later Calvin McGhee became the Chief.

In 1970, at the death of Chief Calvin McGhee, his son, Houston, Became the Chief. In 1973 an Eastern Creek Unity Conference was held, Chief Hoston McGhee was recognized as Chief of the entire Creek Nation East of The Mississippi. He appointed Wesley Thomley of Pensacola, Florida as Chief of The Creek of Florida, and Neil McCormick of Cairo, Georgia as Chief of The Creek of Georgia.

The Creek Nation East of The Mississippi holds Annual Celebrations—Fourth of July Pow-Wow in Cairo, Georgia, Labor Day Pow-Wow in Pensacola, Florida, Thanksgiving Pow-Wow in Poarch, Alabama.

They are represented in The Alabama Commission on Indian Affairs, and have achieved recognition by The United States Bureau of Indian Affairs.

THE CHOCTAW INDIAN REMNANT

The Choctaw Nation by 1830 had ceded most of its land base to The United States Government. Under pressure by the Federal Agents, The Choctaw Tribal Council finally agreed to relocate to the Indian Territory, which is present-day Oklahoma.

Part of the agreement was that those who wished might remain and become citizens of The State of Mississippi, and citizens of The United States of America. Some 3,000 chose to do so, and remained in their homeland.

This group that remained was granted Federal recognition in 1945 as The Mississippi Band of Choctaw Indians. They are today, The Choctaw of The Philadelphia Reservation, which is some 18,000 acres scattered across eight counties in east central Mississippi.

CHOCTAW RESERVATION
Neshoba, Newton, Leake, Scott, Jones, Attala, Kemper,
and Winston Counties, MISSISSIPPI
Choctaw Tribe
Tribal Headquarters: Pearl River, Neshoba County, Mississippi 39350

Federal Reservation
Population: 3,294 (BIA 3/72)

LAND STATUS	Total Area: 17,819 acres
Tribally Owned:	17,381 acres
Allotted:	209 acres
Government Owned:	229 acres

Reservation lands are checkerboarded with non-Indian lands. At the time of the 1830 removal of the Choctaw to Oklahoma, 104,320 acres were awarded to those remaining. By 1918, only one of the 163 sections remained in Indian ownership. The U.S. Government sponsored a land-purchase program and acquired 16,805 acres in seven counties. The title is held in trust by the United States. The tribe is continuing its effort to purchase additional land.

HISTORY

The Choctaw were one of the most powerful tribes in what is now the Southeastern United States. The first white man to encounter them, Hernando de Soto, fought a fierce battle with the Choctaw in 1540. The Indians, although defeated, terrorized the Spanish. After 1700, the Choctaw Tribe was caught between and cleverly divided by the French and English. After 1780, the tribe was caught in a similar situation between United States and Spanish interests. Between 1763 and 1830, the Choctaw signed a series of eight treaties which ceded most of their land to the United States. The Treaty of Dancing Rabbit Creek, in 1830, provided for the removal of the tribe to Oklahoma, including a provision allowing those so choosing to remain in Mississippi. The last group to move left Mississippi in 1903, and, from then until 1916, the remaining Choctaw were largely forgotten. A series of epidemics brought the tribe to the attention of the U.S. Senate, which prompted an investigation resulting in appropriation of Federal funds for schools and services to the tribe.

CULTURE

The tribe is and has been predominantly agricultural, raising crops typical of the area: squash, beans, and corn. The Choctaw dislike war and prefer to settle disputes over the table. Their game of stickball, an often deadly sport, was used to settle differences between tribes. The tribe is democratic and places women in a prominent, rather powerful, position. A part of the Mound Builders' culture, the Choctaw are the builders of the famous "Nanih Waiya," or Mother Mound, from which the first

Choctaw are said to have been born. Choctaw all learn their own language first and English in school so that most of the tribe is at least bilingual.

GOVERNMENT

The Choctaw Tribe adopted a constitution in 1945 under the 1934 Indian Reorganization Act. A 16-member council representing the seven major towns on the reservation is elected every other year. This council elects a chairman and a vice chairman, not necessarily from its own members. A secretary-treasurer is also elected. The council meets four times annually, with additional meetings called when necessary. The chairman is a full-time employee of the tribe.

TRIBAL ECONOMY

The reservation land consists of low, rolling sandy hills. Most of the land, 13,900 acres, is forest land. The remainder is used for agriculture and homesites. The tribal income is derived primarily from forestry and usually averages about $40,000 annually. The tribe organized a land enterprise which operated under tribal authority to develop and utilize land. It is now a profitmaking organization. Indians go to nearby towns for shopping and consumer services. The Choctaw operate an arts and crafts shop in Philadelphia.

MOWA CHOCTAW INDIAN

Another Band of Choctaw remained in the forest areas of Washington and Mobile Counties. In 1979 an Act of The Alabama Legislature created the Mowa Band of Choctaw and established a fourteen member Commission in Mobile and Washington Counties. Today they are organized as The Mowa Band of Choctaw Indians with a Tribal Agency at McIntosh, Alabama. They have achieved recognition by The State of Alabama and are represented in The Alabama Commission of Indian Affairs. They are working toward recognition by The United States Bureau of Indian Affairs.

THE CHEROKEE INDIAN REMNANT—THE EASTERN BAND OF CHEROKEE INDIANS

The Cherokee Nation made much effort to reach an agreement whereby they could remain in their native homeland, but to no avail. Finally, the United States Government sent an Army under the command of General Winfield Scott to drive the Cherokee out of their homeland to The Indian Territory west of The Mississippi River.

There were some Cherokees who by this time had become citizens of The United States, and as such were to be allowed to remain. Many other Cherokees were so opposed to Removal to the West that they hid out in the rugged mountains and caves in the hope of remaining.

In a skirmish with some of these, some United States soldiers were killed. After much effort to round up all the rebel group, with little success, it was decided that if Tsali and his sons voluntarily turned themselves in to be court-martialled, the others might remain. Eventually those who hid out and remained and those who had become citizens banded together. Today they are The Eastern Band of Cherokee of The Qualla Reservation in, and around Cherokee, North Carolina.

The Qualla Boundary
Cherokee Indian Reservation

About 1,000 Cherokee remained in North Carolina. Some were citizen Indians who had assisted the army, and others were fugitives who had been given freedom when Tsali, the Cherokee martyr, surrendered to the soldiers. Tsali had killed an American soldier, but surrendered so that others who had fled to the mountains could go free. Still others were allowed to remain because of the uncertainty of constitutional rights of white males married to Cherokee women.

During this same period William H. Thomas was campaigning for Cherokee rights in Washington, and buying land for the establishment of a Cherokee preserve.

In 1866 North Carolina recognized the Cherokee as residents, and the money due them was released to pay off debts on the land which Col. Thomas had purchased. In 1876 the first official survey of Cherokee lands was conducted and the Qualla Boundary established. In 1924 all American Indians were granted U.S. citizenship.

Their land is held in trust by the federal government . . . they can trade their land amongst themselves, or lease it to private individuals, but it cannot be sold to non-Indians.

The Qualla Boundary is better known as the Cherokee Indian Reservation, and is located in the tip of Western North Carolina adjacent to the Great Smoky Mountains National Park.

Cherokee Today

There is an enrollment of approximately 8,500 Eastern Cherokee, and the Reservation covers over 56,000 acres. A trust relationship is maintained with the government, but the Tribe has a large degree of self governing authority.

The governing body consists of an elected 12-member Tribal Council

(2 representatives from each of six townships); a principal chief, vice chief, and executive advisor. Elections for the Council are held every two years and the Chief is elected every four years.

The tribal government is deeply involved in education, health, and other community services. There are up to date school facilities, an ultra-modern hospital, and improved housing for tribal members. Theirs is a modern, well developed community, but they maintain a strong link with their past.

They manage the Qualla Arts and Crafts Mutual, an organization of their craftspeople, and a Fish and Game Management program. The Cherokee language and alphabet (the alphabet or syllabary was developed by a Cherokee, Sequoyah) is taught in the schools.

There is an annual Cherokee Fall Festival where games handed down from their ancestors are played, the most well-known of which is Cherokee stick-ball. In attractions such as "Unto These Hills", Oconaluftee Indian Village, Museum of the Cherokee Indian, Cherokee Cyclorama and Wax Museum, and the Center of Cherokee Heritage, their past is preserved and their story told to the thousands of visitors who come to Cherokee each year.

CHEROKEE RESERVATION

Cherokee, Graham, Jackson, Macon, and Swain Counties, NORTH CAROLINA
Eastern Band of Cherokee
Tribal Headquarters: Cherokee, North Carolina 28719

Federal Reservation
Population: 4,880 (BIA 3/72)

LAND STATUS

Total Area: 56,573 acres
Tribal Land in Trust: 56,573 acres

The United States Congress transferred Cherokee lands to Federal Government trust in 1925 at the petititon of the tribe. Conflicting possessory titles to landholdings interfere with efficient land use and management.

HISTORY

The Cherokee, a powerful Iroquoian tribe, once held all of the southwest Allegheny Mountain region in Virginia, Tennessee, Alabama, the Carolinas, and Georgia. The United States Government waged war on the Cherokee from about 1820, resulting in the removal of the tribe by United States forces in 1835. The march to the new land in Oklahoma resulted in the death of many members and is known to the tribe as the "Trail of Tears." A number of the survivors of the wars refused to move west of the Mississippi. Since 1889, the Eastern Band of Cherokee has operated as a recognized tribe under a North Carolina State Charter.

CULTURE

Evidence indicates that the Cherokee originally lived north of the south Allegheny region. The tribe adopted a form of government in 1820 modeled on that of the United States. Several years later, Sequoyah, a mixed blood, invented the Cherokee alphabet, enabling the Cherokee to read and write their language. The Cherokee Nation was divided into two factions, one favoring and one opposing the Treaty of Removal of 1835.

GOVERNMENT

The Cherokee Band is governed by a principal chief and his assistant, each elected for 4 years, and a 12-member council elected for a term of 2 years. The tribal business and credit committees form the executive branch of the tribal government.

TRIBAL ECONOMY

The average tribal income is $400,000 per year. Fifty percent of this is derived from taxes. The remainder comes from forestry and business ventures. The tribe employs 22 permanent and 19 seasonal workers. Tribal associations and cooperatives include the Cherokee Boys Club, Cherokee Planning Board, Cherokee Tribal Water and Sewer Enterprise, Fish Management and Wildlife Enterprise, Qualla Housing Authority, and Community Club Council.

Commercial/industrial establishments on the reservation include the Boundary Tree Lodge and Motel, which is tribally owned. The Oconaluftee Indian Village and Historical Pageant is owned and operated by the Cherokee Historical Association. Three private companies, White Shield of North Carolina, Saddlecraft, Inc., and Vassar Corporation, are also on the reservation. There are numerous tourist businesses in Cherokee.

THE LUMBEE INDIANS

In the early 1700's, as the first white colonists moved across North Carolina they found a people living in the area, that some called "Croatans", an English speaking people who appeared to be part Indian, who thought and spoke of themselves as Indians.[1]

In 1885, when the General Assembly of North Carolina first recognized the Indians of Robeson County area and gave them status as Indians, they were called Croatans by the white population. This word, Croatan, was found on a tree in the area of the ill-fated Raleigh Colony, and was thought to be a key to what happened to the colonist.

In 1887, the General Assembly authorized the establishment of a normal school for the Indians of Robeson County. In 1911 the General Assembly referred to them as Robeson County Indians, and in 1913 as The Cherokee Indians of Robeson County. In 1953 the General Assembly designated them Lumbee Indians. The term, Lumbee, comes from the Lumber River area where most of them lived.[2]

Some hold the view that the Lumbee Indian can trace their origin to the Raleigh's Lost Colony at Roanoke. This is the nearly universal oral tradition of the Lumbee Indians themselves. Others hold they have a link with the Cherokee Indians.

According to Lumbee tradition they are decendants of the ill-fated Raleigh Colonist who intermarried with the Hatteras Indians of coastal North Carolina, and the Eastern Sioux. Many of the surnames of the Lumbee are the same as those of the Raleigh colonists.[3]

The Lumbee Indians of Robeson County is today the largest Indian group east of the Mississippi River. They have about 40,000 members, with an average family income of $5,400 and an average 10th grade education. They live in 14 agricultural communities, traditionally tied to strong local churches and schools. They have established a strong agricultural land base and have taken advantage of economic opportunities that have been available to them. They established the first Native American Bank. The Lumbee have the largest Native American United Methodist Church in the whole connection in the nation. It is The Prospect United Methodist Church with a membership of 775. The Lumbee have 12 Native American United Methodist Churches in The North Carolina Conference of The United Methodist Church.

Culturally, the Lumbee Indian do not have visible patterns that anthropologists would recognize as the normal Indian patterns. Professor Adolph L. Dial, Lumbee Historian at Pembroke State University, says, "The important cultural characteristics of the Lumbee Indians are love of land, respect for elderly wisdom, individualism, and spirituality (Christian and Native). All Native Americans uphold the scaredness of the Mother earth."

THE SEMINOLE INDIANS

BIG CYPRESS RESERVATION
Hendry County, FLORIDA
Seminole Indian Tribe
Tribal Headquarters: Hollywood, Florida 33024

Federal Reservation
Population: 343 (BIA 3/72)

HOLLYWOOD RESERVATION
Broward County, FLORIDA
Miccosukee and Seminole Indian Tribe
Tribal Headquarters: Hollywood, Florida 33024

Federal Reservation
Population: 430 (BIA 3/72)

LAND STATUS — Total Area: 42,700 acres
Tribally Owned: 42,700 acres

All land is tribally owned. There have been no individual allotments. In addition to the reservation, the State of Florida has set aside approximately 104,000 acres adjoining the Big Cypress Reservation called the Florida State Indian Reservation, jointly administered by the Seminole Tribe (northern portion) and the Miccosukee Tribe (southern portion). The Seminole enjoy hunting and fishing rights of this land, most of which is swamp.

LAND STATUS — Total Area: 104,000 acres

The State of Florida has set aside approximately 104,000 acres, including 60 rented from Miami, for the use and benefit of the Seminole and Miccosukee Indians of Florida. These lands are administered jointly by the Seminole Tribe (northern portion) and the Miccosukee Tribe (southern portion). Although much of the land on the State reservation may not be developed, all Seminole enjoy hunting and fishing rights there. The land on the State reservation, outside of the conservation area of the Central and Southern Florida Flood Control District, will, in time, be developed and utilized by the Indians of Florida. There are no houses or commercial buildings on the State reservation now. One or two members of the Seminole Tribe may have permits to run small numbers of cattle in limited acreage. However, much of this land is under water most of the year.

The reservation land can be reached by State Highway 84 or the Big Cypress Cross Road maintained by the Bureau of Indian Affairs.

LAND STATUS — Total Area: 35,805 acres
Tribally Owned: 35,805 acres

All land is tribally owned. In addition to the three Seminole reservations, the State of Florida has set aside approximately 104,000 acres adjoining the Big Cypress Reservation called the Florida State Indian Reservation, jointly administered by the Seminole Tribe (northern portion) and the Miccosukee Tribe (southern portion). The Seminole enjoy hunting and fishing rights on this land, most of which is swamp.

HISTORY

The people who came to be known as "Seminole" (the name means "runaways") were Yamasee, driven from the Carolinas in 1715; Hitchiti-speaking Oconee from the Apalachicola River; and Creeks fleeing Georgia after the Creek War—all of whom were fugitives from the whites. Their ranks were swelled by fugitive slaves who found refuge and freedom among the Indians. Attempts by owners to recover these slaves led to Andrew Jackson's campaigns in 1814 and 1818. The Seminole were united by the hostility and fear they felt toward the young United States. In 1821, Florida was annexed by the United States, and pressure by white settlers for Seminole lands and farms led to an attempt in 1832 to remove the Indians west of the Mississippi by force. The wife of their chief, Osceola, was seized as a fugitive, and bloody warfare followed as the Seminole fought bitterly. When Osceola was captured under a flag of truce, some of his warriors fled into the Everglades. Later, a portion of the tribe were transported to Oklahoma where they formed one of the Five Civilized Tribes. A truce with the United States was finally signed in 1934. Another treaty was concluded in 1937.

CULTURE

With the withdrawal of troops, the Seminole continued to live in scattered locations and pursue a nomadic existence, mostly by hunting and fishing. They lived in small houses built with cypress poles and thatched with palmetto leaves. Their clothing is colorful and elaborate; deerskin leggings have been replaced by cloth pants. The tunics and overblouses are laboriously fashioned from small strips of different colored material all sewed into long rows and then stitched together. Seminole folk art, including dollmaking, are still followed. The turban, once the headdress of every Seminole brave, has been replaced by the 10-gallon hat. Seasonal Green Corn and Hunting Dances are still performed during festivities.

GOVERNMENT

The Seminole Tribe's constitution was ratified in 1957. The tribe has an elected five-member tribal council as its governing body. All problems relating to government, law and order, education, welfare, and recreation are handled through standing committees. Authority for the development and management of tribal resoures has been delegated to the Seminole Tribe, Inc., a federally chartered corporation. Non-Indian committeemen are appointed by the board of directors to act as honorary consultants for development.

TRIBAL ECONOMY

The annual tribal income for all three Seminole reservations is $500,000. Ten percent of this is derived from forestry, 25 percent from farming, 30 percent from business, and 35 percent from other sources. There are over 100 tribal employees. The Seminole Tribe has a housing authority, a development company, a village and crafts enterprise, and land development, recreation, and cattle improvement enterprises. In addition, the tribe raises mink.

MICCOSUKEE RESERVATION

Dade County, FLORIDA
Miccosukee Indian Tribe
Tribal Headquarters: Homestead, Florida 33030
Federal Reservation
Population: 430 (BIA 3/71)

LAND STATUS Total Area: 333.3 acres

The tribe holds, on a 50-year permit from the Bureau of Indian Affairs and the National Park Service, a strip of land 5½ miles long and 500 feet wide, containing 333.3 acres. This land, known as the Tamiami Trail, is not available for industrial or commercial development. Three tracts of land 600 feet by 65 feet were dedicated in perpetuity by the State of Florida for the sole use and benefit of the tribe. This land is similar to trust land and is available for industrial and commercial development. Presently being developed are a grocery store, service station, and a restaurant. The Florida State Indian Reservation, dedicated in perpetuity to the tribe by the State, is uninhabited. A court decision recently placed the land in a trust status. Future plans call for a campsite in this area.

HISTORY

The Miccosukee Tribe is politically, but not linguistically or ethnically, separate from the Seminole Tribe of Florida. Its history is the same as that for the Seminole. The Seminole were originally immigrants from Georgia and North Carolina who moved across the border into Florida to escape the clash of Spanish and British interests. Their ranks were swelled by fugitive slaves who found refuge and freedom among the Indians. Friction over recovery of these fugitives led to Andrew Jackson's campaigns of 1814 and 1818. The United States Government in 1832, in possession of Florida, attempted to remove the Seminole west of the Mississippi by force. The seizure of Chief Osceola's wife precipitated war. During the war, Osceola was captured under a flag of truce. Later, a portion of the Seminole were removed to Oklahoma, but about 150 fled into the Everglades. In 1937, when a treaty was signed between the Seminole and United States, the Miccosukee did not join.

CULTURE

The Miccosukee led a nomadic life hiding out from United States troops for long periods in their history. They survived by hunting and fishing, building small shelters with wooden frames and palmetto-leaf roofs. Their homes today are being replaced with more modern units. Their dress is both colorful and difficult to make, being constructed from many strips of different colored material. Folk arts still exist, and the seasonal Green Corn and Hunting Dances are performed. Most of the Miccosukee have retained their Indian religion, whereas the Seminole are largely Christians.

GOVERNMENT

The Miccosukee Tribe was officially organized on January 11, 1962, with the adoption of a constitution and bylaws pursuant to the Indian Reorganization Act. There is no direct connection with the Seminole Tribe organization, although blood relationships exist. The governing body of the tribe is composed of four matrilineal clans, and the business committee is composed of one member from each clan elected for a 3-year period of office. Membership in the tribe is open to Indians of Florida Seminole blood who make formal application for membership.

TRIBAL ECONOMY

The income of the tribe averages $4,300 annually, 95 percent from grazing and right-of-way leases and 5 percent from business. There are four full-time tribal employees. The tribe owns and operates the Miccosukee Restaurant and Tiger's Indian Village.

MATTAPONI RESERVATION

King William County, VIRGINIA
Mattaponi Indians (Powhatan)
Tribal Headquarters: Box 178, West Point, Virginia 23181

State Reservation
Population: 75 (tribal est. 1/73)

LAND STATUS Total Area: 125 acres

Title to the reservation was granted to the Mattaponi in 1658 by the colonial Virginia House of Burgesses. The reservation is located on the Mattaponi River, near Wakema, Virginia. Any qualifying person may obtain permission from the tribal council for land use.

HISTORY

The term "Powhatan" refers to the former confederacy of Virginia's Algonquian tribes and to their most famous chief, whose proper name is Wahunsonacock, and whose daughter, Pocahontas, saved the life of Captain John Smith. At the time the Jamestown settlers arrived, the Powhatan Confederacy had about 200 villages, 160 of which were noted on Smith's map. The Indians were at first friendly to the whites, but were soon driven to hostility by the continued exactions required of them. Under Opechancanough, an uprising was planned which, in 1622, nearly wiped out the English settlements, destroying every one except Jamestown, which was forewarned by an Indian convert. Reprisals followed against the Indians, and, in 1625, a thousand Indians were defeated at the great battle of Pamunkey. Other massacres of Indians, including the raid under Nathaniel Bacon in 1676, effectively decimated the tribe. By 1705 there were only 12 villages left, and Pamunkey, with 150 people, was the only one of importance. The greatest problem the Mattaponi face today is maintaining status as a tribe.

CULTURE

The Powhatan practiced an animistic religion and believed in immortality. Their houses were built with saplings whose tops were bent over and tied and then covered with bark and sided with woven mats. These dwellings could hold several families. They were advanced in agriculture and cultivated maize (corn), beans, pumpkins, fruit trees, and several varieties of roots. They computed by the decimal system. Typical crafted items were clay pots and pipes and ceremonial clothing of woven turkey feathers. Some basketry and beadwork are still done today. The tribal organization has endured, although the Indian language was extinct by the end of the 18th century, and most of the culture has been lost. Hunting and fishing are still important.

GOVERNMENT

The tribe is governed by a chief and five-member council. The chief, secretary, treasurer, and clerk are all elected at large and serve for 4-year terms.

TRIBAL ECONOMY

There is no tribal income. At present there are no industrial establishments on the reservation. The tribe owns and operates a small arts and crafts shop. There is also a museum on the reservation.

PAMUNKEY RESERVATION
King William County, VIRGINIA
Pamunkey Indians (Powhatan)
Tribal Headquarters: Pamunkey, Virginia 23086

State Reservation
Population: 35 (tribal est. 1/73)

LAND STATUS Total Area: 800 acres

The Pamunkey Reservation was established in 1677 by the Virginia House of Burgesses on the Pamunkey River, 20 miles east of present-day Richmond. The States provides minimal services to the reservation, principally the upkeep of roads running to Pamunkey.

HISTORY

The term "Powhatan" refers to the former confederacy of Virginia's Algonquian tribes and to their most famous chief, whose proper name is Wahunsonacock, and whose daughter, Pocahontas, saved the life of Captain John Smith. At the time the Jamestown settlers arrived, the Powhatan Confederacy had about 200 villages, 160 of which were noted on Smith's map. The Indians were at first friendly to the whites, but soon driven to hostility by the continued exactions made upon them. Under Opechancanough, an uprising was planned which, in 1622, nearly wiped out the English settlements, destroying every one except Jamestown, which was forewarned by an Indian convert. Reprisals followed against the Indians, and, in 1625, a thousand Indians were defeated at the great battle of Pamunkey. Other massacres of Indians, including the raid under Nathaniel Bacon in 1676, effectively decimated the tribe. By 1705 there were only 12 villages left, and Pamunkey, with 150 people, was the only one of importance.

CULTURE

The Powhatan practiced an animistic religion and believed in immortality. Their houses were built with saplings whose tops were bent over and tied and then covered with bark and sided with woven mats. These dwellings could hold several families. They were advanced in agriculture and cultivated maize (corn), beans, pumpkins, fruit trees, and several varieties of roots. They computed by the decimal system. Typical crafted items were clay pots and pipes and ceremonial clothing of woven turkey feathers. Some basketry and beadwork are still done today. The tribal organization has endured, although the Indian language was extinct by the end of the 18th century, and most of the culture has been lost. Hunting and fishing are still important.

GOVERNMENT

The Indians practice self-government and are not taxed by the State. They elect a chief, a seven-member council, clerk, and treasurer. These officers serve for 4 years and make the laws for the tribe.

TRIBAL ECONOMY

Ther is no tribal income. There are no industrial establishments on the reservation, although there is an arts and crafts shop that is widely known for its craftwork and artifacts. It includes a small museum. The only important mineral resource is clay, which is used in pottery making.

Much of the 'Remnant' data is Courtesy of The United States Department of The Interior.

CATAWBA INDIANS

The Catawba are refugees of the Neutor Nation of Niagars and the Eries of Lake Erie. They fled sometime in the mid 1600's because of conflict with the Connewange Senecas. They fled first to Virginia, but later moved on into the Carolinas.

In the era of The American Revolution, the Catawba, whose population had been some 5,000 in the early 1600's, contracted small-pox. Their numbers were greatly reduced. They invited the Cheraw Indians to form a union with them. The union was composed of about an equal number of Catawba and Cheraw. They lived in great harmony.

This picture of John Smith and Pocahontas is one scene of a mural in The Birmingham Public Library. Pocahontas was a good friend of the English settlers and is credited with saving the life of Captain John Smith. Later she married John Rolfe and her decendants are to be found in many areas across the nation, including Alabama. The Pocahontas community near Carbon Hill is testimony of that family line coming to Alabama too.

Schoolcraft says, "Among the causes which tended to diminish the numbers of the Catawba nation, may be mentioned their wars and skirmishes, on their own account, and their adhesion to the military fortunes of their white friends; the ravages of the small-pox; the intemperate use of ardent spirits, by all ages and both sexes; the loss of their game, by the encroachments of the white hunters; the assassination of King Hagler, by a few Shawnees, about 1760 (so important is the life of an individual sometimes to a whole people); the fact of their being encircled on every side, and mixed in with a vastly more powerful and energetic race, whereby a distressing sense of inferiority and depression has been kept up among them; and, added to all, impolitic legislation, which gave them permission to lease their lands for long periods, securing to them a miserable subsistence, which exempted them from labor."

In the year 1735 the nation had in reservation only thirty acres of their large and fertile territory, not a foot of which was in cultivation. Many of the Catawbas marched under the Colonial Flag. They offered themselves to march under the command of Colonel Washington. The Catawbas were always ready to engage in the American cause, and always acquited themselves like brave soldiers. Ramsay, in The History of South Carolina, invoked the people of South Carolina to cherish this small remnant of a noble race, always the friends of the Carolinians, and ready to perish all for their safety. They never have shed a drop of American blood, nor stolen property to the value of a cent.

POWHATAN INDIANS
Nansemond Tribe

There were numerous estimates relative to the size of Powhatan's so called Confederacy, the number of tribes, population, number of bowmen or warriors and villages.

Powhatan was approximately 60 years old in 1607 and he died in 1618 at the age of about 70.

Powhatan inherited six tribes and added 25 or more by means of conquest or intimidation which means he had possibly 30 or more tribes under his control. There were about 161 villages with a population estimated to be about 14,000 of which 2,500 were bowmen.

Contrary to some popular beliefs, the Indians in the Coastal Virginia area lived in wigwams. They were made by placing saplings in the ground in two rows and by bending them to form an arch and tying them together, formed the frame of the dwelling—called a wigwam. The frame was covered with bark panels, weed or fiber mats and at times animal skins.

For the most part, the Indians wore very little clothing and the early settlers were amazed at their ability to survive the elements so well. While their clothing was skimpy, they bathed much more frequently than did the English settlers.

The women used tatoos much more than the men but they both enjoyed ornaments for body decorations.

The warriors kept the hair on the right side short, chopped close or shaved to avoid entanglement with their bows. Being close to the water and not having metal implements, they made great use of shells for necklaces, ornaments, tweezers, various tools and household utensils.

At the end of the first 100 years, the population of Powhatan's Confederacy had decreased in numbers from

14,000 Indians down to 1,200±
2,500 bowmen down to 200-300

The primary causes for this rapid decline have been given as smallpox, measles, venereal diseases, and warfare. The Indians had very little immunity against the diseases brought over by the colonists.

The general uprising by the Indians in 1622 and again in 1644 ended the so called Indian era in Virginia.

The first reference to the Nansemond Tribe was made in 1585 by an advance party from the expedition led by Sir Grenville and Ralph Lane that had landed in the Roanoke Island area of North Carolina.

The main village of the Nansemonds was placed in the Reeds Ferry area on the Nansemond River.

The Nansemond Tribe was one of the three largest under Powhatan's control. It had an estimated population of 750-1,000 of which 250-300 were bowmen or warriors.

In 1608 the Jamestown settlement was suffering a severe food shortage. John Smith sent parties of men to the Nansemond River to bargain for food but with little success. The colonists then took the corn by force and burned the Indian's dugout canoes and wigwams. As the colonists gradually moved up the Nansemond River and occupied more Indian land, the Nansemonds moved farther inland. The Nansemonds again sold their reservation land in 1744 in order to buy other land still farther inland. Their last 300 acres of reservation land, located in Southhampton County on the Nottaway River, was sold in 1791/2.

When the tribe moved inland, it split and the second group of Christianized Indians moved and eventually settled in the Bowers Hill, Deep Creek area on the fringe of the Great Dismal Swamp.

Many direct descendants of that group still live in that area and some live on land that has been in the family since the late 1600's and early 1700's.

It is that group from which the members of the resurrected Nansemond Indian Tribe are descended.

Even though the Nansemonds in the Bowers Hill area were informally organized with a "designated" chief—they pulled back and maintained a very low profile due to the severe racial strife that continued to plague them through the 1920-1950's and is not forgotten by those who experienced it. That is worthy of a course of study in Virginia Indian history.

In 1984, the descendants of the Nansemonds decided to regroup and reorganize.

The progress made towards that objective is listed as follows

a. First meeting was held July 1984 at the Indiana United Methodist Church
b. Adopted bylaws in August 1984.
c. Elected Tribal leaders in November 1984.
d. Received charter from the State Corporation Commission in December 1984.
e. Installed our Tribal leaders in January 1985. Chief Oliver Adkins of the Chickahominy Tribe officiated at the installation of the following Nansemond Tribal leaders:
   Chief—Earl L. Bass
   Assistant Chief—Oliver L. Perry
   Councilmen—Kenneth P. Bass
   Stephen D. Bass
   Alvin L. Bond
   William K. Langston
   Joseph F. Weaver
   Secretary—Christine B. Langston
   Treasurer—Frances P. Woodard
   Honorary Post Chief—Albert Bass
f. House Joint Resolution 205 was passed by the General Assembly in February 1985, recognizing the Nonsemond and granting official recognition by the Commonwealth of Virginia.
g. Received Certificate of Recognition from Gov. Robb in July 1985
h. On July 28, 1985 we will
   (1) Have a memorial service to honor our ancestors Rev. Wm. E. Kube will perform the service.
   (2) Mr. Bateman, Supt. of Public Schools, City of Chesapeake, will dedicate a marker on the site of the one room Indian school that was located on the grounds of the Indiana United Methodist

Church. The school was known as Indian Public School #9.

(3) Present an original copy of House Joint Resolution 205 to Mr. Scalf, City Manager, City of Chesapeake.

(4) Receive a letter of recognition from Mr. Scalf, City Manager, City of Chesapeake

(5) Delegate V. Thomas Forehand, Member of the House of Delegates and a co-sponsor of HJR-205 will read the letter and certificate of recognition from Gov. Robb.

(6) Dr. Helm C. Rountree, Associate Professor of Anthropology, Old Dominion University, will give a brief, chronological history on The Trail of the Nansemonds.

That concludes a very brief, condensed tracing of the Nansemond history over the past 400 years, as I see it.

O.L.P.
7-21-1985

Included here, courtesy of Assistant Chief Oliver L. Perry, Sr.

LAND STATUS Total Area: 800 acres

The Pamunkey Reservation was established in 1677 by the Virginia House of Burgesses on the Pamunkey River, 20 miles east of present-day Richmond. The States provides minimal services to the reservation, principally the upkeep of roads running to Pamunkey.

HISTORY

The term "Powhatan" refers to the former confederacy of Virginia's Algonquian tribes and to their most famous chief, whose proper name is Wahunsonacock, and whose daughter, Pocahontas, saved the life of Captain John Smith. At the time the Jamestown settlers arrived, the Powhatan Confederacy had about 200 villages, 160 of which were noted on Smith's map. The Indians were at first friendly to the whites, but soon driven to hostility by the continued exactions made upon them. Under Opechancanough, an uprising was planned which, in 1622, nearly wiped out the English settlements, destroying every one except Jamestown, which was forewarned by an Indian convert. Reprisals followed against the Indians, and, in 1625, a thousand Indians were defeated at the great battle of Pamunkey. Other massacres of Indians, including the raid under Nathaniel Bacon in 1676, effectively decimated the tribe. By 1705 there were only 12 villages left, and Pamunkey, with 150 people, was the only one of importance.

CULTURE

The Powhatan practiced an animistic religion and believed in immortality. Their houses were built with saplings whose tops were bent over and tied and then covered with bark and sided with woven mats. These dwellings could hold several families. They were advanced in agriculture and cultivated maize (corn), beans, pumpkins, fruit trees, and several varieties of roots. They computed by the decimal system. Typical crafted items were clay pots and pipes and ceremonial clothing of woven turkey feathers. Some basketry and beadwork are still done today. The tribal organization has endured, although the Indian language was extinct by the end of the 18th century, and most of the culture has been lost. Hunting and fishing are still important.

GOVERNMENT

The Indians practice self-government and are not taxed by the State. They elect a chief, a seven-member council, clerk, and treasurer. These officers serve for 4 years and make the laws for the tribe.

TRIBAL ECONOMY

There is no tribal income. There are no industrial establishments on the reservation, although there is an arts and crafts shop that is widely known for its craftwork and artifacts. It includes a small museum. The only important mineral resource is clay, which is used in pottery making.

Much of the 'Remnant' data is Courtesy of The United States Department of The Interior.

XV

HOPE!

The great Drama of the American Indian or Native American is by no means ended! It may have appeared in the 1830's, following the Removal Act of 1830, that the final curtain was falling on this noble race. I am sure those who plotted this tragedy thought they had succeeded. And I am sure thousands of those who plodded along the 'Trail of Tears' into exile from their beloved homeland-place of their birth and sacred place of burial grounds of their ancestors felt the end had indeed come! For many thousands, whose shallow graves lined the removal trails, (including the dear wife of that great and noble Chief of The Cherokee, John Ross.), the end did come through the lack of food or ample clothing against the bitter and severe weather, the ravages of disease or epidemics, or the butt of a gun of an impatient or calloused soldier.

In some cases death, even in such agonizing ways, would have been kinder and easier than surviving to face the slow, and deeply agonizing and dehumanizing loss of hope. The loss of hope has devastating effects on any people. The American Indian with all his strength was no exception, in fact, human history would indicate that no people are excepted, from such tragedy, under such circumstances.

Speaking on such loss of hope Alexis de Tocqueville in Democracy in America says, "The social tie, which distress had long since weakened, is then dissolved; they have no longer a country, and soon they will not be a people; their language perished; and all traces of their origin disappear. Their nation has ceased to exist except in the recollections of the antiquaries of America and a few of the learned of Europe."[1]

Some one hundred years set in that can be characterized as virtually hopeless for these noble people who had been so ruthlessly disenfranchised and driven from their homeland. This period saw widespread alcoholism and conflict that evidenced this hopelessness. The amazing part of this drama is there was a remnant that would not give up and die! I believe in this story of survival is one of the greatest, noblest, nothing short of micraculous-Dramas of human history! They sought to hang on, keeping alive some consciousness of their rich and noble heritage, and daring to believe a new era would dawn in which hope would flourish! Melvin Thorn of the National Indian Youth Council says the Indian has kept his culture, while other peoples have lost theirs in the melting pot.[2]

Senator James Abourezk of South Dakota, Chairman of The American Indian Policy Review Commission, has summarized the Indian's plight this way, "In the past 200 years American Indians have been experimented with, involuntarily shifted from one location to another, robbed of their land and water, their political power, and at times, even their freedom. If the Indian people are ever to assume a normal place in American society, the Commission belives there must be some restoration of political power to the tribes. That includes the recognition that Indian tribes must necessarily control their own affairs since control from the outside always results in both manipulating of and deprivation for the Indian."[3]

James Adair argues at great length that the Indians are the "Lost Tribe of Israel", or at least the cousins of the pre-Hebrew stock. Thus therein would be part of the basis of the appeal of the drama of the oppression and persecution of the Jews. Peter Farb says, "There are strong parallels between the hope for salvation among the Jews and the hopes of Indians who followed native prophets, between the early Christian martyrs and the Indian prophets." Particularly fascinating, is the way in which Jews and early Christians have served as models for oppressed peoples from primitive cultures far from the Near East. Almost wherever the White missionary has penetrated, primitive peoples have borrowed from his Bible those elements in which they saw a portrayal of their own plight; and most often this has been an identification with the Jews. Because of such identification, some primitive peoples have claimed descent from one of the ten lost tribes of Israel. In their yearning to escape from servitude, they have found a model in Moses, whose name is a popular cognomen among many colonial peoples. They regard the arrest and execution of a native on charges of being a rebel against white authority in the same terms as the trials undergone by the Hebrew prophets or the passion of Jesus.[5]

In his book, *Include Me Out,* Colin Morris says, "The Church exists to report an Event (The Christ Event) by reenacting it."[6] What does that have to say to the American Indian? It has to do with instilling or giving birth to Hope! The re-enacting of The Christ Event proclaims: Hope Thou In God!—that is, in God we find a basis for Hope! In the reality of God, in God's Covenant with man, in God's Faithfulness—there is Hope!

There are many elements of importance in the Christian Theology of Hope. But here I want to underline three: 1.) God is love, 2.) Each individual is important to God, and 3.) God moves among us and through us to build community. Thus the re-enacting of The Christ Event is in part the building of community—building bridges of understanding and acceptance, building cooperative, and supportive relationships, etc. Much of the Hope so vital to the Indian is in Community—where each is both giver and receiver!

Harold DeWolf in *Christian Mission in Theological Perspective* says, "Mission is of the very nature of the Christian faith." A goal of Christian Mission is to build Community. Community in the Christian sense is where persons and their welfare is of ultimate concern. It is a togetherness where each is important and each can be a participant in the decision making process, in the responsibilities, and in the returns or fruits thereof.[7]

Many things are helping give birth to Hope among the Indian. One of these is God is moving among us stirring us, whom He calls as Prophets, to cry out, "Let My people go!" And from many places—classrooms, pulpits, books, magazine articles and stories, editorials, and such television programs as 'Roots', demonstrations or 'marches', and person to person witness—the cry rings forth, "Let My people go!"

Then, there are those who have given themselves to training and developing the capacities of the Indian to be able to respond when doors of opportunity open. Hope for the Indian lies in better education, better understanding of the Indian by the Government and general population, accepting the Indian as a fellow human being and realizing the importance of allowing the Indian to find pride in their heritage—allowing them to be Indian.[8]

Closely related to Hope is the longing for, the search for, the commitment to 'Self-Determination'. As we note this longing and need of the American Indian, and its great importance to him as an individual, and as a people, we would do well to remember 'Self-Determination' is the root from which Democracy grew! A government of the people, by the people, and for the people had its birth eons ago—no one knows when or where the first occurred—but we do know its birth was in part among the American Indian. We do know the highest form of that Democracy among the Indians was the League of the Iroquois. The basis of its birth was 'Self-Determination'!

This attitude or human drive is so strong an instinct, so deeply imbedded in the Indian, that when denied by the overpowering presence and might of white men it virtually destroyed them. Here, it seems to me, is the answer to the degradation—including widespread alcoholism and poverty—that became such a blight among the Indians. The loss of 'Self-Determination'—denied him by the white men—caused the loss of Hope and resulted in a tragic and pathetic state of being!

Thus 'Self-Determination' is vital to the Indian, but it is also vital to all men for it is the root from which Democracy will continue to draw its life and strength!

Robert Burnette, a respected leader of the Rosebud Sioux, in *The Tortured Americans* says, "Initially, in the interests of justice, I would urge a congressional investigation into the entire field of Indian affairs. Such an investigation not only would reveal the abuses of the BIA, uncover scandals that would make Teapot Dome seem petit larceny in comparison, and afford satisfaction to the hitherto helpless Indian victims, but also would mobilize public opinion in favor of overdue reforms.

Next, I would recommend that the Bureau of Indians Affairs be abolished, and in its place be established a Federal Indian Commission, directly responsible to the President. It would resemble bodies like the Federal Power Commission and the Securities Exchange Commission, its prime responsibility would be to protect the Indians' trust lands. It would be a watchdog agency.

Then I would suggest that Congress enact what might be called "The Fair Indian Act", which would include the following provisions:

First, all elected tribal officials shall be subject to the existing laws that apply to elected federal and state officials. These would include, for example, conflict of interest laws, and statutes under which one could enter federal court to defend the right to run for office and right to vote laws.

Secondly, elected tribal officials shall be held accountable for any federal or tribal funds appropriated, loaned, or borrowed, and records of such transactions shall be available to the public.

Thirdly, all Indians shall have the right to seek redress beyond the tribal courts—that is, in the federal courts system, right up to the Supreme Court, (Mrs. Blue Horse and Norma Jean Le Roy's children, among countless cases, would then have the opportunity to balance the wrongs done them, instead of suffering, as they did).

Fourthly, the Indian people shall have the means to impeach any elected tribal official who violates the laws. Now only the tribal council can recall an elected official. (Since 21 councilmen sat idly or fearfully by while the Valandra administration illegally indebted the tribe for more than $700,000 and spent more than $2 million of federally appropriated funds in defiance of the tribal laws and the OEO regulations, the need for this reform is especially pressing.)

Finally, federal activities having to do with the health, education, and welfare of Indians shall be assumed by the Department of Health, Education, and Welfare, where they belong."[9]

We can learn from history—from our weaknesses or mistakes and from our strengths. One of the greatest mistakes the church made in the early days of missions among the Indian was to work toward changing the Indian into the European ways. This approach was based on Indian ways are savage and he needs to be civilized—which generally meant to be like the whites. The Church's mission would have succeeded much more then and now by recognizing the strengths and values of the Indian, and also recognizing the place and values of their religion or faith. The beliefs of the Indian deserve a place among the varieties of beliefs and religions the world has known. The basis for their beliefs can be found in spiritual well-being, not material possessions. The American Indian theology should be represented in the highest councils of Christian theology in the world.[10]

One of the great strengths of the past mission effort was the use of Native Americans in the leadership of the ministries. Greater effort seems to be forthcoming to call forth, develop, and use Native leadership. There are indications of a healthy (hopeful) trend in this direction as we see efforts to get more persons from the Indian communities into schools, training events, consultations, workshops or seminars, and seminaries.

Josephine Wildcat Bigler, field representative for National Program division of The General Board of Global Ministries of the United Methodist Church, says there is great need for indigenous leadership development. The Native American Linkage Group gathers Native American Church leaders from around the country for training, resourcing, and for dialogue with the National Division Staff.[11]

WE CELEBRATE THE AMERICAN INDIAN

We Celebrate The American Indian as Conquerors of every area of this vast and varied hemisphere—from the frozen north, to the great heights of the Rockies, to the dry deserts, and the primevial forests. They brought forth a successful and good existence. They were—they are—Survivors.

We Celebrate their great and noteworthy achievements—snowshoes—canoes—styles of shelter—agriculture, etc. that enabled them to survive and to conquer their environments.

We Celebrate their Community Life. They developed a highly civilized and organized community. As a more settled society evolved they gave much time and energy to the development of the arts. Artistic expression was evidenced in pottery and crafts, and in their ceremonial life. They developed a society of law and order through the work and influence of The Council House and The Great Council Fire.

We Celebrate their Faith. A great and strong concept of The Great Spirit as Giver and Sustainer of life evolved. Out of this Faith evolved a great tenacity—a great Spirit of Hope! I wear a Coosada Medalion around my neck tonight, a symbol of that Great Spirit of Hope!

(Brief remarks delivered by the author to The Regional School of Missions of The United Methodist Church at Huntingdon College in Montgomery, Alabama).

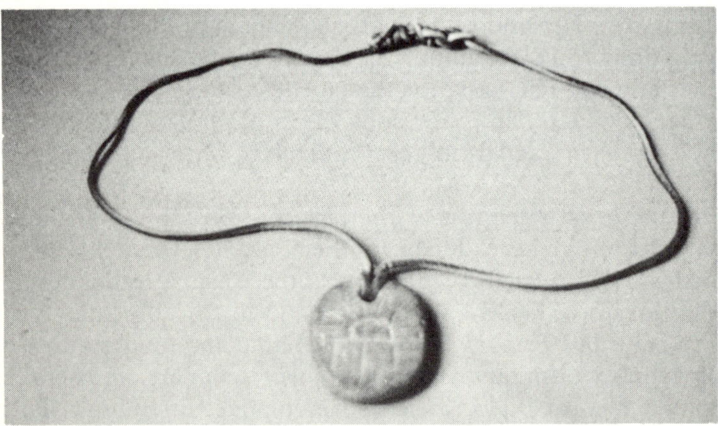

Medallion—Symbol of Hope—I found on the Coosa River at what I believe to be an ancient site of The Coushatta People.

XVI

SOUTHEAST STATES ESTABLISH INDIAN AGENCIES

Southwest Alabama Commission on Indian Affairs

In 1978, during The Fob James Administration, a new direction was set with The American Indian. The Alabama Legislature established the first ever Indian Agency for the State of Alabama—The Southwest Alabama Commission on Indian Affairs. Dr. Leonard Hudson was named Chairman of The Commission, and Jennie Lee Dees, the former Executive Director of The Creek Tribal Agency at Poarch, was named The Executive Director of The Alabama Indian Affairs Commission. The office was funded with Comprehensive Education Act money.

The Commission worked to find funds to help meet needs of the Indians of Alabama. They sought funds for scholarships for Indian youth. They worked to find markets for Indian crafts, etc. Efforts were made to develop Centers of Indian Culture, and to promote a tourist trade and Indian Crafts Trade Fair. Efforts were also made toward doing joint projects with The Tennessee Indian Council and The North Carolina Indian Affairs Commission.

This office opened in Octboer of 1980 and closed, in part, for lack of

Serrated points from the author's collection.

operating funds in October of 1981. There was also a concern with a problem—The Commission was begun on the basis that The Poarch Creeks were the only Federally and State recognized group in the state, and several others were seeking such recognition.

In May, 1984 The Alabama Legislature passed an Act establishing The Alabama Indian Affairs Commission. Jane Weeks was named as The Executive Director of The Alabama Indian Affairs Commission.

The State Agencies of The Southeast that deal with American Indian Concerns are:

Alabama Indian Affairs Commission
339 Dexter, Reese Building, Suite 113
Montgomery, Alabama 36104
(205) 261-2831

State of Tennessee
Department of Human Services
400 Deaderick Street
Nashville, Tennessee 37219
(615) 741-3241

Council of Native Americans of South Carolina
4801 Colonial Drive, P. O. Box 21916
Columbia, South Carolina 29221
(803) 754-7711

North Carolina Commission of Indian Affairs
P. O. Box 27228
Raleigh, North Carolina 27611
(919) 733-5998

INFORMATION ABOUT AMERICAN INDIANS

When Europeans first arrived on this continent, there were in what is now known as the United States of America, approximately one million Indians. By 1900, due to disease and warfare, the Indian population had been reduced to less than 300,000. Today, their number is only 1.4 million. Indians live in every state in the Union; only 28% of all Indians live on reservations. Almost ½ of all Indians in the United States today live in urban areas.

Indians have the lowest life expectancy of any group in the United States and suffer the highest rates of unemployment. They fall well below the national average in income, housing and education.

The average person of the Southeast thinks of the native inhabitant of this area as a half-naked treacherous savage whose principal occupation was to use the scalping knife and the tomahawk. The more truthful story of Indians, however, is the story of a people whose confidence was betrayed by the White race from its arrival under the Spaniards in the 15th Century and later by other Europeans who found their way to the New World. The resulting conflict of interest between the two races culminated finally in the Indian Removal Act, which all but annihilated the Indian race as it had once existed.

After the passage in 1830 of the congressional act called Indian Removal Act, the government of the United States was supposed to negotiate with Eastern tribes for their relocation to the West of the Mississippi River. Between 1832 and 1843, virtually all of the Eastern Tribes were either removed to land significantly reduced in size or were, in fact, physically removed to the Western Section of the United States. We now know, of course, the terribly tragic story of the Trail of Tears in which the Cherokees, Creeks and Choctaws suffered and died. In order to survive, many Indians escaped or were befriended by settlers and were assimilated into White society and still live in small pockets of Indian communities all over the South, and, many are here in the State of Alabama.

Alabama ranks 10th in the nation in Indian population. Many historians tell us that at least ¼ of Alabama's population may count Indian ancestry. Today Alabama's Indian Community numbers just under 14,000 and all have not been identified.

Congress did not grant full citizenship to American Indians until 1924. Life for Indians between 1830 and 1924 was extremely difficult. Because it was illegal for an Indian to be off reservations, a non-Indian could shoot an Indian and there was no penalty under the law for the offense. Alabama passed laws, as did many Southern states, which prohibited an Indian from bringing suit against a White or from giving testimony against a White in a court of law. Many Indians were dispossessed because of these laws and cheated out of lands, goods and crops.

The same laws which prohibited Black children from going to school with White children also barred Indian children from BOTH schools, *if* they claimed their Indian heritage. In Alabama there were no federal Indian Schools. Many children were educated by White Christian churches who wished to educate and assist Indian peoples.

Today's Indian peoples seek to share their heritage with their children and with members of the non-Indian community.

Courtesy of ALABAMA INDIAN AFFAIRS COMMISSION, Suit 113, 339 Dexter Avenue, Montgomery, Alabama 36130, Telephone: 261-2831

XVII

THE SOCIETY FOR THE PRESERVATION OF AMERICAN INDIAN CULTURE

LINDY MARTIN'S DREAM BECOMES REALITY

In 1980 I met Dr. H. L. "Lindy" Martin, a Cherokee Indian, Dean of Student Affairs at Samford University in Birmingham, Alabama, and he shared with me his dream of beginning The Society for The Preservation of The American Indian Culture. I assured him of my interest and willingness to help as a 'founding member'. Early in 1981, Dr. Martin called a group together at Samford University, and with some sixteen members formed SPAIC. In about one year there were some 500 members.

A major concern of SPAIC is the economic development of the Indian community. A concern is to help the Indians attain self-sufficiency. It is the intent of SPAIC to help Indian Tribes, Bands, and groups obtain state and federal recognition, and thereby funds. This is most important where

Calumet or 'Peace Pipe' made by a Cherokee Indian recently, a piece of a trade pipe, a Hopewell Platform Pipe, and trade pipe made in Dublin, Ireland.

educational and health services are needed. Effort of the group is being directed toward identifying and preserving ancestral sites of the area. SPAIC is much interested in encouraging, and developing native skills such as basketry, beadwork, pottery, etc. and developing markets for the sale of the same. This will greatly help the Indian toward self-sufficiency.

One of the first projects of The Society, SPAIC, was to promote an Indian Craft Trade Fair at Western Hills Mall.

The second significant event of SPAIC was to sponsor The Symposium on The American Indian at Samford University. The speakers for the occasion were Dr. H. L. Martin, James Manesco, Dr. Carey Oakley, Franklin Phillips, and Mary Jo Deavors.

The paper I delivered on "Indian Ceremonies: Significant Part of America's Heritage" is printed hereafter as it appeared in the spring 1981 Newsletters—Council Fires—of The Society for the Preservation of the American Indian Culture.

Indian Ceremonies: Significant Part of America's Heritage

By Franklin Phillips

Indian ceremonies and rituals evolved out of their struggles and experiences. These ceremonies, like their other customs, varied from group to group. We will look at some of the most common ones.

One of the greatest, most significant rituals among the Indians of the Southeast was the Green Corn Dance. The ritual evolved with agriculture, especially with the evolvement of maize agriculture. It involved three distinct elements: rejoicing, feasting, worship or thanksgiving.

When the corn or maize was ripe, usually early in July, the Chief would send the word around that the time of the Busk or Green Corn Dance has come! A day was set for all to gather for their great Annual Celebration! It was a great time of rejoicing and celebrating, games of chunky and ballplay, dancing and fellowship, and family reunions! Then comes a high moment of celebration, a great feast in which maize or new corn is the central part. There is also a time of extinguishing old fires and starting new ones from the Sacred Hearth of the Temple.

Then we come at last, some three to seven days into the Busk, to the truly high moment, a time of worship or thanksgiving. Usually some old and honored man of the tribe will step forward and in a most solemn mood will take a great puff from his calumet, and then holding the stem toward the sun offer a few puffs to the Great Spirit. The climax of the Busk is the acknowledgement of the gift of corn from the Great Spirit, the Giver and Sustainer of Life!

I believe this celebration by the Powhatan was a most important influence on the Pilgrims in beginning their Thanksgiving celebrations. There is some indication that one of the Pilgrim's Thanksgiving celebrations was held about the same time as the Powhatan held their Busk.

Thus, I believe all Americans can relate to and appreciate this significant ceremony of Indian heritage!

The calumet is a pipe for smoking tobacco. But it is far more than that. It was of great significance to the Indian. It was a medium of communing with the Great Spirit, as used in the Busk. It was similarly used in private meditation or worship.

The calumet was also used between persons and groups. The calumet was used in the making or pledging of a pact or agreement. It was used to seal or pledge a friendship or to pledge peace and goodwill. The various groups or states of the Iroquois, I am sure smoked the calumet to seal the government of the League of the Iroquois, symbolized by the Wampum Belt (holding hands in unity). Also, William Penn in a treaty with the Indians.

The great example of this ceremony took place here in Alabama, or in the area that became Alabama. In 1702, Bienville and his exploring party in looking for a site to develop a fort and settlement encountered a group of interested or curious Indians. The chiefs of the Indians (probably Maubilian, Choctaw, Alabamos, etc.) greeted Bienville's party and invited them to smoke the calumet. I believe there is great significance here, for first it was saying we want to welcome you, we will help you find a good site for your village, and we will work out a mutually beneficial relationship, the basis of a good trade relationship. Surely, this fine response of the Indian opened the area to an influx of settlers.

I believe this gesture of friendship and goodwill to be the birth of Alabama!

In the summer of 1966, I spent a good many hours with Dr. Herscher of the Archaeology Department of the University of Georgia in the excavation of Burnt Indian Village. One of the most impressive parts of that experience was Dr. Herscher showing me the evidence of the Council House in that little village.

In this house, the elders of good standing, met regularly to discuss the concerns of their people. This was virtually universal among the Indian. This Council House relates to the Great Council Fire in which chosen leaders, like Representatives and Senators, met to discuss issues and concerns and make decisions for the larger group of several villages, state, tribe, or confederacy.

I believe in the Council House and the Great Council Fires mankind witnessed the birth and evolvement of democracy. I further believe these were very significant influences on men like Thomas Jefferson and Benjamin Franklin and on the evolvement of The United States of America!

(Paper presented by the author in a Symposium on The American Indian held at Samford University.)

SPAIC—Martin Plan for Indian Self-Sufficiency

Listed below are suggestions for Indian tribes, groups, and communities to aid in becoming self-sufficient.

1. Every effort should be made to encourage the government to honor its trust agreements, treaties, and financial assistance as long as it is needed to help Indian people.
2. Public Law 93-638 should be studied very carefully by Indians. The opportunity for contracting services will aid if properly negotiated and handled in the self-sufficiency process. Proper contracts utilizing Indian manpower can be a valuable tool.
3. Special attention should be given to the establishment of Indian owned and operated businesses that are necessary in the community. That is; household goods, clothing, and other necessities make for business possibilities.
4. Tribes, groups, and communities should determine if they want to develop *tourism* as a business possibility. Attention should be given to be sure that Indians get the benefit of revenues generated by tourist attractions. Pow-Wow Celebrations to be listed on State Brochures.
5. Each tribe or group should *establish a Tribal Industrial Development Board.* This *Board would seek business and industry possibilities for the community.*
6. Proper contact and relationship should be made with state development boards and seek their assistance in bringing some of their business and industrial discoveries to Indian communities.
7. *Nationally Indians should work together to identify their needs* to the top industries in the country and ask that they consider bringing their expansion factories to areas where Indians live.
8. Each *Indian community* should examine the possibility for developing an *industrial park.* Legal ramifications relative to charters or agreements should be worked out so that prospective businesses would not be turned off by unnecessary red tape.

Tourism promoted thru Pow-Wow Celebrations.

9. *Each tribe or community* should carefully *assess* the *resources,* both *human and natural,* and determine how they could be best used to aid the people.
10. *Private foundations* have money available for humane projects that will aid in *research, training,* and *implementing plans* that will especially help needy people. These groups can be identified and the information passed on to Indian groups.
11. Indian leadership should meet with the Mission leadership of churches dedicated to helping Indian people. These groups should be encouraged to spend more of their efforts and programs in career planning and training as a part of meeting spiritual needs.
12. There are organizations in America, such as Save the Children, that are dedicated to helping Indian people. These groups can be identified and utilized in maintaining self-sufficiency.
13. There must be a cooperative effort on the part of all Indians to share their successes, information, expertise, and human resources with all Indian people. It is the purpose of the Society for the Preservation of American Indian Culture to gather this information and share it with all Indian groups.

Use Your Camera To Record
The Ancient Way Of Life At Oconaluftee Indian Village.

Typical home during the 18th century

The ancient art of making dugout canoe

Grinding corn

Cherokee design basket weaving

Art being created with colorful Venetian beads

Hunting with blow gun

Seven-sided Council House

Beautiful Botanical Gardens

Pictures of Oknaluftee Indian Village promoting tourism.

SPAIC Sponsors Southeastern Indian Arts & Crafts Fair

SPAIC sponsored the Southeastern Indian Arts & Crafts Fair on March 19, 20, & 21 at Western Hills Mall. Artists and crafts-people representing the Mississippi Band of Choctaw Indians, the Eastern Band of Cherokee Indians, the Creek Nation East of the Mississippi, the Jackson County Cherokees, Muskogees of Pike County, the Mowa Band of Choctaw Indians, and Echotas presented exhibits and sold their products. Beadwork, basketry, leathercraft, jewelry, pottery, and needlework were shown.

The Pearl River Social Dancers from the Choctaw Reservation in Mississippi performed traditional dances at 4:00 p.m. and 7:30 p.m. on Friday and at 11:00 a.m. and 3:00 p.m. on Saturday, and the Creek dancers from Atmore, Ala. performed also.

We are looking forward to making this an annual event.

S.P.A.I.C. ECONOMIC DEVELOPMENT PLAN

With reference to progress with the S.P.A.I.C. development plan, the following has been accomplished:

1. The Chief Executive Officers of the Fortune 500 companies have been contacted concerning the possibility of locating appropriate industries in Indian communities. They have also been asked to furnish "on loan" executives to serve as consultants to tribes interested in economic development.
2. Models representing successful economic development programs are being compiled for distribution upon request to interested Indian groups. Currently available are: an Industrial Park Model representing the Mississippi Choctaws and a Contract Services Model representing the Cherokee Boys Club of North Carolina. Groups wishing copies of these may contact the National S.P.A.I.C. office.
3. Deans of Agriculture and Heads of Agriculture Experiment Stations in the various states with Indian populations have been contacted by S.P.A.I.C. A favorable response has been received indicating that some tribes are getting assistance. The Schools of Agriculture are making their services available to other agriculturally oriented Indian communities. S.P.A.I.C. will send this information to all tribes or groups who have farming potential.
4. Consultants are now available to present the S.P.A.I.C. self-sufficiency plan and to give assistance in community based economic programs, museums and cultural centers, and contract services. These consultants are also available for area economic development

workshops. Contact the National S.P.A.I.C. office if you desire this service.

S.P.A.I.C. COMMITTEES AND PLANS

Indian Self-Sufficiency and Economic Development:

This committee will help to carry out the S.P.A.I.C. goal of assisting Indian tribes and individuals in economic development, contracts services, agricultural enterprises, and other matters relating to cultural, educational, and economic survival.

American Indian Preservation:

This committee will deal with preservation through museums, archives, sites on and off reservations, and it will give special attention to preserving things of Indian historical significance for all Americans.

Indian Arts & Crafts:

This committee will direct S.P.A.I.C. Indian Arts and Crafts Fairs, help provide markets for Indian made articles, and help preserve this unique trait of American Indians.

Research, Writing, Publications, and Indian Education:

This committee will encourage research and writing concerning all aspects of American Indian life—past and present. It will also give assistance to Indian Education on and off reservations and provide information and assistance to Title IV, The Indian Education Act. It will also assist in the preservation of Indian traditions, ceremonies, and ritualistic activities.

Public Information, Youth Involvement, and Scholarship Programs:

This committee will cover a wide range of activities. It will provide speakers for clubs, schools, and other groups concerning the American Indian. It will also provide information through public media. The committee will give special emphasis to youth programs for American Indians and involve non-Indian young people in assisting to preserve Indian Culture. This group will also raise money for and identify scholarships available for Indian Youth beyond high school.

XVIII

A NEW BEGINNING

The 1980 General Conference of The United Methodist Church resolved: The United Methodist Church and The Native American Peoples shall have a new beginning.

A new beginning for a relationship as old and troubled as that between native peoples in the U. S. and the majority population will require a great deal of work by a great many people. The United Methodist Church has made a new start, committed to developing a growing relationship with Native Americans.

With some 160 churches and missions spread across the country and in every Jurisdiction, the church is learning to listen to the voice of Indian people and has created the realities of a support system that speaks to their spiritual, physical and mental needs. Annual conferences have shown commitment through specific ministries that effect change and nurture development for more than 45 native societies in some 20 annual conferences. And the whole church participates as well in this affirmative process through support for more than 25 Advance Specials that provide direct support (ranging from a children's camping fund in Alaska to the Oklahoma Indian Missionary Conference) and many others that indirectly impact native lives by assisting churches and communities where they may live and worship.

Oklahoma Indian Missionary Conference has some 8,245 members in 110 churches in Oklahoma, Texas, and Kansas. The Yuma Indian Methodist Mission in Arizona is one of the oldest church and community mission projects related to the National Division. There is a community center with a full-time Indian staff, a day care center and a social service program. Children of the Quechan reservation receive professional attention through the Quechan Interim Child Care Center.

The Navajo United Methodist Mission School in New Mexico prepares Navajo children for college in an environment of quality education geared to the service of the Navajo nation. Administered by the National Division in cooperation with the Navajo, the academy headmaster and teaching staff are more than half comprised of Navajo educators.

The United Methodist Seminole Mission in Florida works with the Seminole Nation and its four reservations. A Seminole language preservation program functions along with a day care center, 4-H activities and a women's center. An Indigenous Community Developer, supported in part by the National Program Division of The General Board of Global Ministries, operates from the mission base in Moore Haven in helping the community maintain the integrity of its culture and helping to advocate for its historic rights and claims.

The National Division's office of Urban Ministries also works closely with Native Americans through two programs: Model Development in Urban Ministries and the Native American Urban Mission Consultation. Activities include social service, recreation, urban economic development, mental health service, alternative education and counseling. Major sites include Los Angeles, Phoenix, Seattle, Oklahoma City, Tulsa, Dallas and Minneapolis.

Out of concern that there are some 130,000 Native Americans in the seventeen annual conferences of the nine Southeastern States, and that The United Methodist Church has only five ministries in that area, a commitment was made at the 1980 General Conference to take a hard look at this whole matter. Therefore, it was decided that a Native American Consultation be called in February, 1983 in Washington, D. C. for Native Americans living in the Southeast and Northeast Jurisdictions to explore the needs and concerns of Native Americans. Representatives from the various tribes of Native Americans were invited to attend and participate. Also, Native American leaders of the various boards and agencies of the general church were invited. After an indepth study of identifying and locating Native Americans in the Southeast, who they are, where they are in regards to districts, annual conferences, jurisdictions and general agencies, and who they relate to. The Consultation felt that it was incumbent upon our connectional church to devise a means of ministry among and with the Native Americans of the Southeast.

The Consultation approved a recommendation: "That a Southeastern Jurisdictional Association for Native American Ministries be established. Therefore, The 1984 Southeastern Jurisdictional Conference meeting at Lake Junaluska would be petitioned to establish The Southeast Jurisdictional Association for Native American Ministries. The Petition is as Follows:

Petition

May 15, 1984

Petition to: *The Southeastern Jurisdictional Conference,* The United Methodist Church

Submitted by: *The Southeastern Regional Native American Caucus*

Subject: *Establishing a SeJ Association for Native American Ministries*

Whereas, in the nine Southeastern States of the United Methodist Church, there are 130,000 Native Americans,

Whereas, There are Native Americans in Annual Conferences within the SeJ with NO intentional ministry from the United Methodist Church,

Whereas, the Native Americans of the SeJ are nearly invisible in most Annual Conference, and only three Annual Conferences have established United Methodist Ministries with Native Americans; and

Whereas, there is little or no United Methodist spiritual or social ministries with Native Americans in the SeJ,

Whereas, Native American Ministries have been mandated by the 1980 General Conference to be a high priority,

Whereas, no new Native American congregation has been established in the SeJ in the past ten years, yet the Native American population has increased

Whereas, it is incumbent upon our connectional church to devise a means of ministry with the total Native American Community in the SeJ.

THEREFORE, WE PETITION

That the 1984 Southeastern Jurisdictional Conference, establish an Association for Native American Ministries within the Southeastern Jurisdiction Council on Ministries; and

That the proposed proposal for implementation as recommended by the Southeastern Regional Native American Caucus be approved for use within the Southeastern Jurisdiction Council on Ministries.

Sam Wynn
Vice-Chairperson
SERNAC

Route 1, Box 362
Rowland, NC 28383

I. THE PREAMBLE

There are urgent needs for establishing an organization for Native American ministries within the Southeastern Jurisdiction of The United Methodist Church.

They are:

1. The General Conference of 1984 approved "Developing and Strengthening the Ethnic Minority Local Church for Witness and Mission" as the missional priority.

2. There are 130,000 plus Native Americans in the seventeen (17) Annual Conferences and nine (9) states of the Southeastern Jurisdiction, with little or no intentional ministry from the United Methodist Church. Often these persons are scattered and detached with little or no sense of community, or support from other Native Americans within the Southeast.

3. United Methodist Native Americans desire an opportunity to be in ministry to and with their sisters and brothers, who make up the Native American population within the Southeastern Jurisdiction. Thereby,

enabling proud self-identity, self-determination, self-development and mutual service within the Community of Native Americans.

4. Native Americans of the Southeast have a need for the ministry, and at the same time, have a contribution to make to the mission of the United Methodist Church.

5. Native Americans need to be identified within the larger community and affirmed as persons of worth with a unique contribution to make.

6. United Methodist Native Americans within the conferences of the Southeastern Jurisdiction need an organization through which they can speak to the conferences, Jurisdictional, and General Church Structures.

7. Recognizing the validity of these concerns, The Southeastern Jurisdictional Conference of 1984, approved the creation of The Southeastern Jurisdiction Association for Native American Ministries as one of the ways of responding to these urgent needs.

III. THE PURPOSE STATEMENT

The primary purpose of The Southeastern Jurisdiction Association for Native American Ministries, is to advocate for Native Americans by developing and strengthening existing Native American Local churches; establishing New Congregations; recognize new areas of need for Native American outreach; to build bridges of understanding with Annual Conferences, Districts and Clusters; and to provide a means of witness through sharing and caring. All these are to enable the Native American United Methodist Church for witness and mission to the community and the world.

GOALS:

1. To create an awareness in each Annual Conference that Native Americans exist within their bounds.

2. To enable and develop ministries with Native Americans in each Annual Conference of The Southeastern Jurisdiction.

3. To motivate, train, and involve Native American lay leadership.

4. To recruit, equip and be available for consultation in the assignment of Native American Clergy within and across conference boundaries—in order to create, maintain and expand Native American ministries.

5. To be a broker for Native American and non-Native American lay persons available to be in mission across the Jurisdiction as Short Term or Life-Long Missioners; (e.g., Teachers, Doctors, Nurses, Lawyers, Business and Construction Personnel.)

6. To provide advocacy programming for issues of justice, equal opportunities, development and self-determination within communities, counties, states and the entire southeast.

7. To provide advocacy (programming) for Native Americans within the United Methodist structures of the Districts, Conferences and the Southeastern Jurisdiction.

8. To provide advocacy (programming) for Native Americans by Native Americans within all of the Native American Communities of the Southeast.

IV. FUNCTION

1. To identify and implement Native American concerns as a pilgrimage people of God; and to open the organizational doors through which Native American concerns can be heard and implemented.

2. To identify areas of Native American populations where no ministries have been started.

3. To provide a model of evangelism by revitalization with Native Americans; and establish new congregations and equip the laity and clergy persons for leadership.

4. To hold consultations to identify and develop models of specific ministries with Native Americans that will address the needs of the poor, powerless, and oppressed which will improve the quality of life for future generations.

5. To strengthen the Local Church in its missional outreach, and to be in mission, rather than being objects of mission.

6. To identify and secure financial resources.

7. To aid in the Recruitment, Training and Deployment of Lay and clergy leadership for Native American ministries.

8. To develop a Native American and Non-Native American Lay and Clergy leaders Data Bank, in order that an effective brokerage of human resources may be shared, and skills matched with needs.

9. To foster Inter-Tribal Relationships and Intra-Tribal Community building among the Native American population of the Southeast.

10. To create (settings of) opportunities for other groups to develop awareness of, and sensitivity to the Native Americans in the Southeast.

DIRECTOR
SOUTHEASTERN JURISDICTIONAL ASSOCIATION FOR NATIVE AMERICAN MINISTRIES

Position Description

The Director is the Administrative Officer of the Southeastern Jurisdiction Association for Native American Ministries to the SeJ Association for Native American Board of Directors for the general administration of the SeJ Association for Native American Ministries Program and Policies.

I. General responsibilities for Program and Policy Administration, include the following:

1. Provides data, leadership, and resources for the development and strengthening of Native American ministries in local churches and communities.
2. Assess available resources (local church and community, funds, church related personnel and etc.) in the United Methodist Church.
3. Responsible for consultation with Native American local churches and communities on program assessment, implementation and evaluation.

Promote support, acceptance, and understanding of Native American Ministries by the general church.

Develop awareness of and need of Native American Ministries within the Native American Communities, districts, annual conferences and the general church.

Provide leadership to increase the number of Native American candidates for ordained, diaconal, and other related ministries.

Enlist the cooperation of general church boards, agencies, annual conferences, districts and local churches in providing program resources for the SeJ Association for NA Ministries.

Serve as an advocate to the Southeast for Native American issues and needs.

Develop the SeJ Association for NA ministries for the exchange of ideas and resources.

Encourage self-sufficiency and self-determination of local Native American churches.

Develop a network for communicating with scattered Native Americans across the Southeast.

Design and coordinate Cross-Cultural Programs.

Coordinate activities intended to promote spiritual formation development among churches and professional leadership.

Assist and design Lay Speaking Training Events, aid in the recruitment and develop a Native American leadership data bank.

Establish Outreach to Native American who are unchurched and assist in establishing new Native American congregations and providing leadership in building new churches.

Develop new and emerging Native American ministries.

Address the needs of the poor, powerless and oppressed.

CONSULTATION ON STRENGTHENING AND DEVELOPING NATIVE AMERICAN MINISTRIES

March 7-9, 1986
Methodist College
Fayetteville, N.C.

Leadership Planning Committee from the Southeastern Jurisdictional Association for Native American Ministries.

Dr. G. Ross Freeman, Exe, Dir. SeJ Com.
Dr. I. L. Rucker, Dir., SeJ Com. on Mission and EMC
Rev. S. F. Cummings, Coord., SeJ Asso. of Native American Ministries
Rev. R. L. Mangum, Chp., Program/Research, SeJ Asso. for Native American Ministries
Rev. Chester Brown, Program/Research, SeJ Association for Native American Ministries
Ms. Josephine W. Bigler, Field Rep. Nat. Division
Dr. Evelyn Burry, Board of Discipleship
Dr. Belton Joyner, Finance, SeJ Association for Native American Ministries

Rev. Franklin Phillips, Resource Person, Pastor, N. Ala. Conference
Mr. James A. Jones, Program/Research, SeJ for Native American Ministries
Ms. Juanita Wolf, Leadership Dev. SeJ Association for Native American Ministries
Mr. Tom Queen, Treasurer, SeJ. NAM
Mr. Robby Lowry, Secretary, SeJ. NAM
Dr. Thomas Cloyd, Finance Chr. SeJ. NAM

A CHALLENGE

There are 130,000 plus Native Americans in the Seventeen (17) Annual Conferences and nine (9) states of the Southeastern Jurisdiction with little or no intentional ministry from the United Methodist Church. Often these persons are scattered and detached with little or no sense of community, or support from other Native Americans in the Southeast.

The Call is to United Methodism in our Seventeen (17) Annual Conferences to share God's love in a caring and loving way.

STATEMENT OF PURPOSE

—To celebrate the presence and ministries of Native Americans in the southeast.

—to challenge local churches of the Southeastern Jurisdiction to establish creative relationships with Native American peoples and ministries within annual conferences.

—to challenge communities, congregations and annual conferences to be open and inclusive to Native Americans.

—to share possibilities for developing New Native American ministries.

GOALS

—Participants will identify Native American persons and their presence in all districts and annual conference; their gifts, hopes and concerns.

—Participants will be involved in each Tribe's/group's identification of their specific needs, identify resources, will develop strategies and skills to meet those needs.

—Participants will develop support systems for continuing work in districts and annual conferences.

FELT NEEDS AND CONCERNS OF NATIVE AMERICANS

Help with recognition—Federal, State, and community.
Educational opportunities, and job training.
Training of community, Band, and Tribal Leaders.
Jobs—Jobs—Jobs.
Help with organizational skills.
Training to do genealogy work in getting Tribal Recognition.
Native Skills Development—such as basket weaving, pottery, carving, etc.
Visibility.
Family-life Education.
Help with Ceremonial research, planning, and development.
Financial assistance.
Marketing skills, and opportunities.
Social Services.
Trades, and native skills workshops near large segments of Native population.

(These needs were shared with the author, by Chiefs, leaders, and members of many of the Tribes, Bands, and groups of The Southeast, in preparation for The Consultation on The Native American Ministries.)

Dr. Israel Rucker spoke to The Consultation on Images of Ministries:

We are challenged by a new vision. . . . what the native American Ministries can be now, and in the future. . . .

This vision of what Native American Ministries can be . . . comes in seven images, like those in the book of Revelation:

Let me share these images briefly with you

I. IMAGE

The Native American Ministry is a vital and Significant part of The Body of Christ, and The United Methodist Church. . . .

II. IMAGE

Native American Churches, like most Ethnic Minority Churches are normative, that is, they are the basic units for the beginning pattern of organization and operation of the Church. This should apply at all levels of operation within the United Methodist Church. . . . Ethnic Congregations must be taken seriously.

III. IMAGE

The Native American Church, economically, Socially and theologically must become inclusive in a pluralistic Society. Persons both alike and unlike us, should become one in the Body of Christ . . . from every tribe in this nation . . . LUMBEE, CREE, CHEROKEE CHOCTAW . . . etc. must be welcome to sit down at the welcome table. . . .

IV. IMAGE

NATIVE AMERICAN CHURCHES MUST enter into some form of Cooperative Forms of Ministries if they are to survive.

V. IMAGE

Native American Churches are Smaller in membership, than the Majority Small Membership Church . . . and therefore, must examine the trends in planning for future ministries . . . WE MUST FIND A BETTER WAY OF DOING MINISTRY

VI. IMAGE

The Native American Church is an important part of this Jurisdiction and must continue to improve the quality of life for all people and move all of us toward a just society.

VII. IMAGE

The Native American Ministry has greater social and economic problems and fewer resources to deal with them.

CONCLUSION

Dear friends, it is good to dream dreams, and see heavenly visions, but the time has come for us to rise up, and put our dreams and visions into reality.

Excerpts from
The Challenge of Rev Simeon Cummings

Our commitment to inclusiveness should be visible. Now the task before us is not just to "FIND A FAITH," on "Strengthening and Developing Native American Ministries," but to find and to be open to the Biblical imperative to discover ourselves and own ourselves, and act as *ONE PEOPLE*. There are various ways that we could approach that, but let us consider from the Biblical point of view.

We are one human family, and we are one unique family within the Christian family. We are one family through God's Creative Act. We are all made in the image of God, and God saw everything that he made was good. God created humankind to be one family.

His creative act gives us dignity and worth, and it invalidates any effort to make some persons more valuable than others, and we must begin to, appropriate and to share and to act out the meaning of the human individual and every human gathering.

We are a people who are under the command of God to do Justice. The prophetic message rings loud and clear in the Old Testament, *TO DO JUSTLY*." And Justice in the Old Testament always topples over into Mercy. WE DO NOT deserve MERCY. Justice always topples over into the concern to reach out to those who are the stranger, the widow, the orphan, the weak, the hungry. Justice is always caring and helping the oppressed.

Now, what I am contending is, that fundamental to anything that we hope to do in "Strengthening and Developing Native American Ministries," is for us:

—to become a people who know we are ONE PEOPLE. And to act as ONE PEOPLE, and therefore, our relationship with oneness through Creation, through Sin, through Justice, through Redemption, through incorporation into Christ's humanity must become the foundation of all of us in "Strengthening and Developing Native American Ministries."

But we also have to deal with the fact that the reality about us is that we are a different people. We are diverse people. We are diverse in our gifts, in abilities, in perspectives, in our spiritual experiences as well as in our ethnic heritage. Paul struggled with this when he tried to include two ethnic groups in the churches at Corinth and Rome. People of Jewish heritage and of Gentile heritage. They simply see things differently. And what Paul does is to try to affirm the Gospel as he understands it and then to allow Freedom for those persons to express that Gospel as they can with integrity and with convictions.

What Paul is trying to do is to maintain our oneness and on the other hand, allow for the Diversity. He does that with regards to gifts. By letting people see that the diversity of gifts is an enrichment to the Church. But to understand that it is the ONE spirit that inspires, the ONE God who gives and the ONE Lord who serves.

This is a great lesson for us to learn and profit by. We do not have to let our Tradition, and our Culture separate us but we as the people of God can use the gifts that God has given to us to affirm us as a people of God.

Keynote: SEJANAM—Consultation on Strengthening and Developing Native American Ministries

delivered by Rev. Bushyhead

Director of The National United Methodist Native American Center

Fayetteville, North Carolina
March 8, 1986

I would like to thank the Southeast Jurisdiction for inviting me to participate in the Consultation on Strengthening and Developing Native American Ministries. I especially would like to thank Simeon Cummings for inviting me to speak this morning.

In trying to come up with an appropriate topic for today, I thought and discarded many ideas. I finally settled on a challenge. I come today to bring to you a challenge as you face the task before you. A formidable one, I might add.

The challenge can be found in Ecclesiastes 5:4-5, "when you vow a vow to God, do not delay paying it; for he has no pleasure in fools. Pay what you vow. It is better that you should not vow than that you should vow and not pay." The passage goes on to say "Let not your mouth lead you into sin . . . when dreams increase, empty words grow many . . . "[3]

There has been an emphasis on ethnic ministries development since 1976. What are our accomplishments? What can we hold up to show Native people the United Methodist Church is fighting for them?

Of the 17 Native pastors who have been seminary trained 8 of them come from the North Carolina Conference. That leaves 9 seminary trained Native pastors for the rest of the country. Before we get too comfortable with that figure let's remember there are 17 conferences in the Southeast Jurisdiction. We *must* ask ourselves why we're in such state of affairs. Why do the Native Americans not feel comfortable in our churches?

Rhett Jackson from South Carolina said, "The church is full of racists who have publicly declared their allegiance to Jesus Christ. That should make us weep. The church hasn't changed these people much. Our perceptions about race must be challenged against Christian principles." You can't convert institutions, lasting change happens when individuals change. As we watch new theologies being born we must keep in mind we can not allow our theology to come from a desire to justify our actions.

Fredrick Douglas, during his struggles said, "When I look at Jesus, I see an unwillingness to allow unjust situations to go unchallenged." Bishop Fitzgerald adds, "separatism in the church cannot be defended on biblical grounds except by the most irrational interpretation of the Scriptures."

"It is better that you should not vow than that you should vow and not pay." Can the United Methodist Church deliver on it's promises of intention to the ethnic minorities? Do we really have a desire to develop Native ministries? Those who have never been oppressed can never understand and those who no longer suffer oppression tend to forget. I once heard oppression described in the following fashion: It's like when your nose is broken so many times you'd almost look forward to breaking a foot. Or when you've done so much crying that laughter becomes pain.

There are many reasons for our failure to carry through on our intentions to do things. Sometimes we are tired; sometimes we are confused; sometimes we are not certain of the appropriate action. Often we become discouraged because our actions appear to have so little effect.

All of us have, at one time or another, substituted planning and meetings for our actions. We need to examine ourselves and determine if our continued meetings, our lengthy planning are only sophisticated ways to avoid action.

We return home from conferences, retreats, consultations or some other religious experience, filled with good intentions. We move, convinced, we can combat massive wrongs. We return to ordinary life. And the right time for our heroic action never seems to come. At first, we keep watch for the right opportunity and the right time. But, bit by bit, we fall into our daily routine. Bit by bit we even think our earlier commitment to do something is itself action. Too often, we allow rhetoric to suffice as our action. We convince ourselves that rhetoric *is* action.

The most dangerous enemy of our good intentions is the eroding effect of our "dailiness." We fail to act and the "nothingness" conquers us. While we consider when to begin, it becomes too late.

So we wait, we plan, we think, we develop strategies and nothing changes.

When it comes to action, its been said that most of us are like wheelbarrows—useful only when pushed and too easily upset.

Good intentions are good, only for those who believe they intend to do something. Without follow through those intentions become idle self-grandizements. Remember, stopping at third base adds no more to the score than striking out. As we read in Ecclesiastes, "when dreams increase, empty words grow many . . . "

When you profess to follow Jesus you vow to do God's work. The gospel is real only when its being acted upon. We are not saved by works, only by faith, but faith without works is dead. We cannot have Christianity ala carte. We cannot pick and choose what we want to do and discard the rest. Christianity is not a static thing. It calls for action. Jesus said, go, preach, teach, heal and love. All action words.

As we say we're about strengthening and developing Native American Ministries, do we really know what that means? When we step into various Native reservations and communities to identify and lift up leadership we must understand that leadership within Native communities is obtained differently than that of the other societies and cultures. Leadership is given—earned. It is not a position to be claimed or self-acquired. It has to be given to you by the people seeking to be represented.

People, the most visible and the most vocal, are often recognized as the leaders of Indian people by those on the outside of the community, but are not seen as such by those on the inside. Leaders within the Native communities are ones of quiet dignity and great stature. They are not necessarily those with elective offices or degrees.

They don't seek grandizement or emulation, but most often have both. They seek merely to serve their God and their people.

Sometimes we get our leadership roles mixed up. Leadership is doing for, not having others do for us. Jesus is the epitome of leadership being servanthood. A servant of God and servant of our people.

Jesus made time for the individual. He was personal . . . He healed the blind man in Jerico; the thief on the cross, and chastised his disciples for trying to keep the children from him.

Julia Ward Howe one day was talking to Charles Sumner, a distinguished senator from Massachusetts. She asked him to interest himself in the case of a person who needed some help. The senator answered, "Julia, I've become so busy I can no longer concern myself with individuals." Julia replied, "Charles, that is quite remarkable, Even God hasn't reached that stage yet."

Christianity is one of doing for others. Leadership is not always the one out front. In the Native cultures everyone did their part, performed the tasks they had to perform for the good of the whole.

Christ was a servant-leader. Too often, we want to be boss leaders. We want to give the orders and have others do our bidding. We read in the

Bible where Jesus said, "The greatest among you must be your servant." Perhaps this speaks clearly to the role women have been relegated to in the western culture. Maybe, we men should learn from them the leader-servant role.

Our responsibility of proclamation of Christianity is an awesome responsibility. We must recognize that that proclamation is of ourselves as servants, not the making of servants of others. Christianity is one of doing.

If we want to develop Native ministries we will be making a vow to God of action. We love to pray and need to pray for God's guidance, strength and courage. But prayers can be a cop-out. Instead of us going to help someone we kneel down and pray and ask God to go over and help them. If we can pray for God's help while we're moving to help others we get to do our part and not leave everything to God.

What God needs is action. You get your blessings back in ways you don't understand—in ways you don't need to understand.

If we are going to be successful, if we are going to do any good in the Native communities we must seek out the real leaders, if we're going to learn how to work in these communities we need to learn, to revere those the community reveres. We cannot be afraid of the Native peoples beliefs and spiritual symbolism.

Norman W. Pittenger said, "From ancient times man has been developing symbols to express his experience and faith. The use of these symbols are part of his search for self understanding and understanding of the universe."[4] The Indian youth today know their Native beliefs aren't pagan. They know there are good things in the Native religious ceremonies.

The awareness of "the sacred", the sense of presence and power has been expressed in words that differs from age to age, place to place and culture to culture. The history of religion is the continuing story of the refining of the meaning of such awareness. We must understand and honor their right to want the good from their cultural beliefs. We don't have all the right answers.

Once in the Native American community we must be able to give them a dream. In most of these communities when people wake in the mornings they face another day of trying to stay alive. Not another day of life but another day of mere existence.

For the Native American the mortality rates in relation to the general population is staggering. According to the American Indian Health Care Association mortality rates for; pneumonia and influenza are 64% greater, homicide 68% greater, diabetes mellitus 124% greater, suicides 150% greater, accidents (automobile) 154% greater, alcoholism 451% greater and tuberculosis 500% greater.

With unemployment within Native communities, reservation or urban, anywhere between 40 to 80% and substance abuse in ages documented from 5 years to adulthood, child abuse/neglect, incest, spouse abuse, and suicides are on the rise. Teenage pregnancy is a continual problem. Where is their hope? Where is their dream. If the young is our future where is their future? I pray it's with us. We are called to proclaim the acceptable year of the Lord.

Viktor Frankl, a Jewish doctor who spent time in a Nazi concentration camp, said of people "Everything that was not connected with the immediate task of keeping oneself alive lost its value. A persons character became involved to the point that they were caught in a mental turmoil which threatened all the values they held and threw them into doubt.

"Under the influence of a world which no longer recognized the value of human life and human dignity, which robbed them of their will and made them objects to be exterminated—under this influence the personal ego finally suffered a loss of values."[5]

The three phases Dr. Frankl saw of the inmates reactions to camp life became quite apparent—shock, apathy and lifelessness.

Since the Nazi concentration camps were patterned from their study of the United States reservation system, I think it appropriate we learn from them. The Native Americans, too, went through all the phases Dr. Frankl describes. Shock, or a cultural shock, and apathy and lifelessness.

As Dr. Frankl says, "The prisoner of Auschwitz, in the first phase of shock, did not fear death. Even the horrors of the gas chambers were lost for him after the first few days—after all, they spared them the act of committing suicide. The thought of suicide was entertained by nearly everyone, if only for a brief time. It was born of the hopelessness of the situation, the constant danger of death looming daily and hourly, the closeness of the deaths suffered by many of the others.

"Apathy, the main symptom of the second phase was a necessary mechanism of self-defense. Reality dimmed, and all efforts and all emotions were centered on one task: preserving one's own life."[6]

Dr. Frankl moves on and asks the question, "Does man have no choice of action in the face of such circumstances?" He makes the argument that the experiences of camp life show that man does have a choice of action. Apathy can be overcome, irritability suppressed. Man can preserve a vestige of spiritual freedom of independence of mind, even in such terrible conditions of psychic and physical stress.

Everything can be taken away from a man but one thing: The last of the human freedoms—to choose one's attitude in any given set of circumstances, to choose one's own way.

In the final analysis it became clear that the sort of person the prisoner became was the result of an inner decision, and not the result of camp influences alone. Fundamentally, therefore, any man can, even under such circumstances decide what shall become of him—mentally and spiritually. He may retain his dignity even in a concentration camp or reservation.

It is this spiritual freedom, which cannot be taken away, that makes life meaningful and purposeful.

The feelings of lifelessness (life without future and without goals) caused anything outside the confines of prison to be remote out of reach and in a way unreal. As we walk across a Native community we can see the lifelessness. "Why try?" they ask, "It doesn't matter, anyhow!"

The prisoner who lost faith in the future was doomed. With the loss of belief in the future, they also lost their spiritual hold. It is the responsibility of the church, yours and mine, to help the Native people maintain their spiritual hold. We must give them hope, a goal and an aim for their lives.

Those who know how close the connection between the state of mind and the courage and hope, or lack of them, and the state of immunity of the body will understand that the sudden loss of hope and courage can have a deadly effect.

The loss of courage and the resultant disappointment which overcomes people has a dangerous influence on the powers of resistance.

Therein lies our task when we speak of our desire to develop Native American ministries. Whenever there is an opportunity we must give the Native people a "*why*"—an aim—for their lives, in order to strengthen them to bear the terrible "*how*" of their existence.

Frankl said in the life saving procedure, the right example was more effective than words. The immediate influence of behavior is always more effective than that of words. But at times, a word was effective, too.[7]

In talking with youth around the country I have one standard question I try to make sure is asked. That question is, "Why as a church are we losing our youth?" The main responses I received are 1) the adults of the church tell us what we're supposed to do, but don't do it themselves and 2) when we, the youth, want to get involved there is no time or support from the adults.

That's quite a serious indictment against us adults.

We need to work with the leadership the people know and respect. We need to seek them out, find them and learn from them. Let's not meet for the sake of meeting, or plan for the sake of planning or let us convince ourselves that our planning and meeting is our action and thus our job is complete.

We must link hands and lend each other our support, not just moral or financial support, but ourselves and out talents.

As the local church finds it needs the talents and energies of the individual people, so have we at the jurisdictional and national level found that we are nothing without the work and help of the local churches. Synergy is definitely at work and can create an unstoppable centrifugal force of our cause. With unified efforts and perseverence we need not be aleatory, but can become an accepted integral part of the United Methodist Church.

Dr. Carl Menninger has spoken of the importance of dreams and visions in motivating persons to realize their fullest potential and to enhance the very meaning of their existence.[8]

Henry Cisneros, Mayor of San Antonio says of dreams, "Dream big. See yourself in the future and extend yourself beyond your present expectations. You lose not only by taking a step backward. You lose, also, by failing to take a step forward."

We must continually lift up the needs and hurts of the Native people. I firmly believe that not do so, to remain silent or to do nothing gives tacit sanction to the Church to continue ignoring the cries of the Native people. Proverbs 21:13 says, "He who closes his ear to the cry of the poor, will himself cry out and not be heard."

We're all in ministry. Would that we all could respond as the shoe cobbler did when asked, "what's your business?" He responded, "My business is to extend the kingdom of God. I only cobble shoes to pay the expenses."

To have a successful consultation, what you learn here you must be able to replicate for implementation at home. Leave here with a clear purpose of why you're here and what you will, not what's possible, but what *you will* do when you get home. Come to learn, go forth to teach.

Let's celebrate out ethnicity, not to the extent that we think ourselves too special, but so we never think ourselves not important. We cannot allow our grievances to overshadow our opportunities.

There is a prayer written by a nine year old Native youth, and the things that he believed in, THE FOUR WAYS OF LIFE. They were, his eyes, his ears, his nose and his mouth. He said his hands protects these four ways. Here's what he wrote:

> Lifegiver, Creator of this world
> Give me strength to fight my greatest enemy, which is myself.
> Because, somewhere lately I've been hearing all the bad things and I can remember them
> And I can see the bad things of life,
> I can smell and taste the bad things, and talk about them.

Lifegiver, I know there is good in this world—somewhere
Even someone to learn from
This is why I need your help, Lifegiver
To fight my greatest enemy, which is myself
To help me fight with my four ways of life
To be able to hear the good things
To be able to see the good things
Smell and taste and talk about these good things, of life.[9]

Courtesy of A. Paul Ortega, 1832 Elizabeth Northeast, Albuquerque, NM

"When dreams increase, empty words grow many . . . " in its stead let's say as Isaiah, "Here am I send me."

WHAT DO YOU SAY?

March 8, 1986
SEJ Consultation of Native Americans
Fayetteville, N. C.

Excerpts from The Message of Dr. Rene Bideaux of The Board of Global Ministries.

Introduction:

1) *What do you celebrate* with a people who have known 100s of years of oppression, abuse, and poverty at the hands of your nation and race?
2) *What do you say* to people who have experienced only the worst that a society could offer: disease and drunkenness, firearms and violence, broken friendships and treaties, displacement and removal from home and property?
3) When *this is the legacy* that one has participated in giving to a people, what Word of hope and celebration can I bring? As I sat to work on this sermon, that was the dominant thought.

A. *I turned to the Prophet Joel. 2: 12-27.*[10]

In reading this, I found the Word that I want to speak this morning. It is two fold: *judgement* and *redemption. . . . confession and hope,* if you would.

1. "The time has come for the American people to be delivered from beliefs which gave support to the false promises and faulty policies which prevailed in the relations of the United States government with America's native peoples."

2. Then these "beliefs" are enumerated:
   a. Whites were ordained by God to possess the land.
   b. Natives were poor stewards of nature because they roamed.
   c. Because the white race grew in number and tamed nature and natives, it was superior.
   d. Forceful displacement of natives was necessary to develop a free and new land.
   e. The white civilization offered a better life.
3. These are rather crude, but they have existed and still persist as the foundation that encourages so many injustices in the lives of native people:
4. The Resolution goes on to say: "The Church is called to repentance, for it bears a heavy responsibility for spreading false beliefs and for unjust governmental policies and practices."

B. The heritage that white people have offered the Indian has been disavowal of culture and history and disease, death, violence, broken confidences, and removal from family, home and land. It is there for all to see.
   1. The highest rates of unemployment and poverty in our nation are among the native peoples . . . ranging as much as 88%.
   2. 23% of urban and 33% of rural Indians live below the poverty level. 40% of Native youth drop out of high school.
   3. Most of the 130,000 Native Americans living in the 9 states of the SEJ are scattered, battered, impoverished and with no sense of community, often struggling to be recognized as a people.

II. *The threat of locusts to Judah and the threat of white people to America's natives have been very similar: the plundering of nature . . . violence to family and society.*
   A. The prophet Joel speaks to us today, white Americans and Natives: "It's time to be delivered. . . . "

   Conclusion:
   1) "I'll expose you no longer to the reproach of other nations." (2:19) . . . Its never too late for God to act in the midst of our lives, regardless of how oppressive it might seem.
   2) In this hope let us celebrate the presence and ministries of Native Americans . . . let us challenge and charge local churches, Annual Conferences and our communities to welcome Native Americans. . . . to right the wrongs . . to affirm all God's children.
   3) We have but to acknowledge our brokeness . . . demonstrate an openness to being healed. God will work with us.

a. God's healing takes many forms: advocacy, demonstrating . . . "bugging the system" . . . ministries of compassion.
b. Healing takes place when we become the healers of others. . . . as we take on the image of God: slow to anger/long suffering . . . full of mercy/compassion . . . but are insistent upon justice and dignity—healing takes place.

4) We celebrate the witness of Native Peoples for 100's of years to all who are white and have eyes to see and the ears to hear. The words of Hope for this gathering:

"... I, the Lord, am your God and there is none else.
And my people shall never again be put to shame." (2:27)

1. Even now in the 11th hour this threat to Native cultures can be averted if we truly repent and turn from the disasterous course and beliefs we have been bound to for these many years.
2. Joel is speaking to those who have been unfaithful and who have violated the rights of Native Peoples: repent!

B. Joel is also speaking to those Native peoples who have been broken by unkept treaties, displacement, violence, disease and abuse . . . His Word speaks to the "broken-hearted."
   1. "Fear not . . . I will restore to you the years which the swarming locust has eaten, . . . You shall know that I am in (your) midst . . ."
   2. Joel is speaking/challenging us to turn away from the destructive stances of diffidence, powerlessness, rage, cynicism and defeat. . . . Joel is saying come come back, turn back to reclaim your heritage as God's full heirs.
   3. *Illus*—Navajo Mission School focus on language and culture. . . . academic excellence, Navajo identity and Christian faith are not incompatible.

Courtesy of The SEJ Council of Ministries, and Rev. Simeon Cummings.

One part of The Consultation was to ask each state group to focus on one pressing need in their area. The Alabama group felt the area of greatest need was the high unemployment of the Calcedeaver Choctaw Community.

We made a commitment to work on ideas and Designs for Workshops, etc., to respond to this challenge. We would work in, and through the Aldersgate United Methodist Church.

This church had burned some 1 year previously and was being rebuilt. Mr. Clare Jones of The General Board of Global Ministries served as the architect for the building. Many donations were given by members, friends in the community, churches of the Mobile District, a gift of one-half of the Mission Rally Offering from the Selma District, and grants from the General Board of Global Ministries.

On April 6th, 1986 the members and many friends of The Aldersgate United Methodist Church met to worship God, and to Celebrate the opening of the new building. And truly it was a time of great Celebration with an overflowing crowd from the community and area.

Follow-up at Aldersgate

A Task Force of Rev. Simeon Cummings, Dr. Roy Sublette, Rev. Billy Gaither, and Rev. Franklin Phillips, will meet with the pastor, Rev. George Weaver and the Aldersgate members on the evening of June 8th. We will begin the task of shaping programs, workshops, ministries, etc, that will help meet the most basic needs of this community. We will look at ways to help sharpen skills in making job applications, job hunting, personal appearance, how to present yourself effectively, etc. We will consider the need for adult education programs dealing with remedial reading, cottage industries such as basketry, bead work, pottery etc, and marketing skills. We will consider the need for a workshop on geneology, and on problems and cost of energy. We will look at the possibility of local resources such as The Job Training Partnership Act and The North Baldwin Assessment Center. We will consider means of finding concerned persons and businesses across the area who would be willing to make jobs available and to help place many of these needy persons of the Calcedeaver community in job opportunities.

It is our HOPE that this will be but the beginning of many new ministries that will be evolving across The Southeast meeting the vast needs of The Native Americans of the Southeast!

BIBLIOGRAPHY

Adair, James. *History of The American Indian.* New York: Promotory Press, 1930.

Adams, James Truslow, editor. *Album of American History.* Vol. 1—Colonial Period. New York, New York: Charles Scribner's Sons, 1944.

Akens, Helen Morgan, and Brown, Virginia Pounds. *Alabama Heritage.* Huntsville, Alabama: The Strode Publishers, 1971.

Akens, Helen Morgan, and Brown, Virginia Pounds. *Alabama Mounds to Missiles.* Huntsville, Alabama: The Strode Publishers, 1972.

Baird, W. David. *The Chickasaw People.* Phoenix, Arizona: Indian Tribal Series, 1974.

Baird, W. David. *The Choctaw People.* Phoenix, Arizona: Indian Tribal Series, 1973.

Bartram, William. *Travels.* New Haven: Yale University Press, 1958.

Bassett, John Spencer. *A Short History of the United States.* New York: The Macmillian Co., 1934.

Better Homes and Gardens Heritage Cook Book. Meredith Corporation, U.S.A., 1975.

Bossau, Jean Bernard. Translated and edited by Seymour Feiler. *Travels in the Interior of North America.* Norman, Oklahoma: University of Oklahoma Press, 1962.

Bourne, Edward Gaylord—edited Knight of Elvas. *Narratives of the Career of Hernando de Soto.* New York: Allerton Book Co., 1904.

Brandon, William. *The Last Americans.* New York: McGraw-Hill Book Co., 1974.

Breckenridge, H. H. *Indian Atrocities—Narratives of the Perils and Suffering of Dr. Knight and John Slover Among the Indians.* Cincinnati, Ohio: U. P. James, 1782, 1867.

Brown, William Garrott. *History of Alabama.* New York and New Orleans: University Publishing Co., 1900.

Buchanan, Robert W. and Was, Murray L. *Solving "The Indian Problem" The White Man's Burdensome Business.* New York: A New York Times Book, 1975.

Burnette, Robert. *The Tortured Americans.* Englewood Cliffs, New Jersey: Prentice-Hall, Inc., 1971.

Burt, Jesse and Fergurson, Robert B. *Indians of The Southeast.* Nashville and New York: Abingdon Press, 1973.

Cahn, Edgar S., editor. *Our Brother's Keeper: The Indian in White America.* Washington, D. C.: New Community Press, Inc. 1969.

Cannon, James, III. *History of Southern Methodist Missions.* Nashville, Tennessee: Cokesbury, 1926.

Carter, Samuel, III. *Cherokee Sunset.* Garden City, New York: Doubleday and Co., Inc., 1976.

Catlin, George. *Last Rambles Amongst The Indians of The Rocky Mountains and The Andes.* London. 1968.

Caughey, John Walton. *McGillivray of The Creeks.* Norman, Oklahoma: University of Oklahoma Press. 1938.

Ceran, C. W. *The First American.* New York, New York: Harcourt Brace Jovanovich, Inc., 1971.

Claiborne, J. F. H. *Life and Times of General Sam Dale.* New York: Harper and Brothers, 1860.

Claiborne, Robert. *The First Americans.* Hastings on Hudson, New York: Time-Life Publication, 1973.

Colden, Cadwallader. *The History of the Five Indian Nations.* Ithaca and London: Cornell University Press, 1973.

Corkran, David H. *The Creek Frontier.* Norman, Oklahoma: University of Oklahoma Press, 1967.

Cotterhill, R. S. *The Southern Indians.* Norman, Oklahoma: University of Oklahoma Press, 1954, 1966.

Crockett, David. *David Crockett's Own Story.* New York: Citadel Press. Scranton, Pa.: The Haddon Craftsmen, Inc., 1955.

Cullen, Joseph P. *History of the American Revolution.* Harrisburg, Pa.: Stackpole Books, 1972.

Cushman, H. B. *History of the Choctaw, Chickasaw and Natchez Indians.* Greenville, Texas: Headlight Printing House, 1899.

Debo, Angie. *A History of The Indian of the United States.* Norman Oklahoma: University of Oklahoma Press, 1970.

Davies, Nigel, *Voyagers to The New World,* New York: William Morrow and Co., Inc., 1979.

Debo, Angie. *The Rise and Fall of The Choctaw Republic.* Norman, Oklahoma: University of Oklahoma Press, 1934, 1961.

De Rosier, Arthur H., Jr. "*Destruction of The Creek Confederacy.*" article in *Forked Tongues and Broken Treaties* edited by Donald E. Worcester, Caxton Ltd, 1975.

DeRosier, Arthur H., Jr. *The Removal of The Chocktaw Indian.* Knoxville, Tennessee: The University of Tennessee Press, 1970.

DeWolf, Harold. "Christian Mission in Theological Perspective" Edited by Gerald H. Anderson.

DeTocqueville, Alexis. *Democracy in America.* New York: Alfred A. Knopf, 1945.

Driver, Harold E. *Indians of North America.* Chicago and London: The University of Chicago Press, 1964, 1969.

Editors of The Album of American History. *Colonial America—From the First Settlements to the Close of The American Revolution.* New York: Charles Scribner's Sons.

Editors of Time—Life Books. *The Great Chiefs.* Alexandria, Virginia: 1975, 1977.

Farb, Peter. *Man's Rise to Civilization as Shown by The Indians of North America.* New York: E. P. Dutton and Co., Inc., 1968.

Foreman, Grant. *Indian Removal.* Norman, Oklahoma: University of Oklahoma Press, 1938, 1973.

Fundaburk, Emma Lila. Edited by Mary Douglass Foremans. *Sun Circles and Human Hands.* Luverne, Alabama: Published by Emma Lila Fundaburk, 1957, 1965.

Gibson, Arrell M. *The Chickasaw.* Norman, Oklahoma: University of Oklahoma Press, 1971.

Gray, Daniel Savage. *Alabama—A Place, A People, A Point of View.* Dubuque, Iowa: Kendall-Hunt Publishing Co.

Griffin, John W. *Investigation in Russell Cave.* Washington, D. C.: National Park Service, 1974.

Harris, W. Stuart. *Dead Towns of Alabama.* Tuscaloosa, Alabama: The University of Alabama Press.

Hertzberg, Hazel W. *The Search for An American Indian Identity.* New York: Syracuse University Press, 1971.

Higginbotham, Prieur Jay. *The Mobile Indians.* Mobile, Alabama: Sir Rey's, 1966.

Hudson, Charles M. *Four Centuries of Southern Indians.* Athens, Ga.: University of Georgia Press, 1975.

James, Marquis. *The Life of Andrew Jackson.* Garden City, New York: Garden City Publishing Co., Inc., 1938.

Jefferson, Thomas. Edited by William Peden. *Notes on Virginia.* Chapel Hill, North Carolina: The University of North Carolina Press, 1955.

Johnson, Bobby H. *The Conshatta People.* Phoenix, Arizona: Published by Indian Tribal Series, 1976.

Josephy, Alvin M., Jr. *The Indian Heritage of America.* New York: New York: Alfred A. Knopf, 1968.

Kollock, John. *These Gentle Hills.* Lakemont, Georgia: Copple House Brooks, 1976.

Lazenby, Marion Elias. *Methodism in Alabama.* Published by The North Alabama Conference and Alabama-West Florida Conference of The United Methodist Church, 1960.

Lewis, Anna. *Chief Pushmataha, American Patriot.* New York: Exposition Press, 1959.

Lindsey, Bobby L. *The Reason for the Tears.* West Point, Georgia: Hester Printing Co., 1971.

Luccock, Halford E. *The Story of Methodism.* New York, Cincinnati: The Methodist Book Concern, 1926.

Man, Col. Robert N. "The Cherokee County Heritage" The Cherokee County Historical Society Journal, Vol. III.

Matthews, Pitt Lamar. *History Stories of Alabama.* Dallas, Texas: The Southern Publishing Co., 1924, 1929.

McTyeire, Holland N. *A History of Methodism.* Nashville, Tennessee: Publishing House of The Methodist Episcopal Church, South, 1889.

Moore, Albert Burton. *History of Alabama.* Tuscaloosa, Alabama: Alabama Book Store, 1951.

Morgan, Lewis H. *League of The Ho-De-No-Sau-Nee or Iroquois.* New York: Burt Franklin, 1901.

Morris, Colin. *Include Me Out.*

Moulton, Gary E. *John Ross Cherokee Chief.* Athens, Georgia: The University of Georgia Press.

Muzzley, David Saville. *An American History.* Boston, New York, Chicago, London: Gin and Company, 1911.

National Geographic, LXXII. "America's First Settlers, The Indian" by Matthew W. Stirling, Chief, Bureau of American Ethnology, Smithsonian Institute. Nov., 1937.

National Geographic. "Life 8,000 Years Ago Uncovered in an Alabama Cave" Carl F. Miller, Expedition Leader. October, 1956.

National Geographic. "Russell Cave—New Light on Stone Age Life" Carl F. Miller, Expedition Leader, Russell Cave Expedition. March, 1958.

National Geographic Society. *The World of The American Indian.* Washington. D. C., 1974.

Owen, Marie B. *Our State—Alabama.* Birmingham, Alabama: Birmingham Printing Company, 1927.

Penicant, Andre. *Fleur de Lys and Calumet.* Edited by Richebourg Gaillard McWilliams. Baton Rouge, Louisiana: Louisiana State University Press, 1953.

Pickett, James Albert. *History of Alabama.* Birmingham, Alabama: Birmingham Book and Magazine Company, reprint, 1962.

Pierre, Chief George. *American Indian Crisis.* San Antonio, Texas: The Paylor Company, 1971.

Porter, C. Fayne. *Our Indian Heritage.* Philadelphia, New York, London: Chilton Book Company, 1964.

Posey, Walter B. *The Development of Methodism in The Old Southwest.* Tuscaloosa, Alabama: Weatherford Printing Co., 1933.

Pruche, Francis Paul. *American Indian Policy in The Formative Years.* Cambridge, Massachusetts: Harvard University Press, 1962.

Reader's Digest. *America's Fascinating Indian Heritage.* Pleasantville, New York, 1978.

Rosebud, Yellow Robe. *An Album of American Indian.* New York, New York: Franklin Watts, Inc., 1969.

Schoolcraft, Henry R. *History of The Indian Tribes of The United States.* New York, New York: Lippincott, 1851, 1857.

Sheehan, Bernard W. *Seeds of Extinction.* Chapel Hill, North Carolina: The University of North Carolina Press, 1973.

Soper, Edmund. *The Religions of Mankind.* Nashville and New York: Abingdon, Cokesbury, 1921, 1938, 1951.

Starr, Emmet. *History of The Cherokee Indian.* Oklahoma City, Oklahoma: The Warden Co., 1922.

Stirling, Matthew William. *America's First Settlers, The Indians.* Washington, D. C.: National Geographic Society, 1937.

Summersell, Charles B. *Alabama History for Schools.* Northport, Alabama: American Southern, 1965.

Trennert, Robert A., Jr. *Alternatives to Extinction.* Philadelphia, Pennsylvania: Temple University Press, 1975.

Tyerman, Rev. L. *The Life and Times of The Rev. John Wesley, M.A.* London: Hodder and Stoughton, 1890, MDCCCXC

Vattel, Emmerich. "The Law of Nations or Principles of The Law of Nature"

Vogel, Virgil, Jr. *This Country Was Ours.* New York, Evanston, San Francisco, London: Harper and Row, 1972.

Walthall, John A. *Moundville, An Introduction to The Archeology of a Mississippian Chiefdom.* University of Alabama: Alabama Museum of Natural History, 1977.

Washburn, Wilcomb E. *The Indian in America.* New York, Evanston, San Francisco, London: Harper and Row, 1975.

Weiner, Michael A. *Earth Medicine—Earth Food.* New York: The MacMillian Co., 1972.

Wesley, John. *The Journal of Rev. John Wesley.* London: J. M. Dent & Sons, Ltd. New York: E. P. Dutton and Co., 1906, 1922.

West Anson. *History of Methodism in Alabama.* Nashville, Tennessee: Publishing House Methodist Episcopal Church South, 1893.

Windham, Kathryn Tucker. *Exploring Alabama.* Huntsville, Alabama: The Stode Publishers, 1974.

Woodward, Grace Steele. *The Cherokees.* Norman, Oklahoma: University of Oklahoma Press, 1963.

Woodward, General Thomas S. *Woodward's Reminiscences of The Creek or Moscogees Indian.* Mobile, Alabama: Southern University Press for Graphics, Inc., reprinted 1965.

Worchester, Donald E., edited by. *Forked Tongues and Broken Treaties.* Caldwell, Idaho: The Claxton Printers, Ltd., 1975.

NOTES

1. Marty, Martin E., *Toward a Usable Past*

Preface—

1. Hertzberg, Hazel M. *The Search for an American Identity* (New York: Syracuse University Press, 1971) p 324

2. Worcester, D. H. edited by, *Forked Tongues and Broken Treaties* (Caldwell, Idaho: The Caxton Printers, Ltd., 1975) p 4

Chapter One—Whence They Came?

1. Washburn, Wilcomb E. *The Indian in America* (New York, Evanston, San Francisco, London: Harper & Row, 1975) p 1

2. National Geographic Society: *The World of the American Indian* (Washington, D. C., 1974) p 29

3. Reader's Digest, *America's Fascinating Indian Heritage* (Pleasantville, New York, 1978) p 12

4. National Geographic Society, *The World of The-American Indian* (Washington, D. C., 1974) p 30

5. Ceran, C. W., *The First Americans* (New York, New York: Harcourt Brace Jovanovich, Inc., 1971) p 289

Chapter Two—Who Are They?

1. Muzzey, David Saville. *An American History* (Boston, New York, Chicago, London: Ginn and Company, 1911) p 22

2. Adair, James. *History of The American Indian* (New York; Promotory Press, 1930) p 117

3. National Geographic Society. *The World of The American Indian* (Washington, D. C., 1974) p 14

4. Sheehan, Bernard W. *Seeds of Extinction* (Chapel Hill, North Carolina: The University of North Carolina Press, 1973) p 59

5. Driver, Harold E. *Indians of North America* (Chicago and London: The University of Chicago Press, 1964, 1969) p 5

6. Farb, Peter. *Man's Rise to Civilization as Shown by The Indians of North America* (New York: E. P. Dutton and Co. Inc, 1968) p 227.

Chapter Three—Cave Dwellers—Russell Cave, Trapp Ledge.

1. National Geographic Magazine, October, 1966 "Life 8,000 Years Ago Uncovered in an Alabama Cave", Carl F. Miller, Leader, Smithsonian-National Geographic Russell Cave Expedition p 254-258.

2. Summersell, Charles B. *Alabama History for Schools.* (Northport, Alabama: American Southern, 1965) p 3

3. DeSoto State Park Ranger Doyle Benefield carried me to see some of these cave shelters near DeSoto Falls.

Chapter Four—Roaming Hunters and Foragers.

1. Smithsonian Magazine, February, 1980, "The Mysterious Rise and Decline of Monte Alban", John E. Pfeifer.

2. Claiborne, Robert. *The First Americans* (New York, New York: Time-Life Publications, Hastings on Hudson, 1973) p 41

3. Reader's Digest. *America's Fascinating Indian Heritage* (Pleasantville, New York, 1978) p 24

4. Reader's Digest. *America's Fascinating Indian Heritage* (Pleasantville, New York, 1978) p 24

Chapter Five—Changing Styles of Life.

1. Driver, Harold E. *Indians of North America* (Chicago and London: The University of Chicago Press, 1964, 1969) p 217-218

2. Sun Circles and Human Hands, Southeastern Indians, Art and Industries, Luverne, Al. Emma Lila Fundaburk, Publisher 1957. renewed C. 1985. p. 30-quotation from William E. Meyer, "Indian Trails of The Southeast," Forty-Second Annual Report, Bureau of Ethnology, 1924-25 pp. 735-746

3. Burt, Jesse and Ferguson, Robert B. *Indians of The Southeast Then and Now* (Nashville, New York: Abingdon Press, 1973) p 116-117

4. Moore, Albert Burton. *History of Alabama* (Tuscaloosa Alabama: Alabama Book Store, 1951) p 10

5. Readers Digest. *America's Fascinating Indian Heritage* (Pleasantville, New York, 1978) p 91

6. From Thomas Jefferson's Notes on The State of Virginia, edited by William Peden. C. 1955 The University of North Carolina Press. Published for the Institute of Early American History and Culture-pp 202-203

8. Jefferson, Thomas. *Notes on Virginia* edited by William Peden. (Chapel Hill, North Carolina: The University of North Carolina Press, 1955) p 93

9. Colden, Cadwallader. *The History of The Five Indian Nations* (Ithaca and London: Cornell University Press, 1973) p Dedication page.

10. Colden, Cadwallader. *The History of The Five Indian Nations* (Ithaca and London: Cornell University Press, 1973) p Preface

11. Pickett, James Albert. History of Alabama (Birmingham, Alabama: Birmingham Book and Magazine Co. Reprint 1962) p 677

12. Burt, Jesse and Ferguson, Robert B. *Indians of The Southeast Then and Now* (Nashville and New York: Abingdon Press, 1973) p 68-72

13. Josephy, Alvin M., Jr. *The Indian Heritage of America* (New York, New York: Alfred A. Knopf, 1968) p 107

Chapter Six—Encounter—White Man—DeSoto Expedition.

1. Corkran, David H. *The Creek Frontier.* (Norman, Oklahoma: University of Oklahoma Press, 1967) p 41

2. West, Anson. *Methodism in Alabama.* (Nashville, Tennessee: Publishing House Methodist Episcopal Church South 1893) p 20

3. Brown, William Garrott. *History of Alabama* (New York & New Orleans: University Publishing Co. 1900) p 25

4. Pickett, James Albert. *History of Alabama* (Birmingham, Alabama: Birmingham Book and Magazine Co, Reprint 1962) p 23-25

5. Schoolcraft, Henry R. *History of The Indian Tribes of The United States.* (New York, New York: Lippincott, 1851-1857) Volume 6, p 51

6. Washburn, Wilcomb E. *The Indians in America* (New York, Evanston, San Francisco, London; Harper and Row, 1975) p 28

7. Bourne, Edward Gaylord. *Narratives of the Career of Hernando de Soto* edited by Knight of Elvas, author (New York: Alberton Book Co., 1974) p 81-82

8. Corkran, David H. *The Creek Frontier* (Norman, Oklahoma: University of Oklahoma Press, 1967) p 45

9. Pickett, James Albert. *History of Alabama* (Birmingham, Alabama; Birmingham Book and Magazine Co., reprint 1962) p 420

10. Thomas, Cyrus. *History of North America in Historic Times* (Philadelphia, Penn.: Printed for subscribers only by G. Barrie, 1903) Vol. II, p 317

11. Aken, Helen Morgan and Brown, Virginia Pounds. *Alabama Mounds to Missiles* (Huntsville, Alabama: The Strode Publishers, 1972) p 22

12. Pickett, James Albert. *History of Alabama* (Birmingham, Alabama: Birmingham Book and Magazine Co., Reprint 1962) p 34

13. Pickett, James Albert; *History of Alabama* (Birmingham, Alabama: Birmingham Book and Magazine Co., Reprint 1962) p 27-45

Chapter Seven—Six Significant Indian Nations.

1. Carter, Samuel III, *Cherokee Sunset* (Garden City, New York: Doubleday and Co. Inc., 1976) p map.

2. Pickett, James Albert. *History of Alabama* (Birmingham, Alabama; Birmingham Book and Magazine Co., Reprint 1962) p 28-29

3. Higginbotham, Prieur Jay. *The Mobile Indians* (Mobile, Alabama: Sir Rey's, 1966) p Introduction and p 67-68

4. Penicaut, André. *Fleur de Lys and Calumet* translated and edited by Richebourg Gaillard McWilliams (Baton Rouge, Louisiana: Louisiana State University Press, 1953) p 81-126

5. West, Anson. *Methodism in Alabama* (Nashville, Tenn.: Publishing House Methodist Episcopal Church, South, 1893) p 16

5.a. Debo, Angie—A History of The Indians of the United States (Norman, OK: University of OK Press, 1970).

6. Josephy, Alvin M. Jr. *The Heritage of America* (New York, New York: Knopf, 1968) p 108

Chapter Eight—The "Tombecbee" Country.

1. Penicaut, André. *Fleur de Lys and Calumet* translated and edited by Richebourg Gaillard McWilliams (Baton Rouge, Louisiana: Louisiana: State University Press, 1953) p 60

2. Higginbotham, Prieur Jay. *The Mobile Indians* (Mobile, Alabama: Sir Rey's, 1966) p 42

3. Penicaut, André. *Fleur de Lys and Calumet* translated and edited by Richebourg Gaillard McWilliams (Baton Rouge, Louisiana: Louisiana: State University Press, 1953) p 61

4. Penicaut, André. *Fleur de Lys and Calumet* translated and edited by Richebourg Gaillard McWilliams (Baton Rouge, Louisiana: Louisiana: State University Press, 1953) p 57

5. Penicaut, André. *Fleur de Lys and Calumet* translated and edited by Richebourg Gaillard McWilliams (Baton Rouge, Louisiana: Louisiana: State University Press, 1953) p 61

6. Higginbotham, Prieur Jay. *The Mobile Indians* (Mobile, Alabama: Sir Rey's, 1966) p 42-43

7. The National Geographic Society. *The World of the American Indian* (Washington, D.C., 1974) p 319

7.a. Brown, Virginia Pounds & Akens, Helen Morgan—Alabama Heritage, Strode, Huntsville, Al, 1967, page 27

8. Sun Circles and Human Hands, Southeastern Indians, Art and Industries, Luverne, Alabama, Emma Lila Fundaburk, Publisher, 1957, renewed copyright 1985, p. 30. Quotation from William E. Myer, "Indian Trails of the Southeast," Forty-Second Annual Report, Bureau of Ethnology, 1924-25, pp. 735-746.

Ibid, p. 31, Quotation from Charles C. Jones, Jr., Antiquities of the Southern Indians. New York, D. Appleton & Co., 1873, pp. 243-244.

9. Penicaut, André. *Fleur de Lys and Calumet* translated and edited by Richebourg Gailard McWilliams (Baton Rouge, Louisiana: Louisiana State University Press, 1953) p 165

10. Brown, William Garratt. *History of Alabama* (New York and New Orleans: University Publishing Co., 1900) p 42-43

11. Pickett, James Albert. *History of Alabama* (Birmingham, Alabama: Birmingham Book and Magazine Co., reprint 1962) p. 283

12. Burt, Jesse and Fergurson, Robert B. *Indians of the Southeast: Then and Now* (Nashville and New York: Abingdon Press, 1973) p 116-117

13. Summersell, Charles B. *Alabama History for Schools* (Northport, Alabama: American Southern, 1965) p 106-107

14. Pickett, James Albert. *History of Alabama* (Birmingham, Alabama: Birmingham Book and Magazine Co., Reprint 1962) p 344-345

15. Matthews, Pitt Lamar. *History Stories of Alabama* (Dallas, Texas: The Southern Publishing Co., 1924, 1929) p 53

16. Pickett, James Albert. *Alabama History* (Birmingham, Alabama: Birmingham Book and Magazine Co., Reprint 1962) p 345

17. Pickett, James Albert. *Alabama History* (Birmingham, Alabama: Birmingham Book and Magazine Co., Reprint 1962) p 345

18. Matthews, Pitt Lamar. *History Stories of Alabama* (Dallas, Texas: The Southern Publishing Co., 1924, 1929) p 55

19. Cotterhill, R.S. *The Southern Indians* (Norman, Oklahoma: University of Oklahoma Press, 1954, 1966) p 63

20. DeRosier, Arthur H. *Destruction of the Creek Confederacy* (article in *Forked Tongues and Broken Treaties* by Donald E. Worcester, edited by, (Caxton, ltd. 1975) page 83

21. The Everett Chambliss' are members of my congregation at The First United Methodist Church, Trussville, Alabama

22. Coughey, John Walton. *McGillivray of The Creeks* (Norman, Oklahoma: University of Oklahoma Press, 1938) p 161

23. Cotterhill, R.S. *The Southern Indians* (Norman, Oklahoma: University of Oklahoma Press, 1954, 1966) p 76

24. Pickett, James Albert. *History of Alabama* (Birmingham, Alabama: Birmingham Book and Magazine Co., Reprint 1962) p 373-375

25. Matthews, Pitt Lamar. *History Stories of Alabama* (Dallas, Texas: The Southern Publishing Co., 1924, 1929) p 57

26. Worcester, Donald E. Editor. *Forked Tongue and Broken Treaties* (Caldwell, Idaho: The Caxton Printers, Ltd., 1975) p 37

27. Pickett, James Albert. *History of Alabama* (Birmingham, Alabama: Birmingham Book and Magazine Co. Reprint 1962) p 406

28. Matthews, Pitt Lamar. *History Stories of Alabama* (Dallas, Texas: The Southern Publishing Co., 1924, 1929) p 58

29. Pickett, James Albert. *History of Alabama* (Birmingham, Alabama: Birmingham Book and Magazine Co., Reprint 1962) p 430-431

30. Pickett, James Albert. *History of Alabama* (Birmingham, Alabama: Birmingham Book and Magazine Co., Reprint 1962) p 469-470

31. Pickett, James Albert. *History of Alabama* (Birmingham, Alabama: Birmingham Book and Magazine Co., Reprint 1962) p 470

32. Cotterill, R.S., *The Southern Indians* (Norman, Oklahoma: University of Oklahoma Press, 1954, 1966) p 112-113

33. Akens, Helen Morgan and Brown, Virginia Pounds. *Alabama Heritage* (Huntsville, Alabama: The Strode Publishers, 1971) p 40

34. Pickett, James Albert. *History of Alabama* (Birmingham, Alabama: Birmingham Book and Magazine Co., Reprint 1962) p 465

35. Josephy, Alvin M., Jr. *The Indian Heritage of America* (New York: Knopf, 1968) p 334

36. Pickett, James Albert. *History of Alabama* (Birmingham, Alabama: Birmingham Book and Magazine Co., Reprint 1962) p 403

37. Cotterill, R.S. *The Southern Indians* (Norman, Oklahoma: University of Oklahoma Press, 1954, 1966) p 140

Chapter Nine—The Pressure of White Colonization.

1. Moore, Albert Burton. *History of Alabama* (Tuscaloosa, Alabama: Alabama Book Store, 1951) p 22

2. Moore, Albert Burton. *History of Alabama* (Tuscaloosa, Alabama: Alabama Book Store, 1951) p 23

3. Owen, Marie B. *Our State-Alabama* (Birmingham, Alabama: Birmingham Printing Co. 1927) p 79

4. Indian affairs—Vol. 1, p 846 (This material provided courtesy of The National Archives and History; Washington, D.C.)

5. Indian affairs—Vol. 1, p 847 (This material provided courtesy of the National Archives and History; Washington, D.C.)

6. Indian Affairs—Vol. 1, p 848 (This material provided courtesy of the National Archives and History, Washington, D.C.)

7. Pickett, James Albert. *History of Alabama* (Birmingham, Alabama: Birmingham Book and Magazine Co., Reprint 1962) p 526

8. Indian Affairs Vol. 1, p 851 (This material provided courtesy of the National Archives and History, Washington, D.C.)

9. Pickett, James Albert. *History of Alabama* (Birmingham, Alabama: Birmingham Book and Magazine Co., Reprint 1962) p 531

10. Indian Affairs—Vol. 1, p 851 (This material provided courtesy of the National Archives and History, Washington, D.C.)

11. Pickett, James Albert. *History of Alabama* (Birmingham, Alabama: Birmingham Book and Magazine Co., Reprint 1962) p 537

12. Indian Affairs—Vol. 1, p 854 (This material provided courtesy of the National Archives and History, Washington, D.C.)

Chapter 10—The United States Goes to War on the Creeks.

1. Pickett, James Albert, *History of Alabama* (Birmingham, Alabama: Birmingham Book and Magazine Co., Reprint 1962) p 580

2. Owen, Marie B. *Our State Alabama* (Birmingham, Alabama: Birmingham Printing Co., 1927) p 71

3. Lewis, Anna, *Chief Pushmataha, American Patriot* (New York: Exposition Press, 1959) p 90

4. Moore, Albert Burton, *History of Alabama* (Tuscaloosa, Alabama: Alabama Book Store, 1951) p 27

5. Crockett, David. *Davy Crockett's Own Story* (New York, New York: Citadel Press, Scranton, Pa.: The Haddon Craftsman Inc., 1955) p 78

7. Pickett, James Albert. History of Alabama (Birmingham, Alabama: Birmingham Book and Magazine Co., Reprint 1962) p 590

8. Pickett, James Albert. *History Of Alabama* (Birmingham, Alabama: Birmingham Book and Magazine Co., Reprint 1962) p 594-595

9. Pickett, James Albert. *History of Alabama* (Birmingham, Alabama: Birmingham Book and Magazine Co., Reprint 1962) p 598

10. Indian Affairs—Vol. 1, p 857-860 (This material provided courtesy of the National Archives and History, Washington, D.C.)

11. Indian Affairs—Vol. 1, p 857-859 (This material provided courtesy of the National Archives and History, Washington, D.C.)

12. Pickett, James Albert. *History of Alabama* (Birmingham, Alabama: Birmingham Book and Magazine Co., Reprint 1962) p 599

13. Indian Affairs Vol. 1, p 860 (This material provided courtesy of the National Archives and History, Washington, D.C.)

14. Material courtesy of the National Archives and History, Washington, D.C.)

15. Map—Credit—Moore, A.B.: History of Alabama (Tuscaloosa, Alabama: Alabama Book Store, 1951) p 11

Chapter Eleven—Policies of Co-Existence or Participation—or—.

1. Woodward, Grace Steele. *The Cherokees* (Norman, Oklahoma: University of Oklahoma Press, 1963) p 157

2. United States Statutes at Large. Vol. III, p 516-517 (This material provided courtesy of Congressional Library, Washington, D.C.)

3. Luccock, Halford E. and Hutchinson, Paul. *The Story of Methodism* (New York, Cincinnati: The Methodist Book Concern, 1926) p 307-310

4. Cannon, James III. *History of Southern Methodist Missions* (Nashville, Tenn.: Cokesbury, 1926) p 111

5. Posey, Walter B. *The Development of Methodism in the Old Southwest* (Tuscaloosa, Alabama: Weatherford Printing Co., 1933) p 120

6. West, Anson. *History of Methodism in Alabama* (Nashville, Tenn.: Publishing House Methodist Episcopal Church South, 1893) p 252

7. McTyeire, Holland N. *A History of Methodism* (Nashville, Tenn.: Publishing House of The Methodist Episcopal Church South, 1889) p 581

8. National Archives and History—Old Army-Navy Section says, though Chief Pushmataha wore a General's uniform and was called a General, he was commissioned a Captain for his support of the United States in The War of 1812.

9. West, Anson. *History of Methodist in Alabama* (Nashville, Tenn.: Publishing House Methodist Episcopal Church, South, 1893) p 251

10. McTyeire, Holland N. *A History of Methodism* (Nashville, Tenn.: Publishing House of The Methodist Episcopal Church, South, 1889) p 582

11. United States Statutes at Large—Vol. III, p 516 Indian Civilization Act This material provided courtesy of the National Archives and History, Washington, D.C.)

12. Gibson, Arrell M. *The Chickasaws* (Norman, Oklahoma: University of Oklahoma Press, 1971) p 108-111

13. Lazenby, Marion Elias. *Methodism in Alabama* (Published by the North Alabama Conference and Alabama-West Florida Conference of the United Methodist Church, 1960) p 171

14. Lazenby, Marion Elias. *Methodism in Alabama* (Published by the North Alabama Conference and Alabama-West Florida Conference of the United Methodist Church, 1960) p 171

15. Lazenby, Marion Elias. *Methodism in Alabama* (Published by the North Alabama Conference and Alabama-West Florida Conference of the United Methodist Church, 1960) p 172-173

16. McTyeire, Holland N. *A History of Methodism* (Nashville, Tenn.: Publishing House of the Methodist Episcopal Church, South, 1889) p 580

17. Cannon, James III. *History of Southern Methodist Missions* (Nashville, Tenn: Cokesbury, 1926) p 264

18. Lazenby, Marion Elias. *Methodism in Alabama* (Published by the North Alabama Conference and Alabama-West Florida Conference of The United Methodist Church, 1960) p 173-179

19. Cannon, James III. History of Southern Methodist Missions (Nashville, Tenn.: Cokesbury, 1926) p 268

Chapter Twelve—Removal.

1. Johnson, Bobby. *The Coushetta People* (Phoenix, Arizona: Published by Indian Tribal Series, 1976) p 27

2. Vogel, Virgil J. *This Country Was Ours* (New York, Evanston, San Francisco, London: Harper and Row, 1972) p 103

3. Prucha, Francis P., American Indian Policy in The Formative Years (Cambridge, Harvard Univ Press, 1962, p. 139

3.a. Prucha, Francis P. *American Indian Policy in The Formative Years* (Cambridge, Massachusetts: Harvard University Press, 1962) p 241

4. article, Breckenridge, H.H. *Indian Atrocities-Narratives of the Perils and Suffering of Dr. Knight* (In *This Country was Ours* edited by Virgil G. Vogel. Cincinnati, Ohio: U.P. James, 1782, 1867) p 62-72

5. Farb, Peter. *Man's Rise to Civilization as Shown by The Indians of North America* (New York: E.P. Dutton and Co. Inc. 1968) p 276

6. Farb, Peter. *Man's Rise to Civilization as Shown by The Indians of North America* (New York: E.P. Dutton and Co. Inc. 1968) p 248

7. Farb, Peter. *Man's Rise to Civilization as Shown by The Indians of North America* (New York: E.P. Dutton and Co. Inc. 1968) p 247

8. Farb, Peter. *Man's Rise to Civilization as Shown by The Indians of North America* (New York: E.P. Dutton and Co. Inc. 1968) p 247

9. Farb, Peter. *Man's Rise to Civilization as Shown by The Indians of North America* (New York: E.P. Dutton and Co. Inc. 1968) p 248

10. Trennert, Robert A. Jr. *Alternatives to Extinction* (Philadelphia, Penn.: Temple University Press, 1975) p ppl

11. Letter from President Jefferson to Benjamin Hawkins dated Feb. 1803 (Courtesy of the National Archives and History Washington, D.C.)
12. Ford, Paul Luicester. *Thomas Jefferson Vol. III* (New York and London: G.P. Putnam's Sons, 1904-1905) p 241-249
13. United States Statutes at Large—Section 15, p 283-289
14. American Historical Association Vol. 1, p 244-245
15. Hudson, Charles M. *Four Centuries of Southern Indians* (Athens, Georgia: University of Georgia Press, 1975) p 86
16. Reprinted from *Four Centuries of Southern Indians* by Charles M. Hudson, C. 1975 by permission of The University of Georgia Press
17. America's Fascinating Indian Heritage, (c) 1978 The Reader's Digest Association, Inc. Used with permission.
18. Excerpts from Cherokee Sunset by Samuel Carter III. Copyright c. 1976 by Samuel Carter III, Reprinted by permission of Doubleday & Co., Inc.
19. Cotterill, R.S. *The Southern Indians* (Norman, Oklahoma: University of Oklahoma Press, 1954, 1966) p 238
20. Debo, Angie. *A History of the Indians of the United States* (Norman, Oklahoma: University of Oklahoma Press, 1970) p 106
21. Muzzey, David Saville. *American History* (Boston, New York, Chicago, London: Ginn and Co., 1911) p 265
22. Debo, Angie. *A History of the Indian in the United States* (Norman, Oklahoma: University of Oklahoma Press, 1970) p 106
23. Congressional Record, May 19, 1830—Davy Crockett was outspoken against this bill or act. (Courtesy of the National Archives and History, Washington, D.C.)
24. Reader's Digest. *America's Fascinating Indian Heritage* (Pleasantville, New York, 1978) p 108
25. Foreman, Grant. *Indian Removal* (Norman, Oklahoma: University of Oklahoma Press, 1932, 1956) p 6
26. Foreman, Grant. *Indian Removal* (Norman, Oklahoma: University of Oklahoma Press, 1932, 1956) p preface
27. Foreman, Grant. *Indian Removal* (Norman, Oklahoma: University of Oklahoma Press, 1932, 1956) p preface
28. Moulton, Gary E. *John Ross Cherokee Chief* (Athens, Georgia: University of Georgia Press) p 53
29. Foreman, Grant. *Indian Removal* (Norman, Oklahoma: University of Oklahoma Press, 1932, 1956) p 124
30. Foreman, Grant. *Indian Removal* (Norman, Oklahoma: University of Oklahoma Press, 1932, 1956) p 236
31. Foreman, Grant. Indian Removal (Norman, Oklahoma: University of Oklahoma Press, 1932, 1956) p 28-29
32. DeRosier, Arthur H. *The Removal of The Choctaw Indians* (Knoxville, Tenn.: The University of Tennessee Press, 1970) p 13
33. Foreman, Grant. *Indian Removal* (Norman, Oklahoma: University of Oklahoma Press, 1932, 1956) p 46
34. Baird, W. David. *The Choctaw People* (Phoenix, Arizona: Indian Tribal Series, 1973) p 36
35. DeRosier, Arthur H. Jr. The Removal of The Choctaw Indians (Knoxville, Tenn.: The University of Tennessee Press, 1970) p 131
36. Indian Affairs. "Choctaw Emigration" Claiborne to January 25, 1836 (Courtesy of the National Archives and History, Washington, D.C.

37. United States Senate Files. Twenty fourth Congress, First Session, Report of The Secretary of War (Courtesy of The National Archives and History, Washington, D.C.)
38. Baird, W. David. *The Choctaw People* (Phoenix, Arizona: Indian Tribal Series, 1973) p 38
39. Foreman, Grant. *Indian Removal* (Norman, Oklahoma: University of Oklahoma Press, 1932, 1956) p 69
40. Foreman, Grant. *Indian Removal* (Norman, Oklahoma: University of Oklahoma Press, 1932, 1956) p 69
41. Baird, W. David. *The Chickasaw People* (Pheonix, Arizona: Indian Tribal Series, 1973) p 38
42. Foreman, Grant. *Indian Removal* (Norman, Oklahoma: University of Oklahoma Press, 1932, 1956) p 213-215
43. Foreman, Grant. *Indian Removal* (Norman, Oklahoma: University of Oklahoma Press, 1932, 1956) p 226
44. Brandon, William. *The Last American* (New York: McGraw-Hill Book Co., 1974) p 277 and 281
45. Debo, Angie. *A History of The Indian in The United States* (Norman, Oklahoma: University of Oklahoma Press, 1970) p 102
46. Foreman, Grant. *Indian Removal* (Norman, Oklahoma: University of Oklahoma Press, 1932, 1956) p 146
47. Moore, Albert Burton. *History of Alabama* (Tuscaloosa, Alabama: Alabama Book Store, 1951) p 32
48. Foreman, Grant. *Indian Removal* (Norman, Oklahoma: University of Oklahoma Press, 1932, 1956) p 152
49. Brandon, William. *The Last Americans* (New York: McGraw-Hill Book Co., 1974) p 286
50. Debo, Angie. The History of The Indians in The United States (Norman, Oklahoma: University of Oklahoma Press, 1970) p 95
51. Cotterill, R.S. *The Southern Indians* (Norman, Oklahoma: University of Oklahoma Press, 1954, 1966) p 231-232
52. Mann, Colonel Robert N. The Cherokee County Historical Society Journal. "The Cherokee County Heritage" Vol. III p 99
53. Moulton, Gary E. *John Ross Cherokee Chief* (Athens, Georgia: The University of Georgia Press, 1978) p 96
54. Moulton, Gary E. *John Ross Cherokee Chief* (Athens, Georgia: The University of Georgia Press, 1978) p 96-106
55. Pierre, George, American Indian Crisis (San Antonio, Texas: The Naylor Company, 1971) p 209

Chapter XIII Our National Heritage from The American Indian.

1. Schoolcraft, Henry R. *History of The Indian Tribes of The United States* (New York, New York: Lippincott, 1857) Vol. 2, p 29
2. Editors—*Better Homes and Gardens Heritage Cookbook* (USA: Meredith Corporation, 1975) p II
3. Bassett, John Spencer. *A Short History of The United States* (New York: The McMillian Co., 1934) p 61
4a. Josephy, Alvin M. Jr.—The Indian Heritage of America (New York: Knopf, 1968) p 32
4. Reprinted from Better Homes and Garden Heritage Cook Book, C. Meredith Corporation 1975. All rights reserved.

5. Muzzey, David Saville. *American History* (Boston, New York, Chicago, London: Ginn and Co., 1911) p 147

6. Adams, James Truslow, editor *Album of American History,* Vol. 1-Colonial Period (New York, New York: Charles Scribner and Sons, 1944) Vol. 1, p 19

7. Director of Colonial Park at Jamestown in a letter to me.

8. Adams, Jarner Truslow, editor. *Album of American History,* Vol. Colonial Period (New York, New York: Charles Scribner's Sons, 1944) Vol. 1 p 19-20

9. Adams, James Truslow, *Album of American History* Colonial Period, Vol. 1 (New York, New York p. 19-20

10. Porter, C. Fayne. *Our Indian Heritage.* (Philadelphia, New York, London: Chilton Book Co. 1964) p 2-4

11. Nadover, Saul K. editor. *Washington Papers* (New York, New York: Harper and Brothers, 1955) p 150-151

12. Chief Sealth's quote reprinted by permission from The American Indian by Sidney Fletcher. Copyright 1954 renewed c. 1982 by Grosset & Dunlap, Inc. page 16

13. Muzzey, David Saville. *American History* (Boston, New York, Chicago, London: Ginn and Co., 1911) p 147

13a. Porter, C. Fayne—Our Indian Heritage (Philadelphia, New York, London: Chilton Book Co. 1964) p 3

14. Editors National Geographic Society. *The World of The American Indian* (Washington, D.C., 1974) p 139

15. Weiner, Michael A. *Earth Medicine-Earth Foods* (New York: The Macmillian Co., 1972) p 3

16. Porter, C. Fayne. *Our Indian Heritage* (Philadelphia, New York, London: Chilton Book Co., 1964) p 3

17. Letter of Chief Sealth to President Franklin Pierce in 1855 (Courtesy of National Archives and History, Washington, D.C.)

18. Karen D. Paul Legislative and Natural Resources Branch The National Archives and History said, "Apparently Chief Seattle's speech first appeared in the Seattle Sunday Star of Oct 29, 1887, as part of Dr. Henry A. Smith's account of a meeting between Seattle and Isaac Stevens.

19. Porter, C. Fayne. *Our Indian Heritage* (Philadelphia, New York, London: Chilton Book Co., 1964) p 6

20. Burt, Jesse, and Ferguson, Robert B. *Indians of the Southeast.* Then and Now (Nashville, New York: Abingdon Press, 1973) p 61

21. Bigelow, John editor. *The Complete Works of Benjamin Franklin* (New York and London: G. P. Putnam's Sons, 1887-1888) p 108-109

21a. Porter, C. Fayne—Our Indian Heritage, Philadelphia, New York, London: Chilton Book Co., 1964 p 10

22. Morgan, Lewis H.—League of The Ho-de-no-san-nea or Iroquois (New York: Burt Franklin, 1901) p 32

23. Porter, C. Fayne—Our Indian Heritage (Philadelphia, New York, London: Chilton Book Co., 1964) p 10

23a. Josephy, Alvin M. Jr.—The Indian Heritage of America (New York: Knopf, 1968) p 34-35

24. Josephy, Alvin M. Jr.—The Indian Heritage of America (New York: Knopf, 1968) p 35

24a. Bigelow, John, editor. The Complete Works of Benjamin Franklin (New York: G. P. Putnam, 1887) Vol. II, p 219

Chapter XIV Remnants Remain across The Southeast.

Chapter XV Hope!
1. DeTocqueville, Alexis. *Democracy in America* (New York: Alfred A. Knopf, 1945) p 27
2. America's Fascinating Indian Heritage, (c) 1978 The Reader's Digest Association, Inc. Used with permission.
3. American Indian Policy Review Commission, Chairman, Senator James Abourezk. U.S. Senate
4. Hertzberg, Hazel W. *The Search for an American Indian Identity* (New York: Syracuse University Press, 1971) p 277-278
5. From Man's Rise To Civilization as Shown By The Indians of North America From Primeval Times to the Coming of the Industrial State by Peter Farb. Copyright (c) 1968 by Peter Farb. Reprinted by Permission of the publisher, E. P. Dutton, a division of New American Library.
6. Morris, Colin. *"Include Me Out"* Nashville: Abingdon Press, 1968, p 68
7. Anderson, Geral H. edited by *Christian Mission in Theological Perspective* (Nashville, New York: Abingdon Press, 1967) "The Gospel, The Church, and The Mission", L. Harold DeWolf p 49
8. Pierre, Chief George. *American Indian Crisis* (San Antonio, Texas: The Naylor Company, 1971) p 211-213
9. Burnette, Robert. *The Tortured Americans* (Englewood Cliffs, New Jersey: Prentice-Hall, Inc., 1971) p 151
10. Fassett, Thom White Wolf "Native Peoples and The Alaska Experience" in Response, June 1985 p 14
11. Reaves, Malik Stan "Native American Ministries Today" New World Outlook, Oct 1985 p 23

XVIII.
1. New World Outlook, October, 1985. Reaves, Malik Stan—"Native American Ministries Today" p 23, 26
2. Courtesy of the SEJ Association of Native American Ministries.
3. Scripture—Courtesy of National Council of Churches of Christ in the U.S.A., Division of Education and Ministry, New York, N.Y. © 1972
4. Norman W. Pittenger, *Process Thought and Christian Faith* p 19
5. Frankl, Viktor E., Man's Search for Meaning, Pocket Books a Simon & Schuster div. of Gulf & Western Corp. N.Y. © 1963.
6. Ibid
7. Ibid
8. Dr. Karl Menninger,
9. The Four Ways of Life—Three Worlds (Record Label)
   A. Paul Ortega
   Waltiske
   P.O. Box 243
   Albuquerque, New Mexico 87103
10. Scripture—Courtesy of National Council of Churches of Christ in the U.S.A., Division of Education and Ministry, New York, N.Y. © 1972